D1570981

THE
PEROT
VOTERS

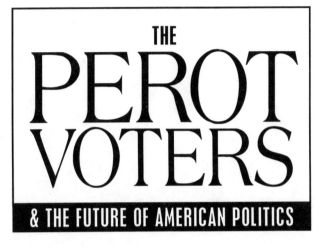

THE PEROT VOTERS

& THE FUTURE OF AMERICAN POLITICS

ALBERT J. MENENDEZ

Prometheus Books

59 John Glenn Drive
Amherst, NewYork 14228-2197

Published 1996 by Prometheus Books

00 99 98 97 96   5 4 3 2 1

Library of Congress Cataloging-in-Publication Data

Menendez, Albert J.
   The Perot voters and the future of American politics / Albert J. Menendez.
      p.   cm.
   Includes bibliographical references.
   ISBN 1–57392–044–4 (cloth : alk. paper)
   1. Perot, H. Ross, 1930–   —Influence. 2. United States—Politics and government—1993–   3. Voting—United States. I. Title.
E840.8.P427M46   1996
324.973'0928—dc20   96–3754
                                                CIP

Printed in the United States of America on acid-free paper

For Shirley

Contents

8 CONTENTS

Acknowledgments

I am grateful for the tireless and skilled assistance of Marie Gore, who helped to improve the manuscript at every stage.

To the late Alice McGillivray, I can only express my appreciation for her thirty years of providing me with election information, often before it appeared in *America Votes*.

To my wife, Shirley, I owe everything that really matters in life, and to her I dedicate this book.

Introduction

The 20 million voters who supported Ross Perot for president in 1992 have already contributed to two major political upheavals: the removal of George Bush from the White House and the installation of a Republican-controlled Congress for the first time in forty years. This book takes a close look at the diverse and broadly based groups of people who voted for Perot in 1992. These voters will have a major, if not decisive, impact on the 1996 election.

Analyzing elections is a lot like detective work. It involves searching for clues to voter behavior in thousands of likely and unlikely places, discarding those that make no sense or lack coherence, and finally discovering patterns and often hidden meanings buried in mountains of data compiled by a myriad of election officials from far and near. Looking at county election data and even better, where possible, at precinct returns from the counties gives the election analyst insights into the ways in which elections shape government policies and may even change the face of history. Such data also reveal the expectations and yearnings of those who choose to exercise their right of suffrage on that quadrennial first Tuesday after the first Monday in November when our democracy ratifies itself and by doing so renews its future.

In the course of things political, there is nothing like a U.S. presidential election. It absorbs our attention (though perhaps less so than a generation ago) and focuses our hopes and dreams—and angers and fears—on fallible human beings (usually two of them) who believe that they can lead us to a promised land.

So who, exactly, voted for Perot and is likely to do so in the future? Let's look at the most recent data.

The Pro-Republican Shift

In the 1994 congressional elections, the Perot voters showed the largest pro-Republican shift of any segment of the electorate. Whereas 51 percent voted Republican in the 1992 congressional races, 67 percent supported the GOP in 1994, a sixteen-point swing. This was clearly the most politically salient factor in the outcome. In the seventy House districts where Perot won 25 percent or more of the presidential vote, Republicans won fifty-one seats to the Democrats' nineteen. This thirty-two-seat majority more than offset the Democratic edge in weaker Perot districts and gave Republicans a comfortable control of the House for the first time since 1952, the year Dwight Eisenhower first won the presidency.

Does this mean that Perot voters are turning Republican? Will they support the likely Republican nominee against President Clinton in 1996? Or would they prefer another run by Mr. Perot?

The evidence suggests that Perot's 1992 supporters would support a second Perot candidacy. And they may be joined by additional voters disillusioned with the present party system.

The Times Mirror Center for The People & The Press released a major survey on September 21, 1994, which indicated that Mr. Perot would receive 20 percent of the ballots in a three-way contest with President Bill Clinton and Sen. Robert Dole. This is an increase of 1 percent over 1992. Perot gained in the poll among Democratic-leaning groups and among those embittered by the present political system. He lost ground among libertarians, enterprisers, and the upper-middle-class segments of the electorate.

The Times Mirror survey has identified certain similarities among voters and classified the electorate into ten categories. Perot's 1992 strength, these researchers found, came from two groups in particular, the new economy independents and the libertarians.

According to the study, the "new economy independents [are] the most important swing voters in the new electorate. Their middle class status seems precarious in the post-industrial economy, and the future uncertain, at best." These voters, who are mostly female and young, are "unreceptive to traditional partisan appeals" and the most supportive of all voters for a third party. Perot ran second to Clinton among them, winning 29 percent of their support. Perot still retains his strength with this group and would win 30 percent support in 1996 if he runs for president again.

Libertarians, 27 percent of whom cast their vote for Perot in 1992, were the second strongest group of Perot supports. Among libertarians Perot ran second to Bush. These voters defected to Perot, according to the Times Mirror survey, partly because "the extremism of the religious right registered as a major source of dissatisfaction." Libertarians are "pro-business, anti-government and anti-social welfare but highly tolerant and moderately environmentalist. They scored very low on religious faith and have a cynical view of politicians." These voters are white, male, highly educated, affluent, and financially secure. They are the most supportive of term limitation of all voters and favor the formation of a third party. However, Perot has slipped in potential support among these voters, possibly because they endorsed the North American Free Trade Agreement (NAFTA) and the General Agreement on Trade and Tariffs (GATT) and are generally pro-internationalist.

Perot voters as a whole, while supporting the Republican positions on many economic issues, have little in common with the Religious Right, which increasingly influences Republican social policy positions. Many Perot supporters still remember with disdain the attacks mounted on their candidate by one Religious Right author, George Grant, who in 1992 had this to say:

> Perot is opposed to any semblance of family values as they are traditionally understood. He is the first presidential candidate ever to have conceived close personal and institutional ties to the grisly abortion industry. The Perots are not simply pro-choice, they are activists with a vested interest in the most radical fringe of the pro-abortion movement.*

The new economy independents and the libertarians typify the kind of politically unique and unpredictable coalition Ross Perot created in 1992.

*George Grant, *Perot: The Populist Appeal of Strong-Man Politics* (Crossway Books, 1992), pp. 97–98.

Voters clearly yearn for substantial change, and are still skeptical that the existing party system can achieve it. A national *Time*/CNN poll conducted in March 1995 shows that support for a third party has reached 56 percent.

*   *   *

Ross Perot is an extraordinary character who emerged as a classic outsider candidate, articulating anti-elitist and anti-establishment values and in the end convincing a fifth of the electorate to follow him. While much has been written about his candidacy and its ultimate appeal—a good deal of it erroneous and misleading—little has been based on actual verifiable data. Many interpretations are derived from analyses of overnight exit polls, which have become a feature of U.S. political life since 1972. As mentioned above, I have researched a wide variety of data to develop the most detailed analysis to date of Perot supporters across the nation.

The data contained in this book come from two primary sources. One is the U.S. Census data, available in printed form or on CD-Rom. *The County and City Data Book* (New York: Gordon Press, 1992) is a particularly good reference for comparative county data on a variety of sources, including per capita income, median family income, educational attainment, and racial characteristics. Ethnic ancestry data have also been useful to this study. The *Statistical Abstract of the United States* (Washington, D.C.: U.S. Government Printing Office, 1992), which is a useful compendium of different phases of census data, has also been occasionally useful.

The county election data are contained in a superb reference series, *America Votes,* edited by R. Scammon et al. (Washington, D.C.: Congressional Quarterly, Inc.), available in twenty-one volumes and covering the presidential, gubernatorial, and senatorial elections from 1952 through 1994. Two companion volumes, *America at the Polls, 1920–1964,* edited by R. Scammon (reprint, Salem, N.H.: Ayer, 1976), and *America at the Polls, 1968–1984,* edited by R. Scammon and A. McGillivany (Washington, D.C.: Congressional Quarterly, Inc., 1988), have also been consulted. These are indispensable and accurate sources for election specialists.

Precinct data that I have cited have been obtained directly from county election offices. Some states publish detailed precinct-level data in regular volumes. I have long utilized the *Pennsylvania Manual* (published since 1867) and the *Wisconsin Blue Book.*

Part One

Who Voted for Perot?

1

General Overview

There has never been a presidential candidate quite like Ross Perot, a man who came out of nowhere to win the support of nearly 20 million voters. This successful Texas businessman who has never held public office, not even on a school board, and who had never been prominent in national politics, received almost one out of five ballots cast.

Here is a man who received enormous support in states west of the Mississippi River but also topped his national average in all six New England states, which are traditional political and economic rivals of the West. He won votes from liberals and conservatives, from Republicans and Democrats. What other independent presidential candidate could have won a quarter of the votes of Mormons and Lutherans and almost as many from nonreligious or secular voters who prefer not to be involved in formal religious activities?

Perot's 19 percent of the vote far overshadows the other major third-party contenders in this century: Alabama Governor George Wallace, who ran a kind of neopopulist campaign and won 13.5 percent in 1968, most of it in his native South; John Anderson, the Midwestern liberal Republican who received almost 7 percent in 1980; and Wisconsin Senator Robert LaFollette, who rode a wave of economic protest from the Midwest to a respectable 17 percent in 1924. Only Theodore Roosevelt, who received 27 percent of the vote in 1912, did better, but one can argue that Roosevelt, a former Republican president for seven years, was seen by voters as a Republican, even the legitimate Republican candidate in that bitter three-way election.* The point I am trying to make is that Ross Perot was probably the strongest *genuine outsider* to win so large a vote in his quest for the nation's highest office.

Who, then, were these millions who placed their faith in an eccentric Texas billionaire who limited his campaign to infomercials, books, and high-toned political debate? Will they vote for him again in 1996? Will others join them, making him an even more formidable candidate? Polls strongly suggest that Perot could indeed be an even stronger contender in the next election than he was in the previous. Some polls have shown him leading President Clinton or any likely Republican. Polls are fickle, however. What really counts is the 1992 vote. Here we can find solid clues to the kinds of voters who responded favorably to the Perot candidacy.

The geography of the Perot vote is revealing. With the exception of his best state, Maine, where he won 30 percent, all of his top-ten states were in the West, including Alaska, Utah, Kansas, Wyoming, Nevada, Montana, Idaho, Oregon, and Minnesota. Perot exceeded his national average of 19 percent in all six New England states, in every western state (except New Mexico and Hawaii), and in Texas, Michigan, Wisconsin, Indiana, Ohio, Florida, and Delaware. In all Perot polled higher than his national average in thirty-one states. (See Table 1)

What do Maine and Utah have in common? Or Alaska, Idaho, and Kansas, for that matter? A certain quirky individualism, to be sure, per-

---

*Actually, it was a four-ring circus, since Socialist candidate Eugene Debs received over 5 percent of the national vote. Roosevelt had fought President William Howard Taft hard for the nomination and had outpolled the chief executive in the primaries, only to have the nomination given to Taft by the party bosses. The Republican party's progressive wing cried foul, and the former president threw his hat into the ring as the Progressive party nominee.

But Roosevelt received his votes almost exclusively from Republicans, then the majority party. He was the official party-designated candidate in California and South Dakota, and the counties he carried were Republican counties. Of the nation's heaviest Republican counties, Roosevelt carried 150 to Taft's seventy-eight. The vote was so divided in sixty-seven staunch Republican counties that Democrat Woodrow Wilson squeaked ahead of them. (In 1916 all of these banner GOP counties backed Charles Evans Hughes against President Wilson.) Still, Wilson held the Democratic vote and, like Bill Clinton in 1992, won the presidency despite receiving a smaller percentage of the total vote than the previous, and unsuccessful, Democratic nominee, William Jennings Bryan.

Table 1
Support for Perot by State

State	% Perot Vote	State	% Perot Vote
1. Maine	30.4	26. Ohio	21.0
2. Alaska	28.4	27. California	20.6
3. Utah	27.3	28. Delaware	20.4
4. Idaho	27.0	29. Florida	19.8
5. Kansas	27.0	30. Indiana	19.8
6. Nevada	26.2	31. Michigan	19.3
7. Montana	26.1	32. Iowa	18.7
8. Wyoming	25.6	33. Pennsylvania	18.2
9. Oregon	24.2	34. Illinois	16.6
10. Minnesota	24.0	35. West Virginia	15.9
11. Arizona	23.8	36. New York	15.7
12. Washington	23.7	37. New Jersey	15.6
13. Nebraska	23.6	38. Hawaii	14.2
14. Colorado	23.3	39. Maryland	14.2
15. Rhode Island	23.2	40. Kentucky	13.7
16. North Dakota	23.1	41. North Carolina	13.7
17. Oklahoma	23.0	42. Virginia	13.6
18. Vermont	22.8	43. Georgia	13.3
19. Massachusetts	22.7	44. Louisiana	11.8
20. New Hampshire	22.6	45. South Carolina	11.5
21. Texas	22.0	46. Alabama	10.8
22. South Dakota	21.8	47. Arkansas	10.4
23. Missouri	21.7	48. New Mexico	10.1
24. Connecticut	21.6	49. Tennessee	10.1
25. Wisconsin	21.5	50. Mississippi	8.7

meates these states. Alaska elected an independent governor in 1990 and Maine did so in 1994. Independent candidates were nearly elected to the U.S. Senate in Utah and Kansas several decades ago. An independent candidate won 34 percent of Utah's vote for governor in 1992. The Perot states have a higher than average percentage of the population that claims English or Anglo-Saxon descent. (Utah and Maine are the nation's most "British" states.) And Perot seems to have done quite well in areas that might best be characterized as "culturally Protestant" rather than in Bible Belt evangelical strongholds. The education/religion axis shows Perot stronger among "cultural moderates" on social and family-values issues, while Clinton swept the cultural liberals and Bush won convincingly

Table 2
Perot's Strongest Counties (Over 500,000 Total Votes)

County	State	% Perot
San Diego	CA	26.3
Dallas	TX	25.8
Maricopa	AZ	25.3
Orange	CA	23.9
King	WA	21.5
Santa Clara	CA	21.4
Middlesex	MA	21.3
Hennepin	MN	21.1
St. Louis	MO	20.4
Ramsey	MN	20.1
St. Louis	MN	20.0
Suffolk	NY	19.9

among cultural conservatives. Perot also did well among those of German, Scandinavian, and French descent. (His French-sounding name may have been worth a few percentage points in New England, but in the Cajun country of South Louisiana, he only won 13 percent of the vote.)

While the Perot vote was largely a small-town and rural vote, with some patches of suburban support and very little big-city support, he did well in some large counties where more than five hundred thousand votes were cast. (See Table 2.) Perot's best showings were in San Diego, where he won 26 percent, his home county of Dallas, Texas, where he won just under 26 percent, and Phoenix, Arizona, where he won 25 percent of the vote. All are Sun Belt cities with a growing population and considerable economic change. Perot did well in traditionally Republican Orange County, California, where he took 24 percent of the vote. He took 21 percent in Silicon Valley (Santa Clara County), California, where many highly skilled high-tech workers live. He won 21 percent in Middlesex County, Massachusetts, a generally middle-income Boston suburb, and 21 percent in Hennepin County, Minnesota, which includes Minneapolis and its adjoining suburbs. Perot also won 20 percent in Ramsey County, Minnesota (St. Paul); St. Louis County (Duluth), Minnesota; and St. Louis County, Missouri, the major suburban county for the city of St. Louis. He also won 21 percent in Washington's King County (Seattle).

Perot did well in both Democratic and Republican areas. His top three large counties were strongly Republican, but the Minnesota, Massachusetts, and Washington counties have been leaning toward the Democrats for a number of years.

Another county where Perot did well was Suffolk, which is in the easternmost part of New York's Long Island and is middle class, conservative, and Republican. In contrast, he did not do well in the various New York City boroughs or in Dade County, Florida. And his support was well below his national average in Detroit, Philadelphia, Chicago, and Oakland. He did reasonably well but just a little below norm in Broward County, Florida (Ft. Lauderdale); Cuyahoga County, Ohio (Cleveland); Allegheny County, Pennsylvania (Pittsburgh); Oakland County, Michigan (Detroit suburbs); Los Angeles, California; and Harris County, Texas (Houston).

There are more than one hundred counties in the United States which recorded between one hundred thousand and five hundred thousand votes in the 1992 election. Perot did quite well in a dozen of them, and all are reflective of his many types of voters. His two best counties in this group were in his home state of Texas—Denton County and Collin County—where he won over one-third of the vote and came in second to Bush. Denton County includes the University of North Texas and is relatively affluent and well educated. Collin County is a prosperous North Dallas suburb. Perot's third-best medium-size county was Snohomish County, Washington, a very middle-class county of moderate educational attainment. Snohomish is a Seattle suburb but is not one of its wealthier areas. *Time* magazine referred to it in the summer of 1993 as a county where people are more likely to drive trucks than Volvos or Mercedes. Perot did very well in Salt Lake County, Utah; New London, Connecticut; Tarrant County, Texas (Fort Worth); and Washoe County, Nevada (Reno). A middle-income Boston suburb (Plymouth County) was Perot's seventh-best county. St. Charles County, Missouri, a middle-to-upper-income St. Louis suburb, was Perot's fifth-best large county. One of the big surprises in Perot's strength was Erie County, New York, the Buffalo area, where he exceeded 27 percent of the vote. The Greater Buffalo area is near the state average in per capita income and education, and is very ethnic and Democratic leaning. Perot nearly beat out Bush for second place. Anoka County, Minnesota, is a middle-income suburb of Minneapolis-St. Paul, and Perot did

Table 3
Perot's Strongest Counties (100,000–500,000 total votes)

County	State	% Perot
Denton	TX	34.0
Collin	TX	33.6
Snohomish	WA	29.2
Salt Lake	UT	28.9
St. Charles	MO	28.5
Anchorage*	AK	28.3
Plymouth	MA	27.9
New London	CT	27.8
Tarrant	TX	27.6
Erie	NY	27.3
Washoe	NV	27.0
Anoka	MN	27.0

*election districts 9–27

very well here. Finally, Perot took nearly 27 percent of the vote in Anchorage, Alaska, a fast-growing community where a considerable portion of the state vote is cast. Anchorage is very prosperous and one of Perot's best showings in an upscale area. (See Table 3.)

Perot also did well in places like Boise, Idaho; Wichita, Kansas; the Kansas City suburbs; Cape Cod; Dakota County; Minnesota (St. Paul suburb); Las Vegas; the Portland, Oregon, suburbs; Reading, Pennsylvania; Vancouver, Washington; the middle-income Los Angeles suburb of Ventura County; and San Luis Obispo County, California. Perot ran strongly in the middle-income suburbs of Denver; in the Cape Canaveral area of Florida; in Pasco County north of Tampa, Florida; in Lorain, Ohio; in traditionally Republican Canton, Ohio; and in Gloucester County, New Jersey. In these areas Perot took nearly a quarter of the vote and proved to be a significant factor.

At the other end of the scale, Perot did poorly in the Bronx, New Orleans, Memphis, Little Rock, Baltimore City, Birmingham, Columbia (South Carolina), Jersey City, San Francisco, Prince George's County (Maryland), and Atlanta (Fulton County) and its nearby suburbs (DeKalb County). Perot did not do well in some of the large population centers. In Maine, Michigan, North Dakota, Oregon, Pennsylvania, Wyoming, Florida, Louisiana, Minnesota, and New York, Perot's worst-county showing was also the largest population center. This includes places like Philadelphia, New Orleans, Baltimore, Miami, Portland, and Detroit. The largest counties in Connecticut, Nebraska, and Nevada were also Perot's second-poorest counties in their states.

The geographic breadth of Perot's strength is one of the more stunning findings of the 1992 election. He did well practically everywhere in certain states. He equalled or exceeded his national percentage of the vote in every county in Delaware, Idaho, Kansas, Maine, Montana, Nevada, New Hampshire, Oregon, and Wyoming. (On the other hand, he failed to equal his national average in any county in Alabama, Hawaii, Mississippi, South Carolina, and Tennessee.)

In addition to these states Perot also ran better than his national average in a majority of counties in Arizona, California, Colorado, Connecticut, Florida, Illinois, Indiana, Iowa, Massachusetts, Michigan, Minnesota, Missouri, Nebraska, New York, North Dakota, Ohio, Oklahoma, Pennsylvania, Rhode Island, South Dakota, Texas, Utah, Vermont, Washington, and Wisconsin. No third-party presidential candidate since 1912 has done that well.

Perot's impact on the election outcome in the states and counties was profound though indirect. This indirect influence has already caused some analysts to ignore or minimize its significance. We should not forget that because of the Perot vote, only one state gave a majority to any candidate: Arkansas for Bill Clinton, and even there the state's governor won just 53 percent of the total vote.

On the county level the Perot impact is even more noticeable. Of the nation's 3,111 counties, only 869, or about 28 percent, gave a majority to any candidate. Bill Clinton won a majority of the total vote in 496 counties, and George Bush was the majority victor in 373 counties. The other 2,242 counties could only muster a plurality for their winner.

And the vote was so competitive that in 501 counties, or 16.1 percent of them, the winning candidate received less than 40 percent of the vote. The majority of counties in Maine, Delaware, Nevada, and Oregon were intensely fought three-way splits. So were more than a third of counties in California, Idaho, Kansas, Michigan, Minnesota, Montana, and Wisconsin. So while Perot did not win nearly as many counties as George Wallace in 1968 or Bob LaFollette in 1924, he energized a much broader following with a potential for the future. (See Table 4.)

Table 4

The Three-Way Split Counties
(Winner won less than 40% of vote)
States with a High Percentage of
Three-Way Competitive Counties

State	% of counties
Maine	75.0
Delaware	66.7
Nevada	52.9
Oregon	52.8
Minnesota	49.4
Montana	42.9
Kansas	39.0
Michigan	38.6
California	37.9
Idaho	36.4
Wisconsin	34.7
Washington	30.8
New Hampshire	30.0
Colorado	28.6
Arizona	26.7
Nationwide	16.1

2

The Economic Distress Factor:
The Revolt of the Middle Class

My study of Perot's strongest counties in all fifty states reveals a significant and almost unvarying conclusion: Perot did best in areas of economic
distress, in which the vote was strongly tied to economic protest. Perot may
also have gained some votes because of the cultural issues. These issues,
like abortion, gay rights, and the environment, helped Perot because he was
seen as a centrist, a "cultural moderate." Clinton was clearly the cultural
liberal candidate and Bush was the cultural conservative one. This left
Perot appealing to voters who were perhaps ambivalent on the cultural issues and who wanted someone to deal with the economic decline they perceived.

My study of the per capita income averages of the highest Perot coun-
ties in all states shows this factor clearly. Only in Texas and Utah, and with
a mixed picture in Rhode Island, did Perot's counties measure slightly
above the state average in per capita income. In a few states—Alabama,
Arkansas, Idaho, Illinois, Indiana, Kentucky, Mississippi, North Carolina,
Oklahoma, South Carolina, Tennessee, Virginia, West Virginia, and
Wyoming—Perot's counties came within 10 percent of the state averages.
In these states Perot's vote was essentially middle class. His voters in the
South seem to have come disproportionately from the middle-income

class, people who migrated to the region and lived in fast-growing suburban or resort communities. Most of the South is locked into a rigid pattern
of racial voting and is culturally conservative in most areas, two factors
which tended to keep the Bush vote high.

In regard to education, in every state, with the possible exception of
Rhode Island where the pattern is mixed, results showed that Perot ran
strongest among voters who were less likely to have a college education
than those in the state in general. College-educated voters, whether prosperous or not, gave a disproportionately large vote to Bill Clinton. This is
because college-educated voters are almost universally liberal on religious, social, and cultural questions, a pattern that has begun to affect
American politics in critical ways during the past twenty to thirty years.
Only in Colorado, Idaho, and Wyoming were Perot's strongest supporters
in the counties nearly as well educated as those in the state.

In some states the Perot voters were clearly economically and educa-
tionally disadvantaged, and hence their support represented a classic
protest vote. In states like Arizona, California, Iowa, Montana, Nebraska,
and New York, the Perot counties were more than 20 percent below the
state average in both per capita income and percentage of college-educated
voters. In a few other states one factor or the other looms large. In Georgia, for example, voters in the Perot counties were only half as likely to
have a college education as all of Georgia's voters. The educational level
of the high Perot counties was decidedly below average in Kansas,
Louisiana, Maryland, Minnesota, New Mexico, North Dakota, Ohio, Oregon, Vermont, Washington, and Wisconsin. (See Table 5.)

Perot's voters were, in general, the middle- to lower-middle-income
portion of the Reagan-Bush coalition, who saw their livelihoods recede
during the Bush presidency. These are the forgotten Americans who lack
the income potential and educational skills to compete in a shrinking,
competitive economy. They are fiercely independent and individualistic
folks, who want their vision of the American dream restored. They want the
economy repaired, no matter what it takes, and they want action taken to
achieve it now, not in the distant future. They are cultural and religious
moderates, who are a bit uncomfortable with ideological extremes and dog-
matic positions on the social issues. In the crunch, though, they will oppose
the Religious Right's attempt to ban abortion or to weaken or destroy pub-

Table 5

The Socio-Economic Distress Factor in the Perot Counties*

State	Ratio Per Capita Income	Ratio College Educated	State	Ratio Per Capita Income	Ratio College Educated
AL	99.6%	76.6%	MT	68.6%	73.1%
AK	—	—	NE	61.3%	63.6%
AZ	78.1%	62.6%	NV	88.3%	87.5%
AR	94.2%	73.1%	NH	92.3%	88.2%
CA	78.0%	79.9%	NJ	89.5%	79.1%
CO	85.4%	95.2%	NM	86.9%	63.6%
CT	85.6%	88.2%	NY	76.7%	63.7%
DE	82.1%	64.6%	NC	92.1%	72.7%
FL	82.8%	73.2%	ND	86.6%	67.6%
GA	80.3%	50.0%	OH	87.3%	66.8%
HA	87.9%	75.1%	OK	90.8%	72.2%
ID	91.2%	98.7%	OR	85.1%	67.0%
IL	91.8%	71.6%	PA	88.2%	70.6%
IN	93.7%	77.4%	RI	105.3%	123.4%
IA	77.4%	70.5%	SC	98.3%	82.8%
KS	84.9%	62.9%	SD	84.7%	79.3%
KY	94.6%	70.0%	TN	92.6%	73.0%
LA	89.4%	64.0%	TX	104.6%	88.2%
ME	81.1%	72.2%	UT	102.6%	83.4%
MD	86.0%	65.2%	VT	82.0%	57.4%
MA	89.5%	89.0%	VA	94.2%	79.6%
MI	80.9%	81.1%	WA	82.1%	68.9%
MN	83.1%	62.1%	WV	98.1%	82.7%
MS	99.5%	82.9%	WI	81.9%	66.6%
MO	87.1%	72.3%	WY	97.4%	91.6%

*These figures represent the average per capita income and college education levels of the strongest Perot counties in each state as a percentage of the average per capita income and college education level of the state. For example, the residents of Perot's strongest Arizona counties had a per capita income that was 78.1% of the state average income.

The per capita income ratio is the average per capita income of the strongest Perot counties as a percentage of the state's per capita income. The college educated ratio also represents the average percentage of college educated adults in the Perot counties as a percentage of the statewide percentage of adults who have a college degree.

lic education through religious strife and through attempts to divert funds to private and sectarian schools. Perot's strongest counties and cities in Colorado and Massachusetts, for example, overwhelmingly opposed referendum proposals in 1986 and 1992 for state aid to private and parochial schools. They also favored abortion rights and gay rights.

Table 6

The Perot Fourteen

The Fourteen Counties Carried by Perot

County	State	% Perot	% Clinton	% Bush
Loving	Texas	46.9	20.8	32.3
San Juan	Colorado	40.4	32.5	26.0
Somerset	Maine	39.0	35.1	25.7
Wabaunsee	Kansas	37.2	25.1	37.0
Moffat	Colorado	36.8	27.2	35.5
Piscataquis	Maine	36.8	33.1	29.6
Waldo	Maine	36.2	34.9	28.3
Storey	Nevada	36.2	32.1	30.2
Somervell	Texas	35.2	30.5	34.0
Irion	Texas	34.9	30.8	34.1
Grayson	Texas	34.8	32.7	32.1
Anderson	Kansas	34.8	32.0	33.0
Trinity	California	34.7	32.6	31.3
Jefferson	Kansas	34.0	32.6	33.0
ALL		36.3	33.2	30.5

1988: Bush—57.2%; Dukakis—42.8%

1992 Turnout Increase—20.0%

The fourteen counties that Perot carried (see Table 6) show many of the characteristics that will be discussed in detail in this book. All of them supported George Bush in 1988 and Ronald Reagan in 1984 by margins 3 percent to 6 percent greater than their overall national average. Even in 1988, though, Bush dropped eight percentage points in these counties, compared to a five-point drop nationally, which suggests that some Perot voters in 1992 were not enthusiastic about Bush in 1988.

The Perot counties were more Republican than the nation in all the presidential elections from 1952 to 1988, except in 1964 and 1976. They supported all the winners except in 1960 when Richard Nixon beat John Kennedy 57 percent to 43 percent. That result shows that these counties are more Protestant and less Catholic than the nation. (Religion was the quiet issue in 1960, and the passions that emanated from it distorted the outcome in many states.)

Perot voters tend to reject candidates they regard as extreme. Thus, Lyndon Johnson decisively defeated Barry Goldwater 65 percent to 35 percent in 1964, despite the GOP leanings of the Perot counties. In 1972 Richard Nixon won a 68 percent to 32 percent sweep over George Mc-Govern. The Perot counties do not respond favorably to strongly ideological campaigns waged by the right or left.

In 1976 these counties gave Jimmy Carter a three-point edge over Gerald Ford. This suggests that Carter's image as an outsider may have helped his candidacy in counties that Perot captured a decade and a half later.

The fourteen Perot counties are preponderately rural. Their average per capita income was 80 percent of the national average, and their residents were only 78 percent as likely to be college educated as all American adults.

One additional source of information is the exit-polling data conducted at sample precincts on election day by a consortium of national television networks called Voter Research and Surveys (VRS). Here are some of their findings, as reported by the *New York Times*.

The typical Ross Perot voter was a white male under age forty-five with a family income of $15,000 to $49,000, a high school education, and residence in the West or New England.

Perot received 21 percent support among men and 17 percent among women. This gender difference held in all regions and among all age groups.

He won 20 percent of whites, 16 percent of Asian Americans, 14 percent of Hispanics, and 7 percent of blacks.

There was a significant age factor in Perot's support. His vote decreased as the voter's age increased. He won 22 percent of voters under age thirty, 20 percent of those thirty to forty-four, 19 percent of forty-five-to-fifty-nine-year-olds, but only 12 percent of voters over age sixty. His inability to draw strongly among older voters is also revealed in his lower-than-average 13 percent support among retirees.

In education and income categories Perot did best in the middle or lower middle, rather than at the top or bottom. He did best among the $30,000 to $50,000 income voters and least well among those above $75,000, though the income differences were smaller than the age differences. Perot did well (21 percent) among union households and the unemployed (20 percent), which were both Democratic-leaning groups, and among Republican-leaning homemakers (19 percent).

Perot did better among main-line, nonevangelical Protestants (24 percent), Catholics (20 percent) and the religiously nonaffiliated (20 percent) than he did among white evangelical and fundamentalist Protestants (15 percent) and Jews (10 percent). Perot did exceptionally well among Mormons (25 percent), Lutherans (25 percent) and Catholics of German descent in the Midwest (24 percent) and of French descent in New England (28 percent). He ran ahead of Bush among French Catholics in New England and ahead of Clinton among Mormons.

As might be expected for an outsider candidate, Perot did much better among voters who called themselves Independents, among whom he won 30 percent, than among Republicans (17 percent) or Democrats (13 percent). He attracted many new voters, winning 22 percent of first-time voters. Perot also won the support of 18 percent of those who had voted for Bush in 1988, 11 percent of Dukakis voters, and 20 percent of the so-called Reagan Democrats.

Ideologically, Perot was slightly more popular among those calling themselves moderates (21 percent) than among self-defined liberals (18 percent) or conservatives (17 percent). Ideology was far less important than independence from traditional party identification in the minds of Perot voters.

When data combining ideology and party leaning are considered, the Perot support can be pinpointed even more precisely. He won 30 percent of voters who call themselves moderate or liberal independents, 29 percent of liberal Republicans, and 28 percent of conservative independents. He also did better than average among moderate Republicans (21 percent). He did least well among liberal Democrats (11 percent), conservative Republicans (14 percent), moderate Democrats (14 percent), and conservative Democrats (16 percent).

The VRS data confirm that Perot supporters were concerned about the direction of the economy, which they perceived as deteriorating. He won 37 percent, tying Clinton, among voters who cited the federal budget deficit as their main concern, and 23 percent of those who said the economy and jobs were the primary issues of concern. Perot voters also cited the need for change and the specificity of Perot's plans for the future.

Perot supporters resembled Clinton's in many respects. Very few of either group cited "family values" or foreign policy questions as significant

Table 7

Perot's Second-Place Showings

Number of Counties Where Perot Ran Second

State	To Bush	To Clinton	Total	State	To Bush	To Clinton	Total
California	0	1	1	Nevada	7	0	7
Colorado	10	9	19	New York	2	0	2
Florida	4	0	4	North Dakota	18	0	18
Idaho	26	3	29	Ohio	3	1	4
Indiana	4	0	4*	Oklahoma	9	4	13
Kansas	61	2	63	Oregon	4	2	6
Maine	0	7	7	South Dakota	3	0	3
Massachusetts	0	4	4	Texas	19	6	25
Minnesota	1	5	6	Utah	19	0	19
Missouri	0	5	5	Washington	0	3	3
Montana	19	4	23	Wisconsin	1	0	1
Nebraska	68	0	68	Wyoming	9	0	9
				Totals	287	56	343

*Perot also tied Clinton for second place in Hancock County.

in determining their votes. Only 8 percent of voters who cited abortion as a major issue voted for Perot, probably since the anti-abortion voters went for Bush overwhelmingly and prochoice voters chose Clinton.

The family financial situation of Perot voters was perhaps the major factor in their voting decision. One-fourth of voters who said their family's financial situation was worse today than four years ago voted for Perot, compared to 18 percent who said their income was the same, and 14 percent whose financial situation had improved. Almost 44 percent of Perot's voters said their family financial situation had worsened, compared to 38 percent who said it was about the same and 18 percent who said it had improved. This was almost identical to the portrait of the Clinton voter (48 percent worse, 39 percent same and 14 percent better). Bush's supporters, in contrast, were prosperous, as 42 percent said they were better off and only 13 percent worse off under his administration.

Perot tied for first place in Morris County, Kansas, and tied for second place in Hancock County, Indiana. He ran second in 343 counties, most of them in rural America. (See Table 7.) He ran second in the majority of counties in Idaho, Kansas, Nebraska, and Utah. The Republican tilt to his vote is once again revealed, since he ran second to Bush in 287 counties and to Clinton in fifty-six counties. (This also points up Clinton's weakness in much of the rural West.) Perot ran second in at least one county in twenty-four states, nearly half the nation.

3

Clues from the Past: The Perot Vote and Previous Third-Party Support

Perot showed unusual strength in counties where voters had in the past supported independent or third-party presidential candidates. His appeal seems to have transcended ideology and regionalism. He scored major successes in areas where George Wallace, John Anderson, and Progressive Republicans like Robert LaFollette and Theodore Roosevelt had received disproportionate support.

George Wallace

Conservative populism is a rather vague and amorphous political philosophy that has never actually developed into a coherent political movement. It best describes the political orientation of a segment of the rural South and West. Surfacing during William Jennings Bryan's three presidential campaigns (1896, 1900, and 1908), this political philosophy can best be described as liberal or radical in economic policy, emphasizing the plight of the little guy against large, impersonal, and often distant economic collectives perceived as oppressing him. These voters, on the other hand, often held very conservative social and cultural views stemming from their

35

evangelical and fundamentalist religious backgrounds, and they were occasionally hostile toward blacks, Catholics, Jews, and immigrant groups of
various kinds. Consequently, in the much more politically sophisticated
and complex political system that has developed since World War II, conservative populists don't quite fit in either party nor can they be pigeon-
holed as standard liberals or conservatives.

In 1968 many supporters of Alabama Governor George Wallace, particularly in the North and West, were really conservative populists. Wallace
promised to "send a message" on behalf of the "average American" who
felt oppressed and ignored. While much of his support was racist in orientation, particularly in his home area of the Deep South, some of it was
more complex and rooted in conservative populism. Wallace also presented himself as a law and order candidate—a position Nixon coopted.

Outside the Deep South and the southern-flavored regions of such
border states as Oklahoma, Kentucky, Missouri, and Maryland, Wallace did
surprisingly well. While his vote is often described as high in certain ethnic neighborhoods of large cities, his real strength remained in rural Protestant areas where most voters are native-born Americans of old English
stock. In parts of the South voters also share these sentiments, particularly
in areas like north Alabama and north Mississippi, west Florida, middle
Tennessee, eastern North Carolina, and the northwestern Piedmont region
of South Carolina. These voters supported Wallace for reasons other than
race, though race and opposition to the civil rights movement were certainly major factors. Many of these regions had gone for Democrat Lyndon
Johnson rather than Republican Barry Goldwater in 1964, which made
them somewhat different from the Old South backlash areas, which had
bolted to Goldwater. Many of the counties in west Florida's conservative
rural panhandle region, for example, had supported liberal-populist Claude
Pepper for the U.S. Senate in 1950 and 1958 while also supporting segregationist candidates for governor throughout the 1950s and 1960s. It is this
unusual combination of sentiments that gave Wallace such an impressive
vote throughout the South and border states, but also a generally unnoticed
and often forgotten vote throughout the West and Midwest.

What does all this have to do with the Ross Perot campaign of 1992?
Perot condemned racism and in one of the national debates made the com-
ment, "If you hate anybody, I don't want your vote." Still, one of the more

Table 8
Perot Strength in High Nonsouthern Wallace Counties
Top Wallace Counties Outside the South and Border

County	State	% Wallace 1968	%Perot 1992
Esmeralda	NV	27.5	37.7
Warren	OH	25.4	21.1
Mineral	NV	24.4	28.2
Clermont	OH	24.1	22.3
Nye	NV	24.1	31.2
Custer	ID	23.0	33.7
Brown	OH	21.7	24.2
Lemhi	ID	21.0	30.8
Alexander	IL	20.8	10.9
Gooding	ID	20.4	28.6

extraordinary findings of this study is how well Perot did in Wallace strongholds outside the South. There were 123 counties in eighteen states where Wallace exceeded his national support of 13.5 percent in 1968. These counties are mostly in Ohio, Idaho, Indiana, Kansas, Illinois, and Colorado. There are also a few counties in Arizona, Delaware, Michigan, Nebraska, New Jersey, New Mexico, Pennsylvania, Utah, Washington, West Virginia, and Wisconsin. In 1992 Ross Perot exceeded his national average in 105 of these counties. In other words, in 85 percent of the counties outside the South where George Wallace did unusually well in 1968, Ross Perot did unusually well in 1992. (See Table 8.)

In some states the highest Perot county was also the highest Wallace county. In Esmeralda County, Nevada, for example, Perot took 38 percent of the vote. This was his best county in the state and he lost to George Bush by only one vote. George Wallace received 28 percent of the votes cast here in 1988, and tiny Esmeralda County was Wallace's best county in the nation outside of the South. The pattern is repeated elsewhere. In certain Colorado counties (Teller, Dolores, and San Juan) Wallace and Perot had some of their best showings in that region. In Idaho the top-four Wallace counties (Custer, Lemhi, Gooding, and Minidoka) were also in the top ten for Perot.

Even in counties where Wallace just missed his 13.5 percent, there are some striking similarities. In Trinity County, California, in the northern part

of the state, Perot was the winner. This was one of the fourteen counties
across the nation that he carried in the 1992 election. It was also Wallace's
best county in the state in 1968. Perot's number-one county in Wyoming,
Sublette, was also Wallace's number-one county. Even in Iowa, where racial
and cultural conflicts were somewhat minimal, Wallace's best county—
Mills County, a Republican stronghold in the southwestern part of the state—
was also Perot's best county. In Kansas, Perot's best county, Jefferson—a
longtime Republican stronghold which he carried, has long had a considerable conservative populist orientation. It was the third-highest county in the
state for Wallace. Wallace's two best counties in Montana, Garfield and Lincoln, both gave Perot more than 30 percent of their votes. Garfield County
was Perot's second-highest Montana county. Perot's best county in New
Jersey, Salem County—a poor area in the southern part of the state with a
somewhat southern orientation—was Wallace's second-best county. Douglas
County, Oregon, the center of the state's logging industry, was Wallace's banner county, and Perot did very well there, winning 27 percent. In Wisconsin
Wallace's best county was Taylor County. It was Perot's fourth-highest
county in the state and one of Perot's best showings in the Midwest. In Utah
both Wallace and Perot came in second in Kane County. This unusual connection between two seemingly unrelated candidacies is an important clue
to understanding the voting behavior of many disaffected Americans.

Even in the Deep South there are occasional connections. As a general
rule Perot did not do well in the Wallace strongholds of the Deep South,
where voters may have seen Wallace solely in terms of racial protest and/or
southern pride. Perot won only 12.5 percent, or about one out of eight
votes, in the top-twenty Wallace counties. These counties are almost all in
rural Alabama and Mississippi except for one small county, Holmes, in
west Florida and Echols in Georgia, a small county on the Florida border.
As it turns out, however, Echols County was Perot's best county in Georgia, giving the Texan 26 percent. Echols County was also Wallace's best
county in the state. Nearby Miller County, Georgia, was Wallace's second-
best and Perot's third-best county. In Holmes County, Florida, Perot won
22 percent, above his national and state averages.

Most of the top Wallace counties in Alabama and Mississippi, however, went for George Bush. In these top-twenty Wallace counties Bush
won 51 percent, Clinton 36 percent, and Perot, as mentioned, 12.5 percent.

Table 9
Perot and the Wallace Vote in the South
Nine Southern States Where Wallace Won a Majority of the
Total Vote in at Least Four Counties.

State	% Perot in Wallace Strongholds (1968)	% Perot Statewide (1992)
AL	13.0	10.8
AR	9.8	10.4
FL	24.2	19.8
GA	18.0	13.3
LA	14.1	11.8
MS	10.8	8.7
NC	14.0	13.7
SC	15.0	11.5
TN	12.3	10.1

Table 10
1992 Presidential Vote in the 1968 Wallace Strongholds

Locations	% Bush	% Clinton	% Perot
Top 20 counties (all states)	51.1	36.4	12.5
Strongest Wallace Counties			
By State:			
MS	54.7	34.5	10.8
SC	49.8	35.2	15.0
AL	49.0	38.0	13.0
LA	44.8	41.1	14.1
FL	43.0	32.8	24.2
NC	40.2	45.8	14.0
GA	38.7	43.3	18.0
TN	37.7	50.0	12.3
AR	31.8	58.4	9.8

But it may be worth noting that Perot did better in eighteen of these twenty counties than he did in the states of Mississippi, Alabama, Florida and Georgia. So even in this region of the nation, where racial voting and religious conservatism have shaped the political culture in recent years, Perot did slightly better in the Wallace counties than he did statewide. For example, Perot's fifth-best Alabama county, Dale, was in the top-twenty Wallace counties in the entire nation and the top-ten in Alabama. George County, Mississippi, was Perot's fifth-best county in that state and Wallace's second-best county in the entire nation, giving Wallace 91 percent of its 1968 ballots. George County is also unusual in that 15 percent of its 1992 vote went for right-wing splinter parties, suggesting that right-wing individualism is still strong there. In summary, Perot ran stronger in the top Wallace counties in most southern states than he did in counties where Wallace was weaker. (See Tables 9 and 10.)

There were a few areas where there was not a strong connection between Perot and Wallace. This was particularly true in southern Illinois in the so-called Egypt counties of Alexander, Pulaski, and Massac. These were Wallace's best counties in 1968 and they were the three worst Perot counties in 1992. The same was true to some extent in the Wallace strongholds in southwestern Ohio and in the blue-collar suburbs of Cincinnati (Warren and Clairmont counties), where Perot did not do quite as well as Wallace. But looking at the pattern in national terms suggests a strong coincidence of political interest, stemming perhaps as much from what voters read into candidates as from what candidates themselves espouse. Perot was clearly a man for all seasons. Voters apparently read into him what they wished to see and projected some of their beliefs onto his candidacy. This is one explanation for why he did so well at various ends of the spectrum, winning a higher than average vote, for example, among conservative Mormons and Lutherans, and among the more liberal nonreligious voters.

John Anderson

Not only did Perot do well in counties that gave disproportionate support to George Wallace in 1968 but he attracted a great many votes in counties where John Anderson had achieved his best returns in 1980. In the top-fifty Anderson counties—all in New England or the West—Perot equalled or exceeded his national support level in 92 percent of them (46). Only in three college-oriented counties in Iowa and Illinois and in Windham County, Vermont, did Perot fall short. But in most of the others, Perot did very well, including a victory in San Juan County, Colorado, and support in excess of 30 percent in Colorado's Summit and Eagle Counties. Moreover, Perot was stronger than Anderson in forty-six of the fifty Anderson bailiwicks. So even where Anderson polled strongly in 1980, Perot did better in 1992.

These Perot-Anderson counties tended to vote Democratic in 1992, partly as a result of the Perot appeal. George Bush carried only three of the counties, while Bill Clinton won forty-six of them and Perot, one. Four years before, Bush had carried twenty-five of them. Ronald Reagan won forty-six of them in 1984 and forty-one of them in 1980. Even in 1976 Gerald Ford carried thirty-five of these counties, which was a better showing in defeat than Bush had achieved in victory in 1988.

Voters who were attracted to Anderson were disproportionately well educated, had high incomes, and were often involved in high-tech or entrepreneurial enterprises. Historically, they were likely to be liberal or moderate Republicans, though some liberal Democrats had also opted for Anderson rather than Carter. The Republican party's ties to the Religious Right, its increasing unpopularity among environmentalists, and its economic record caused strong erosions in those areas where Anderson received his greatest support. Even in 1988 George Bush could win only half of these counties, far fewer than such losing GOP candidates as Gerald Ford in 1976, Richard Nixon in 1960, and Thomas Dewey in 1948 had won. Twenty-one of these fifty counties switched from Reagan in 1984 to Dukakis in 1988. By 1992 the erosion was complete.

John Anderson's supporters might best be described as liberal populists, who placed considerable trust in participatory democracy. George Wallace's supporters were conservative populists, particularly in the West, and while neither had much in common, both were disproportionately attracted to the Perot candidacy. Perhaps their independent spirit was a common factor. Individuals who are willing to break with the established pattern of the two-party system are perhaps more inclined than other voters to remain open to third-party alternatives in the future.

Perot's voter appeal had almost a fusion quality about it, an ability to attract quite different kinds of voters to a specific cause or for a specified goal. Wallace voters were largely conservative southern or western Democrats in transition to the Republican party. Anderson voters were generally progressive Republicans in transition to the Democratic party, which is the reason that about 70 percent of them (including Anderson himself) voted for Mondale over Reagan in 1984, according to network exit polls. (There are no data for 1988, but I would guess Anderson voters would have supported Dukakis overwhelmingly.)

By no means did a majority or even a plurality of Anderson or Wallace voters support Perot in 1992, but it is likely that more than 25 percent of both sets of voters did so. I would guess that 30 percent of Anderson voters supported Perot, while 65 percent wanted Clinton, and 5 percent voted for Bush. (My estimate for nonsouthern Wallace voters would be Bush, 40 percent; Clinton, 35 percent; and Perot, 25 percent.)

One final clue to the kind of coalition that Perot built comes from another third-party candidate in 1980: Ed Clark of the Libertarian party. Clark's appeal, such as it was, was strongest in the West and among young male and affluent voters. Alaska was his main stronghold, where he won almost 12 percent of the total vote and ran ahead of Anderson. Clark ran second to Ronald Reagan in District 6, a rural area north of Anchorage. This political unknown outpolled President Jimmy Carter in this individualistic outback. In 1992 this area (now District 28) was Ross Perot's number-one Alaska stronghold. Perot carried the area with 40 percent to Bush's 35 percent and Clinton's 22 percent.

Perot clearly appeals to voters who want alternatives to the two-party system and who favor structural reforms in it, e.g., term limitations. His appeal to Alaska conservatives and to Anderson-type liberal independents suggests considerable potential trouble for both the Democrats and Republicans.

The Progressive Republican Tradition

The old Progressive Republican tradition in the Midwest and Far West emphasized government intervention in the economy to bring about greater social justice and equality of opportunity, opposed monopolies, and favored various reforms in political life. Progressive Republicans were suspicious of foreign-policy entanglement and opposed to U.S. military intervention overseas except when the nation was threatened. The heroes of this tradition were President Theodore Roosevelt and Wisconsin Senator Robert LaFollette, both of whom were supported enthusiastically in the 1912 and 1924 presidential elections.

While all this may seem a distant memory from the perspective of 1992, it is not irrelevant. There is a surprising continuity in U.S. politics, especially in stable regions like the small-town West, where voters have long memories, and long-established political habits die hard, if at all.

Thus, in 1992, it should not be surprising that Perot did exceptionally well in the bastions of Progressive Republicanism. Of the 109 counties in eleven states (Idaho, Iowa, Minnesota, Montana, Nebraska, Nevada, North Dakota, South Dakota, Texas, Washington, and Wisconsin), which supported *both* Roosevelt in 1912 *and* LaFollette in 1924, Perot exceeded his national vote-support average in 91.7 percent of them (100). Perot's support topped 30 percent in seventeen of these counties, and was near 30 percent in many others. He ran second in a number of them.

Voters in strongholds of Progressive Republicanism moved en masse to the Democrats in 1932, when Franklin D. Roosevelt carried all 109 of these counties. But as early as 1936, a few of them drifted back to the Republicans, and more did so during the era of Eisenhower's modern Republicanism. Since the 1960s elections in these counties have been closely contested between Democrats and Republicans but, in common with much of small-town America, voters in these areas have leaned somewhat to the Republicans.

When the GOP nominates candidates seen as reactionary or incompetent, however, voters from this tradition will refuse to support them. Bill Clinton won fifty-seven of these counties to George Bush's fifty-two. This was especially true in Wisconsin and Minnesota, but also to some degree in Montana, Washington, and South Dakota. The combined anti-incumbent vote for Clinton and Perot swept over the old Roosevelt-LaFollette basin like a tidal wave, leaving George Bush the clear majority winner in only eight of the 109 counties.

It may be that Perot's relative success among these voters had something to do with their willingness to buck the two-party system earlier in the century. But it may just have something to do with Perot's unique combination of policy positions, since these Progressive Republicans did not respond enthusiastically to recent third-party nominees George Wallace or John Anderson (though Anderson had pockets of support).

William Lemke

On some issues there was a similarity between the Perot campaign and that of the 1936 Union party candidate, William Lemke of North Dakota. Lemke was a kind of populist, nationalist, and isolationist who won 2 percent of the national vote against Franklin Roosevelt and Alfred Landon. In a dozen or so counties, populated largely by German Catholics and Scandinavian Lutherans, Lemke won 16 percent to 21 percent of the vote. In all twelve of those counties, Perot exceeded both his national and statewide average vote.

In North Dakota Lemke's vote was more of a hometown phenomenon than an ideological one. He won a third of the vote in Burke and Williams counties, and a fourth or more in another eight counties. His North Dakota support was also disproportionately Norwegian and German. Perot also did well, exceeding his state and national support in ten of the twelve strongest Lemke counties in North Dakota. Perot's average support in the Lemke counties of North Dakota was 26.7 percent, compared to 23.1 percent statewide.

Certain demographic and economic factors, intrinsic to the changing American economy of the 1980s and 1990s, also played a role in predisposing certain groups toward the independent candidacy of Ross Perot.

4

Other Clues to High Perot Support

High Population Growth

One final clue to areas where Perot's support exceeded his national average was his unusual strength in another traditionally Republican region: the high population growth areas.

In all regions of the country, Perot's vote exceeded 19 percent in those counties where the population grew the most during the 1980s. This suggests that Perot did well among voters who do not have strong political roots or attachments as they move to different counties or regions. Perot's support reached 28 percent in the south central (mainly Texas) region and topped 25 percent in the bustling Northwest, the staid and stable Midwest, and the booming Southwest. But he also received 23 percent of the votes cast in the high-growth areas of the Northeast and 20 percent in similar areas of the Southeast. Nationally, he received one-fourth of the vote in the fastest-growing counties which, since the 1960s, have always been more Republican than the nation. And while Bush edged Clinton by about 40 percent to 35 percent, the strong competitive majority normally given to Republican presidential candidates in high-growth areas almost vanished in 1992. Bush ran only two percentage points above his national average in counties where Republicans usually run ten points or more ahead of their national support. (See Table 11.)

Table 11
Perot's Support in High Population
Growth Areas by Region*

Region	% Perot
South Central	28.4
Northwest	27.1
Midwest	25.8
Southwest	25.1
Northeast	22.9
Southeast	19.7
Nation	24.9

*This geographical breakdown was devised by Mark T. Mattson in his *Atlas of the 1990 Census* (New York: Macmillan, 1992). It is slightly different from the U.S. Census Bureau's classification.

The Migration Factor

As we have seen, Perot seemed to do unusually well in those regions of the country where a large portion of the population were born elsewhere, or were recent migrants. This lack of community roots turns up as a curious factor in the level of support given to Perot. Consider this fact: Perot exceeded his national average in *all ten* states that have the lowest percentage of their population born in the state. In contrast he exceeded his national vote in only three* of the ten states with the highest percent of its population born there, and he barely did so in Michigan. (See Table 12.)

Perot also received an impressive 26.2 percent of the votes cast in the top-ten, high-growth retirement counties, reaching 31.3 percent in Mohave County, Arizona, which has the highest growth rate of retirees of any U.S. county.

*Wisconsin, Michigan, Ohio

Table 12
Percent of Population Born in State of Residence, 1990
Nation: 61.8 percent

State	%	State	%
Pennsylvania	80.2	Texas	64.7
Louisiana	79.0	Georgia	64.5
Iowa	77.6	Oklahoma	63.5
Kentucky	77.4	Rhode Island	63.4
Mississippi	77.3	Kansas	61.3
West Virginia	77.3	Montana	58.9
Wisconsin	76.4	Vermont	57.2
Alabama	75.9	Connecticut	57.0
Michigan	74.9	Hawaii	56.1
Ohio	74.1	New Jersey	54.8
Minnesota	73.6	Virginia	54.2
North Dakota	73.2	New Mexico	51.7
Indiana	71.1	Idaho	50.6
North Carolina	70.4	Delaware	50.2
South Dakota	70.2	Maryland	49.8
Nebraska	70.2	Washington	48.2
Missouri	69.6	Oregon	46.6
Tennessee	69.2	California	46.4
Illinois	69.1	New Hampshire	44.1
Massachusetts	68.7	Colorado	43.3
Maine	68.5	Wyoming	42.6
South Carolina	68.4	Arizona	34.2
New York	67.5	Alaska	34.0
Utah	67.2	Florida	30.5
Arkansas	67.1	Nevada	21.8

The Farm Vote

Perot did quite well among farmers and those who earn their income from manufacturing. In a study of representative counties of both types, the percentage of people who voted for him went beyond his national average. Perot won 21.2 percent of the vote in the twenty-five counties where the highest percentage of the population is engaged in agriculture. These twenty-five counties, located in twelve states, often move somewhat against the national trend, though they have given majorities to most Republican presidential candidates since 1940. Only Harry Truman in 1948 and Lyndon Johnson in 1964 were able to eke out small majorities. And, in Johnson's case, his 52 percent of the vote was a good deal below his national strength. In fact, no Democrat has run stronger among farmers than among all voters since 1932. The Democrats' image as the party of urban and multicultural interests has tended to depress the party's fortunes among the largely white Protestant farm community. Adlai Stevenson in 1956 and Harry Truman in 1948 came close to achieving parity among these voters. In Stevenson's case, there was a full-fledged farm revolt against Eisenhower's farm policies, personified by Secretary of Agriculture Ezra Taft Benson.* In his 1960 campaign against John F. Kennedy Nixon equalled Eisenhower's vote, owing to the intense anti-Catholicism in rural areas.

Since the late 1960s, farm areas have favored the Republicans, though Jimmy Carter, a Georgia peanut farmer himself, won 49 percent in 1976, which fell only 2 percent short of his national support. George Wallace received 13.7 percent in 1968, which was equal to his national vote, though his support was regional. Southern farm counties gave Wallace 45 percent, while those in the Midwest and West gave him only 8 percent. Southern farmers also backed Carter in both 1976 and 1980, but he ran poorly among nonsouthern farmers.

In 1988 Bush won easily, 60 percent to 40 percent over Dukakis, though Dukakis made a ten-percentage-point gain over Mondale among Western farmers compared to a meager two-point gain among southern farmers.

In 1992 Bush fell to 48.3 percent in these counties while Clinton won 30.5 percent and Perot 21.2 percent, the latter exceeding his national average. Perot's farm support was high in the West and Midwest, where he received 25.4 percent, more than Clinton's 23.9 percent. Bush still held a majority, with 50.7 percent. Southern farmers were only half as likely to support Perot, who won 13.6 percent compared to Bush's 44 percent and Clinton's 42.4 percent. These regional tilts to the Perot vote were clearly evident among farmers and agricultural workers.

One warning emerges from the data. Clinton's western farm support—less than one out of four votes—was the lowest level received by a Democratic presidential candidate since 1924. Perot's second-place showing was the strongest support for a third-party candidate since Robert LaFol-

---

*Farm income declined during the Eisenhower years, and farmers felt neglected by Eisenhower's pro-big-business policies.

lette's outstanding 1924 vote in these areas. Clinton may have suffered because of attacks on his draft record, personal life, or cultural liberalism.

Indeed, Clinton dropped nearly as many percentage points (9.5) as did Bush (11.7 percent) in the nation's premier farm counties. This dissatisfaction allowed Perot to take Democratic as well as Republican votes in the farm belt.

The Manufacturing Vote

Perot won almost 21 percent of the votes cast in the twenty-five counties in sixteen states where the highest percentage of the work force is engaged in manufacturing. His vote in these counties came entirely at the expense of Bush, who declined from 63.2 percent to 42.5 percent. Clinton and Dukakis both received 37 percent. Perot stressed jobs and castigated the Bush administration for allowing so many U.S. jobs to be lost to foreign competition. That message hit home to a considerable number of voters in the manufacturing belt.

Perot received almost 31 percent of the vote in Sagadahoc County, Maine, and 29 percent in Box Elder County, Utah (where Bush had topped 80 percent in 1988). Perot's 28 percent in Elk County, Pennsylvania, was his highest statewide support, while his 24 percent of the vote in Kendall County, Illinois, represented his second-best county showing. And his 22 percent in Hancock County, West Virginia, a Democratic Catholic stronghold, was his third-best result in the mountain state.

In all, Perot made a strong national showing among voters whose livelihoods are closely linked to manufacturing and who had supported recent Republican presidential candidates.

The German-Americans

Perot scored major gains among German-Americans, who reside mostly in the rural Midwest, have modest socioeconomic status, and a progressive populist heritage, which favors government that works on behalf of average Americans to achieve justice and fairness. German-Americans, who may number nearly 60 million people, are America's largest ethnic group, though they are so well integrated into American life one hardly notices them as a political force anymore. Their curious blend of progressivism in domestic affairs and isolationism or protectionism in foreign policy made them ideal recruits for the Perot campaign.

In the past, German-Americans were likely to be the progressive Republicans, who soured on the GOP in the 1920s, bolting to Robert LaFollette in 1924 and even to Democrat Al Smith in 1928. Religion shaped the 1928 vote, and, while Smith did not win a majority of the German vote, he came close, sweeping the Catholics and winning a surprising Lutheran vote. Only among the non-Lutheran Protestants (Reformed and Methodist voters generally) did Hoover win convincingly.

Germans went to Roosevelt by a landslide in 1932 and by a somewhat reduced margin in 1936, as some conservatives switched to Alf Landon. Many German Catholics voted for Lemke, the extreme-right candidate, who received 2 percent nationally but almost 20 percent in some Catholic German counties.

In 1940 Wendell Wilkie, himself a German American from Indiana, won a landslide against FDR throughout Teutonic America. His vote reached 93 percent in McIntosh County, North Dakota, for example, and he gained up to 50 percentage points in other German areas. Thus were German Americans expressing their fear of and opposition to another war with Germany. This revolt against the Democrats has continued for a half century. While Harry Truman did much better in 1948 than FDR in 1940 or 1944, carrying some of the German Catholic counties, the Democratic vote has lagged behind the national norm. Dwight Eisenhower, of Swiss-German ancestry, won 75 percent of the German American vote. Nixon led Kennedy easily. And though German Catholics favored JFK, the Massachusetts senator did not run as strongly as Al Smith. Only in 1964 did German voters desert Goldwater, and Johnson became the first Democrat since FDR in 1936 to win their vote. Jimmy Carter did unusually well in 1976, but extremely poorly in 1980. Reagan and Bush, on the other hand, swept through the German-American communities with ease.

In 1992 economic revolt was again in the air, and George Bush lost ground to Ross Perot throughout German America. In the forty strongest German-American counties, Perot won a solid 25.4 percent of the vote, while Bush was reduced to a plurality of 43.7 percent and Clinton limped in with 30.9 percent. Bush's vote was the lowest since Goldwater, and Clinton's vote ranked below the normal Democratic support among these voters. Clinton carried only seven of those counties, which was more than Dukakis's three, but Clinton's popular vote declined, especially in places like Carroll County, Iowa, where he received 3,800 votes to Dukakis's 5,437.

German Americans had voted 60 percent to 40 percent for Bush over Dukakis in 1988. Thus, when the 1992 vote was tallied, Bush dropped sixteen points and Clinton dropped nine points. So even with a decline in strength, Clinton was relatively stronger than Dukakis, gaining about 3.6 percent. Clearly, a majority of Perot's German voters had supported Bush in the previous election. Turnout increased 11.4 percent in most German counties, a bit below the national increase of 14 percent for voters going to the polls in 1992.

Looking at the German-American vote from a different perspective reveals the depth and breadth of the Perot constituency. There are fifteen states that have a significant number of well-defined German-American counties and where the statewide population ranks high in German-Americans. Perot did well in all of these states. (See Table 13.) In all but South Dakota, where his German-American support was equal to his statewide support, Perot received a higher percentage of the German-American vote

Table 13
German-American Vote by State

State	% Perot in German Counties	% Perot Statewide	Difference
Colorado	25.1	23.3	+1.8
Illinois	20.3	16.6	+3.7
Indiana	20.9	19.8	+1.1
Iowa	22.6	18.7	+3.9
Kansas	31.7	27.0	+4.7
Minnesota	28.1	24.0	+4.1
Missouri	25.7	21.7	+4.0
Montana	29.2	26.1	+3.1
Nebraska	28.4	23.6	+4.8
North Dakota	27.1	23.1	+4.0
Ohio	25.1	21.0	+4.1
Pennsylvania	20.4	18.2	+2.2
South Dakota	21.8	21.8	0
Texas	23.0	22.0	+1.0
Wisconsin	24.9	21.5	+3.4

than the overall statewide percentage. The German-American vote was 4 percent or more higher than the total state support in Kansas, Minnesota, Missouri, Nebraska, North Dakota, and Ohio. Furthermore, Perot exceeded 25 percent among Germans in these six states plus Colorado and Montana. Nowhere did he fall below 20 percent, even in his weakest states, Illinois and Pennsylvania. Perot's strongest showing among German-Americans came in Kansas, where he won 31.7 percent and ran second to Bush. He also ran second to Bush in Nebraska and almost did so in North Dakota.

Perot clearly cut into the Bush vote. Only in Texas did German-Americans give a majority to Bush, though Bush had won a majority in fourteen of the fifteen states in which this group played a significant role in 1988. In five states (Iowa, Kansas, Minnesota, Missouri, and Montana) Bush's vote plummeted below 40 percent.

Bill Clinton did not do particularly well, either. He edged Bush only in economically hard-hit Iowa, but he had poorer support in the Hawkeye State than Dukakis, where a majority of German-American Perot voters had supported the former governor of Massachusetts in 1988. Clinton failed to win even 40 percent among this ethnic group in any state, and less than 30 percent in Nebraska, North Dakota, Ohio, and Texas.

Among their other attributes, German-Americans are highly religious in a formal sense. The vast majority of residents of these counties belong to some church—usually Lutheran, Catholic, United Church of Christ, or Methodist.

Conservative Populism

Another kind of conservative populism—separate from the support for George Wallace—is represented, in the minds of many voters at least, by Harry Truman and Barry Goldwater. Counties that supported both the Democratic winner in 1948 and the Republican loser in 1964 can be said to exhibit conservative populist characteristics. (For this analysis the South has been eliminated, because race and civil rights issues were the overshadowing issues in that region in 1964, and the Truman counties that defected to Goldwater in places like Georgia, west Florida, and south Virginia demonstrated a political dynamic quite different from other regions.)

There were, in fact, thirty-two counties in thirteen states from Arizona to Maryland that supported Truman and Goldwater. In these, Ross Perot exceeded his national support in 85 percent of them (27 counties) and even topped 30 percent of the vote in five. George Bush won a majority in only ten, mostly in Oklahoma, and Bill Clinton carried two in Arizona. Perot garnered considerable support in these swing counties, and he ran second in fourteen of them.

One can argue that most Truman supporters who were alive in 1964 voted for the Democratic standard-bearer Lyndon Johnson. But not all voters have a coherent ideology; many are attracted by personality, style, and instinctive symbolism. President Truman, though he was the incumbent in 1948, was the underdog who structured his campaign as a fight for the oppressed common man against the economic establishment. And that appeal worked in countless small towns and farming areas in the less prosperous regions of the country.

Barry Goldwater, though his views were far to the right of Truman's, was seen by some as an outsider willing to challenge a new liberal establishment. Various kinds of issues go into the mix called conservative populism, including an aggressive U.S. posture in foreign policy and a disinclination to help minority groups at home.

The Daniel Elazar Thesis

In his book *The American Mosaic: The Impact of Space, Time and Culture on American Politics*, Daniel J. Elazar writes:

> The national political culture of the U.S. is itself a synthesis of three major political subcultures. These subcultures jointly inhabit the country, existing side by side or sometimes overlapping one another. All three are of nationwide proportions . . . yet each subculture is strongly tied to specific sections of the country, reflecting the streams and currents of migration that have carried people of different origins and backgrounds across the continent in more or less orderly patterns. . . . These cultural patterns give each state its particular character to help determine the tone of its fundamental relationship, as a state, to the nation.*

---

*Daniel J. Elazar, *The American Mosaic: The Impact of Space, Time and Culture on American Politics* (Boulder, Colo.: Westview Press, 1994), pp. 229, 282.

Elazar, director of the Center for the Study of Federalism at Temple University, defines his three regions as moralistic, individualistic, and traditionalistic.

The moralistic political culture roughly coincides with upper New England, the upper Midwest, and the Pacific Coast region. Elazar says,

> The moralistic political culture emphasizes the commonwealth conception as the basis for democratic government. . . . In the moralistic political culture both the general public and the politicians conceive of politics as a public activity centered on some notion of the public good and properly devoted to the advancement of the public interest. Good government is measured by the degree to which it promotes the public good and in terms of the honesty, selflessness and commitment to the public welfare of those who govern.*

The individualistic political culture, found in the Mid-Atlantic, Midwest, and lower New England regions, "emphasizes the conception of the democratic order as a marketplace. It is rooted in the view that government is instituted for strictly utilitarian reasons."†

The traditionalistic political culture is based in the South and the southern-oriented states of Oklahoma, Kentucky and West Virginia, as well as Arizona and New Mexico. About them Elazar observes, "The traditional political culture is rooted in an ambivalent attitude toward the marketplace coupled with a paternalistic and elitist conception of the commonwealth. It reflects an older precommercial attitude that accepts a substantially hierarchical society as part of the ordered nature of things."‡

The Elazar thesis is an intriguing and stimulating way of looking at politics, though it is not without its flaws. Elazar admits that many states are themselves in flux and exhibit characteristics across the tripartite lines he has established. Illinois and Ohio, for example, have counties that exhibit different cultural characteristics.

Applying the 1992 presidential vote to this paradigm or model reveals some striking findings, especially as it pertains to the Perot vote. (See Tables 14 and 15.)

---

*Elazar, *The American Mosaic*.
†Ibid.
‡Ibid.

Table 14
States Classified by the Elazar Thesis

Moralistic (17)	Individualistic (17)	Traditionalistic (16)
California	Alaska	Alabama
Colorado	Connecticut	Arizona
Idaho	Delaware	Arkansas
Iowa	Hawaii	Florida
Kansas	Indiana	Georgia
Maine	Illinois	Kentucky
Michigan	Maryland	Louisiana
Minnesota	Massachusetts	Mississippi
Montana	Missouri	New Mexico
New Hampshire	Nebraska	North Carolina
North Dakota	Nevada	Oklahoma
Oregon	New Jersey	South Carolina
South Dakota	New York	Tennessee
Utah	Ohio	Texas
Vermont	Pennsylvania	Virginia
Washington	Rhode Island	West Virginia
Wisconsin	Wyoming	

Perot did best in the moralistic political culture, receiving 22.1 percent of the ballots cast. He did least well among the traditionalists, with 16.4 percent, and his support was average, at 18.6 percent, in the individualistic states.

In sharp contrast to Perot, Bush did best in the traditionalistic culture, winning 42.3 percent and edging out Bill Clinton by one percentage point.

Bill Clinton's strongest support came in the individualistic culture, where he won 45.3 percent and beat Bush by nine percentage points. Clinton's vote had the best overall shape, since he also defeated Bush by eight points in the moralistic culture. Clinton's vote varied least within these three regions of political culture. Only four percentage points separated his best and worst regions. Perot's vote varied by almost six percentage points, while Bush's vote varied by almost seven and a half points, clearly indicating that Bush's political base had narrowed to one type of political culture.

These 1992 results indicate how much American politics has changed in the past several decades. At one time the moralistic culture was the most likely to be Republican; today, it is least likely to be so. Considering the

Table 15
Presidential Vote by Political Culture

Type of Culture	% Perot	% Clinton	% Bush
Moralistic	22.1	42.9	34.9
Individualistic	18.6	45.3	36.1
Traditionalistic	16.4	41.3	42.3

Republican party's historic image as a moralistic party, prone to supporting abolitionism, Prohibition, and, now, school prayer and the banning of abortion, this is surprising. It may be that moralism is seen differently by the electorate. The Republican brand of moralism is highly privatized and directed toward personal morality and individual ethical behavior. Republicans are far less likely to support "moralistic" economic and public policies, relating to public ownership of utilities, regulations on business enterprises, or restrictions on commercial profit. It may also be likely that voters in the moralistic culture see the Republicans as more likely to be corrupt in the public realm. This is not the place to apportion partisan blame, but most historians regard three Republican national administrations, those of Grant, Harding, and Nixon, as the most corrupt. Some would argue that the Iran-Contra scandal and an unusual number of cabinet resignations during the Reagan-Bush years are symptomatic of continuing problems in the Republican camp. Many voters, on the other hand, like to emphasize Democratic scandals in some large cities, statehouses, and in Congress. The Republicans, however, have fallen to a historic low in the moralistic culture where Perot was found to be most attractive. Perot's relative weakness in traditionalistic areas may relate partially to the stronger political-party traditions in that group.

Elazar forecasts "an overall shift of American national political culture in a moralistic direction. This shift is evidenced by the new standards of public and private rectitude demanded of politicians."*

---

*Elazar, *The American Mosaic*, p. 285.

Part Two

Perot's Impact on the 1992 Election

1

Perot and the Republicans

There is no doubt that Perot's candidacy harmed the Republicans more than the Democrats. Consider the following facts as evidence:

• The fourteen counties that Perot carried had all gone for Bush in 1988. This time around, Bush ran third in the aggregate vote. Bush dropped twenty-seven percentage points and the Democrats, now represented by Clinton, lost ten percentage points, compared to their 1988 showing. The total voter turnout shot up by 20 percent.

• There were 181 counties in which Perot's vote was approximately 30 percent or higher, but where he was not the winner. In these counties he captured 32.2 percent of the vote, second to Bush's 36.3 percent. Bill Clinton won 31.5 percent in these areas. Bush's support declined twenty-three percentage points from 1988 while the Democrats led by Clinton lost nine points. Only ten of these counties had supported Dukakis in 1988, while in 1992 forty-two went for Clinton. The higher the Perot vote, the greater was the damage to Bush.

• Of the twenty-six counties in which Bush dropped from first place in 1988 to third place in 1992, Perot received 34 percent of the total vote and carried seven of the counties. Clinton captured 37 percent, winning nineteen counties, while Bush plunged to 29 percent.

Table 16
Presidential Vote Change 1988–1992
in Perot County Strongholds

State	% Change in Republican Vote	% Change in Democratic Vote	State	% Change in Republican Vote	% Change in Democratic Vote
AL	−17.3	+ 1.6	MT	−22.3	−10.8
AK	NA	NA	NE	−19.2	−13.0
AZ	−25.6	− 3.6	NV	−29.2	− 4.5
AR	−25.8	+ 9.5	NH	−26.7	+ 1.6
CA	−21.9	− 7.3	NJ	−21.3	0
CO	−25.7	− 7.5	NM	−19.8	− 1.0
CT	−20.8	− 6.6	NY	−19.5	− 9.8
DE	−22.5	− 1.0	NC	−17.9	+ .4
FL	−27.3	− .7	ND	−20.6	−11.8
GA	−23.2	+ 3.4	OH	−22.0	− 6.2
HA	−11.3	− 6.6	OK	−18.9	− 9.7
ID	−24.0	−10.0	OR	−16.7	−13.1
IL	−22.4	− 1.2	PA	−21.0	− 3.7
IN	−20.6	− 5.0	RI	−17.3	− 8.0
IA	−12.9	−12.7	SC	−16.9	+ 2.0
KS	−22.5	−12.0	SD	−17.0	−11.3
KY	−17.0	− 2.9	TN	−21.1	+ 6.9
LA	−13.4	− 2.7	TX	−25.7	− 8.3
ME	−29.8	− 8.0	UT	−26.8	− 7.6
MD	−20.3	+ .4	VT	−23.8	− 3.5
MA	−19.9	− 7.0	VA	−19.4	+ 1.5
MI	−24.5	− 3.9	WA	−18.0	−10.6
MN	−19.0	−11.8	WV	−16.4	− 4.2
MS	−16.4	+ 2.2	WI	−16.4	−11.6
MO	−22.0	− 8.4	WY	−25.5	− 2.9

• In all fifty states the strongest Perot counties showed a greater decline for Bush than for the Democrats, even in Iowa, where Clinton did not do as well as Dukakis. (See Table 16.) Bush's vote share in these counties plummeted more than twenty-five percentage points—compared to his 16 percent decline nationally—in the Perot strongholds of Arizona, Arkansas, Colorado, Florida, Maine, Nevada, New Hampshire, Texas, Utah, and Wyoming. Bush's vote share also dropped more than sixteen points in the high Perot counties in all the other states except Hawaii, Iowa, and Louisiana. In other words, the Perot strongholds in forty-seven states were more anti-Bush than all U.S. voters taken as a whole.

Table 17
335 Staunch Republican Counties Since 1948

State	Number	Perot at or Above 18.9%	Bush Majority	State	Number	Perot at or above 18.9%	Bush Majority
CA	5	5	1	NM	1	1	0
CO	3	3	0	NC	9	0	9
FL	8	7	0	ND	7	7	2
ID	12	12	2	OH	5	4	3
IL	23	15	0	OK	9	9	5
IN	13	11	5	OR	2	2	1
IA	7	4	4	PA	4	3	3
KS	38	38	7	SD	14	10	7
KY	19	0	19	TN	20	0	11
MD	1	0	1	TX	1	1	1
MI	3	2	1	UT	12	9	9
MN	3	3	0	VA	16	1	9
MO	16	13	0	WA	2	1	0
MT	10	10	0	WV	4	1	1
NE	52	51	32	WI	3	3	0
NV	3	3	0	WY	9	9	2
NH	1	1	0	TOTAL	335	239	135
						71.3%	40.3%

• Perot showed unusual appeal to conservative Republican voters in the nation's most loyal Republican counties. There are 335 counties in thirty-three states that have supported every GOP presidential candidate since Thomas E. Dewey in 1948. Perot exceeded his national average vote (18.9 percent) in 239 of them, or 71.3 percent of these true-blue Republican areas. In fact, he carried two of them, Wabaunsee and Jefferson counties in Kansas. Even more significantly, perhaps, was the fact that Democrat Bill Clinton carried twenty-one of the counties. In all twenty-one, the Perot vote kept the Clinton vote below 50 percent. There is no doubt that anger against Republican economic and cultural policies was widespread among traditional Republican voters. In almost two dozen counties that rejected Lyndon Johnson (and Franklin D. Roosevelt, for the most part), voters preferred Bill Clinton.

• Of the 335 staunch Republican counties, only 135 (40.3 percent) gave Bush a majority of the total vote. (See Table 17.) If the Clinton and Perot vote had been combined—or if they are combined in 1996—three out of five of the most Republican counties in the nation would have rejected

Table 18
Perot's Top 25 Republican Strongholds

County	State	% Perot
Wabaunsee	KS	37.2*
Arthur	NE	36.9
Jackson	KS	34.7
Rooks	KS	34.4
Pottawatomie	KS	34.4
Garfield	MT	34.3
Harper	KS	34.1
Jefferson	KS	34.0*
Coffey	KS	33.6
Sibley	MN	33.5†
Linn	KS	32.8
Chase	NE	32.4
Woodson	KS	32.4
Sublette	WY	32.2
Grant	ND	32.1
Douglas	NV	31.8
Hayes	NE	31.7
Golden Valley	ND	31.6
Graham	KS	31.5
Pawnee	NE	31.3
Perkins	NE	31.3
Red Willow	NE	31.2
Clay	KS	31.2
Hitchcock	NE	31.2
Elbert	CO	31.1

*Perot carried the county.
†Clinton carried the county.

Bush carried all other counties.

a Republican president. As it was, Clinton was the first Democrat in this century to carry several of these counties.

• In thirty-nine rock-ribbed Republican counties, Perot attracted more than 30 percent of the vote. Neither John Anderson in 1980 nor Robert LaFollette in 1924, both life-long Republicans, did nearly this well in the loyal Republican areas of the country. (See Table 18.)

• The only Republican areas that remained impervious to the Perot challenge were those dominated by religious conservatism, racial divisions, or Civil War loyalties.

Another source of Perot strength are those counties that might best be regarded as postwar Republican growth counties. There are twenty-four counties in seven states (Florida, Idaho, Montana, Nevada, North Carolina, Utah, and Virginia) that broke with their Democratic heritage and supported Dewey in 1948. They have remained loyal to Republicans ever since, backing even such losing candidates as Goldwater, Ford, and Bush in 1992. Perot performed well in these counties, bettering his national average in sixteen of them. In general Perot did well except in North Carolina and Virginia. He ran second to Bush in eight of these counties, particularly those in Utah, Nevada, and Idaho. Some of these Republican convert counties showed up among the best Perot counties in their states. Indian River County, Florida, one of the smaller, more WASPish counties on the Gold Coast,* was Perot's fifth-best county in Florida. Matthews County, Virginia, on the Northern Neck,† was Perot's second-best county in the Old Dominion.

Two of these Dewey-convert counties gave such a large vote to Perot and Clinton that they defected to Clinton. San Diego, California, and Palm Beach, Florida, both went Democratic for the first time since 1944. Perot won 26 percent in San Diego and 19 percent in Palm Beach. Clinton also had a strong following in these normally Republican areas.

Perot and the Reagan Converts

Ross Perot showed considerable strength among those voters who tended to vote Republican (in political jargon they *trended Republican*) during the Reagan years. These folks, many of whom had leaned toward the Democrat until the 1980s, defected to Perot in considerable number, particularly in the West and Midwest.

There are 238 counties in twenty-one states in which the Democratic vote declined by *more than half* between 1976 and 1984. Perot surpassed his national average in 130 (54.6 percent) of them. There was a strong regional pattern to the Perot vote among Reagan-era Republican converts. In

---

*The Gold Coast is the northern-oriented retirement and resort area on Florida's lower Atlantic coast from Palm Beach County to Dade County.

†The Northern Neck is a rural area in northern Virginia.

seventy-eight of seventy-nine counties outside the South, Perot performed better than he did nationally. In the South (and Oklahoma) he exceeded his national percentage in only fifty-two of the 159 counties, or about a third of them.

When the Perot vote in these 238 counties is compared to the states in which they are located, the pattern is somewhat different. Perot did better in 172 of these counties (72.3 percent) than he did statewide. Regionally, there was a reversal of the comparison with the nation, since Perot was weakest overall in the South. In the southern counties Perot ran stronger in 75 percent of these newly Republican areas than he did in the states as a whole. Outside the South, Perot's vote exceeded the state average in 63 percent of these counties.

Any way you look at it, Perot made a dent in the Reagan-Bush coalition. These 238 counties are overwhelmingly white, Protestant, and populated mostly by people of Anglo-Saxon or old-stock American descent. They are largely rural, with a few suburban or exurban counties around Atlanta, Dallas, Birmingham, and Jacksonville included. Several are in the Piedmont region of South Carolina.

In 1992 Bush still carried 215 of these counties, compared to twenty-one for Clinton (all in Georgia, Florida, Arkansas, and Oklahoma) and two for Perot (in Texas). Bush won a majority of the vote in only 115 counties, fewer than half of them.

Ronald Reagan's popularity can be seen in this statistic: All 238 counties were carried by Reagan in 1984, mostly by landslide margins. Eight years before, 127 of them (53.4 percent) had gone for Democrat Jimmy Carter.

Perot's ability to win votes from different sectors of the electorate can be seen in Texas. Of the forty-two Texas counties that showed enormous Republican gains during the 1980s, twenty-one had gone for Jimmy Carter in 1976. These were "defectors" to the GOP in the 1980s. The other twenty-one counties had supported Gerald Ford and became even more Republican during the 1980s. Perot received about the same level of support in both types of counties. He carried one of the Carter defectors and averaged 22.2 percent of the vote. But he also carried one of the old line Republican counties and averaged 21.5 percent in it. He topped 30 percent of the vote in three counties in each category, but also received below-aver-

Table 19

Perot's Strength in the Reagan Convert Counties

State	Number of Reagan Convert Counties	Number of Counties Where Perot Exceeded His National Average	Number of Counties Where Perot Exceeded His State Average
Alabama	10	0	9
Arkansas	8	0	7
Colorado	4	4	4
Florida	15	13	12
Georgia	49	6	48
Idaho	10	10	4
Kansas	27	27	12
Louisiana	3	0	3
Mississippi	6	0	5
Montana	1	1	1
Nebraska	23	23	21
Nevada	2	2	2
North Carolina	4	1	3
North Dakota	3	3	3
Oklahoma	13	12	9
South Carolina	6	0	6
South Dakota	3	2	2
Texas	42	19	15
Utah	4	4	1
Virginia	3	1	3
Wyoming	2	2	2
Totals	238	130	172
Percentage	—	54.6%	72.3%

age support in about half of the counties in each category, where the Republican trend of the 1980s held firm in 1992.

Many of the Perot voters may have supported Carter in 1976 because the Georgia governor was seen as an outsider who would challenge "politics as usual." When he disappointed them, they embraced Ronald Reagan twice and, to a lesser extent, George Bush in 1988. (See Table 19.)

2

Perot and the Democrats

While Perot's primary support came from Republicans, Independents, and those somewhat to the right of center on economic issues, he had a strong appeal to moderate Protestants, to secular voters, and to certain kinds of Democrats. This Democratic support could cause trouble to Clinton if the Democrats who voted for Perot do not return to the fold in 1996.

There are thirty-seven counties in sixteen states that the Democrats have carried in every election since World War II, including the disastrous campaigns of Stevenson, McGovern, and Mondale. In eleven of these counties Perot exceeded his national vote, so those counties must be considered danger signals for the Democrats. Perot's best showing among what might be labeled "yellow dog Democrats" (loyalists) is in Columbia County, Oregon, where the Texan took 29 percent of the vote and ran second to Clinton. A county with similar characteristics in voter profiles is Gray's Harbor County, Washington, where Perot also came in second to Clinton, winning 27 percent of the vote. While this may not appear terribly dangerous at first, it is important to note that Clinton failed to receive a majority in these two Democratic strongholds. Clinton's vote percentage was the lowest for a Democrat since Al Smith lost the counties in 1928.

There were six staunch Democratic counties in Minnesota which gave

Table 20

Perot's Strong Showings Among Yellow-Dog Democrats

County	State	% Perot	Perot Rank
Columbia	OR	29.2	2nd
Gray's Harbor	WA	27.4	2nd
Itasca	MN	24.7	3rd
Deer Lodge	MT	22.9	2nd
Cottle	TX	22.9	3rd
Lake	MN	22.6	3rd
Red Lake	MN	21.4	3rd
Carlton	MN	20.4	3rd
Ramsey	MN	20.1	3rd
St. Louis	MN	20.0	3rd
Greenlee	AZ	20.0	3rd

Perot a much higher vote than expected: Itasca, Lake, Red Lake, Carlton, Ramsey, and St. Louis. Clinton still won majorities in Carlton, Lake, Ramsey, and St. Louis, but his percentage fell to the low fifties. He failed to win majorities in Itasca and Red Lake, where his percentage slipped into the forties. These counties, which have not gone Republican since the 1920s, are solidly working class and contain many voters of Scandinavian and Eastern European descent. Carlton County is a Finnish stronghold and has voted Democratic since Roosevelt in 1932. Ramsey is the liberal Catholic stronghold of St. Paul, which has not supported a Republican presidential candidate since 1924. Red Lake County is a French Canadian rural county. As in many other French Canadian counties throughout New England, Perot did unusually well, cutting into both Democratic and Republican bases of support. St. Louis County (Duluth) is a working class area with many voters of Finnish and Yugoslavian ancestry. Here Perot's fifth of the electorate included many Democrats.

Lake County is one of Minnesota's more unusual counties. Early in the century it went Socialist for president, but its strong Protestant identity gave it to Herbert Hoover in both 1928 and 1932. In one of the more bizarre results in the nation, this old Socialist bailiwick was the only county in Minnesota to stay with Hoover against Roosevelt in 1932, though more than 20 percent of voters preferred Socialist Norman Thomas. Roosevelt won the county by a landslide in 1936, and it has remained Democratic ever since. But Perot's 23 percent was a noticeable defection from the Democrats.

Perot won 23 percent in Deer Lodge County, Montana, a historically Irish Catholic area in the depressed copper region. Clinton still won a comfortable 60 percent, and George Bush ran a poor third here. Cottle County, Texas, is a county of poor whites, and one of the few non-Hispanic Texas counties that has been Democratic since 1932. Perot won 23 percent here to Clinton's 53 percent. Perot almost bested Bush for second place.

Finally, an old rural Democratic bastion, Greenlee County, Arizona, which has never voted for a Republican since Arizona entered the Union in 1912, gave Perot 20 percent, Clinton 43 percent, and Bush 37 percent. The county, while depressed economically and Democratic from longtime sentiment, is somewhat culturally conservative. Recent Democrats have not done very well. Mondale and Dukakis did not win by large margins, and Mondale's support was worse than McGovern's. Clinton's 43 percent is the worst showing since the 1920s. This could hint at problems for Democrats in the future in the rural west. (See Table 20.)

In other parts of the country staunch Democratic counties in Texas, Scandinavian Douglas County, Wisconsin, Logan County, West Virginia, seven Civil War Democratic strongholds in Kentucky, and North Carolina's Northampton and Orange Counties gave Perot little support. Neither did Boston, Detroit, Saint Louis, Philadelphia, or New York City. In these Democratic areas there was not an appreciable defection to Perot, and Democratic fortunes look safe.

3

Perot and the Voter Turnout Increase

In forty states the Perot strongholds experienced a higher percentage gain in the presidential vote than the state as a whole. In other words, in counties where Perot received his highest percentage of the vote, the increase in voter turnout was higher than that in the state as a whole. This was particularly true in Colorado, Illinois, Georgia, Alabama, Tennessee, Texas, and Virginia. The high pro-Perot turnout damaged Republicans most in Colorado and Texas. Perot clearly energized a segment of the electorate that had been politically indifferent. (See Table 21.)

In the state of Maine, for example, the highest percentage of the eligible population voted in the 1992 presidential election. An impressive 72 percent of Down Easters voted, compared to 55.2 percent nationwide and only 41.9 percent in Hawaii, which had the lowest turnout. Only 50 percent had voted in 1988.

Traditionally, Western states have had higher turnouts in national elections, and Minnesota (second), Montana (third) and Wisconsin (fourth), ranked in the top ten, as did the Dakotas, Oregon, Alaska, and Iowa. Vermont, a politically aware state, had the fifth-highest turnout. The upper Midwest has always been a stronghold of citizenship consciousness.

In contrast, the South has been the politically apathetic region, owing

71

Table 21

Presidential Vote Increase 1988–1992 in Perot County Strongholds

State	Perot Counties % Change in Voter Turnout	Entire State % Vote Change in State Turnout	State	Perot Counties % Change in Voter Turnout	Entire State % Vote Change in State Turnout
AL	+34.7	+22.5	MT	+ 6.4	+12.3
AK	N.A.	+29.2	NE	+ 5.4	+11.5
AZ	+34.8	+26.9	NV	+40.9	+44.6
AR	+16.5	+14.9	NH	+21.1	+19.3
CA	+21.8	+12.6	NJ	+14.5	+ 7.9
CO	+30.1	+14.3	NM	+ 0.5	+ 9.3
CT	+17.1	+12.0	NY	+10.9	+ 6.8
DE	+20.4	+15.9	NC	+21.0	+22.4
FL	+27.8	+23.5	ND	– 1.6	+ 3.7
GA	+41.3	+28.3	OH	+14.6	+12.4
HA	+21.1	+ 5.2	OK	+14.5	+18.7
ID	+21.4	+17.9	OR	+22.7	+21.7
IL	+23.1	+10.8	PA	+18.1	+ 9.3
IN	+ 8.0	+ 6.3	RI	+15.4	+12.1
IA	+10.7	+10.5	SC	+29.0	+22.0
KS	+12.3	+16.5	SD	+ 5.9	+ 7.4
KY	+18.9	+12.9	TN	+33.9	+21.2
LA	+12.1	+ 9.9	TX	+32.8	+13.4
ME	+28.0	+22.4	UT	+15.1	+15.0
MD	+25.8	+15.8	VT	+22.1	+19.1
MA	+ 9.3	+ 5.4	VA	+27.9	+16.8
MI	+21.8	+16.5	WA	+21.2	+22.7
MN	+20.8	+12.0	WV	+ 6.2	+ 4.7
MS	+ 6.0	+ 5.4	WI	+18.4	+15.5
MO	+21.7	+14.2	WY	+19.6	+13.6

perhaps to racial conflicts, low income and education, one-party politics, and a certain isolation from the policies of the federal government. Except for Hawaii and Nevada, most of the bottom ten states in voter turnout in 1992 were in the South, even though all three presidential candidates resided in the region! Texas, home to both President Bush and Ross Perot, was tied with California for forty-sixth place. New York has also been experiencing declining turnouts, ranking forty-first.

There are some interesting, if inexplicable, variations within regions. In the Pacific Coast area, Oregon (eighth) and Alaska (ninth) had very high turnout rates, while Washington was near midpoint (twenty-third) and Cal-

Table 22

Percentage of Voting-Age Population Who Voted in 1992

State	%	State	%
Maine	72.0	Illinois	58.9
Minnesota	71.6	Rhode Island	58.4
Montana	70.1	New Jersey	56.3
Wisconsin	69.0	Alabama	55.2
Vermont	67.5	Delaware	55.2
North Dakota	67.3	Indiana	55.2
South Dakota	67.0	Pennsylvania	54.3
Oregon	65.7	Arizona	54.1
Alaska	65.4	Arkansas	53.8
Iowa	65.3	Kentucky	53.7
Idaho	65.2	Maryland	53.4
Utah	65.1	Mississippi	52.8
Connecticut	63.8	Virginia	52.8
Nebraska	63.2	Tennessee	52.4
New Hampshire	63.1	New Mexico	51.6
Kansas	63.0	New York	50.9
Colorado	62.7	West Virginia	50.6
Wyoming	62.3	Florida	50.2
Missouri	62.0	North Carolina	50.1
Michigan	61.7	Nevada	50.0
Ohio	60.6	California	49.1
Massachusetts	60.2	Texas	49.1
Washington	59.9	Georgia	46.9
Louisiana	59.8	South Carolina	45.0
Oklahoma	59.7	Hawaii	41.9

ifornia (forty-sixth) and Hawaii (fiftieth) were gripped by apparent apathy. (See Table 22.)

There is a strong connection between turnout of voting-age population and support for Perot. Perot's vote exceeded his national average in nine of the top-ten turnout states, falling just slightly short in Iowa. Indeed, Perot's vote was greater than it was nationally in twenty-three of the top-twenty-five high-turnout states (92 percent). This certainly suggests that his candidacy motivated some eligible voters to cast their ballots when they would otherwise have ignored the election altogether. In contrast, Perot's vote exceeded his national showing in only four of the ten states with the lowest voter turnout.

Nationwide, the turnout has been declining in every presidential election since 1964. The 1992 electoral participation represented the first increase since the hotly contested Kennedy-Nixon race of 1960.

Presidential Vote Increase from 1988 to 1992 by State

This measurement differs somewhat from the voter turnout based on the voting-age population. (That measurement is important because it takes into account the failure of many eligible people even to register to vote, let alone to actually cast a ballot. This is why that figure for eligible voters increased only five percentage points between 1988 and 1992.)

This category compares the actual number of votes cast for president in each state for the last two presidential elections. The overall increase in 1992 was a stunning 14 percent, the highest since 1952. Almost 13 million more people cast ballots in the exciting three-way battle in 1992 than in the comparatively dull 1988 contest, which had the lowest voting-age turnout since 1924.

The actual increase in voter turnout takes into account both greater interest in the campaign on the part of the voters and population growth within the states during the previous four years. Nevada had the highest percentage increase in its total vote, a whopping 44.6 percent rise. Alaska, Georgia, Arizona, Florida, Washington, Alabama, Maine, North Carolina, and South Carolina were the top-ten states in this category. Perot exceeded his national average in six of them, failing only in four southern states. This is not surprising, since Perot's vote increased most in high-growth counties *within* states, rather than just in the high-growth states. And when we examine precinct-level data, we discover that Perot generally did best in those regions *within* the counties that experienced the greatest population growth. (See Tables 23 and 24.)

Table 23

Percentage Increase in Total Presidential Vote from 1988 to 1992 by State

State	% Increase	State	% Increase
Nevada	44.63	Mississippi	14.23
Alaska	29.18	Wyoming	13.63
Georgia	28.26	Texas	13.39
Arizona	26.89	Kentucky	12.88
Florida	23.45	California	12.59
Washington	22.68	Ohio	12.43
Alabama	22.46	Montana	12.29
Maine	22.42	Rhode Island	12.05
North Carolina	22.37	Connecticut	11.98
South Carolina	21.96	Minnesota	11.98
Oregon	21.72	Nebraska	11.50
Tennessee	21.17	Illinois	10.77
New Hampshire	19.26	Iowa	10.52
Vermont	19.06	Louisiana	9.94
Oklahoma	18.73	Pennsylvania	9.34
Idaho	17.89	New Mexico	9.34
Virginia	16.75	New Jersey	7.87
Kansas	16.53	South Dakota	7.43
Michigan	16.50	New York	6.80
Delaware	15.94	Indiana	6.33
Maryland	15.78	Mississippi	5.40
Wisconsin	15.49	Massachusetts	5.35
Utah	14.99	Hawaii	5.19
Arkansas	14.85	West Virginia	4.65
Colorado	14.34	North Dakota	3.66

Nationally: 14.00

Table 24

The Perot Voters—1992

Total: 19.7 Million

1988 Vote	Millions of Voters	%	% Voters
Bush	8.8	44.7	65.7
Dukakis	4.6	23.3	34.3
Did not vote	6.3	32.0	—

Perot attracted many new, first time, or previously disillusioned voters. About one-third (32 percent) of his voters had not voted in 1988. Of those who did, almost 66 percent chose Bush over Dukakis.

Part Three

State-by-State Summary of Perot's Support

ALABAMA

1992 Presidential Election Results	
ELECTORAL VOTES*:	9 (Bush)
TOTAL VOTE:	1,688,060
BUSH:	804,283 (47.6%)
CLINTON:	690,080 (40.9%)
PEROT:	183,109 (10.8%)

Perot's Alabama showing was one of his poorest; he won just under 11 percent of the vote in one of the few states in the country that backed George Bush enthusiastically. Perot's Alabama vote followed a distinctive pattern. Six of his top-ten counties were in the northern part of the state, centered in Huntsville (Madison County). This part of the state, which is almost all white, has a different political heritage from the rest of the state. In the past, it displayed a distinct populist trend, often opposed the Old South Democratic establishment, and went for Herbert Hoover in 1928 because of his strong support for Prohibition. In much of the modern era, though, it was more loyal to the Democratic party. Adlai Stevenson did well here in the 1950s, for example, and Kennedy won in 1960. It has gone Republican in recent times, but Perot won a good 15 percent to 17 percent of the votes here and cost Bush his majority in these counties. Perot's fourth-best showing was in Madison County, the state's wealthiest county, with many high-tech workers and a reasonably well-educated electorate.

Perot also did well in a few south Alabama counties, such as Baldwin County, a conservative suburb of Mobile and Alabama's primary Gulf Coast resort area. He received a respectable vote in Elmore County, a suburb of Montgomery, and in Dale County, a George Wallace stronghold in the southeastern part of the state. His Alabama counties were also distinctly middle class, with per capita income almost equalling the state average.

---

*There are a total of 538 electoral votes, a sum equal to the total number of senators (100) and representatives (435) in Congress, plus three votes from the District of Columbia. A presidential candidate who receives the plurality of the popular vote in a particular state wins all of the electoral votes of that state. A candidate needs a majority of 270 electoral votes to be elected president.

ALASKA

1992 Presidential Election Results	
ELECTORAL VOTES:	3 (Bush)
TOTAL VOTE:	258,506
BUSH:	102,000 (39.5%)
CLINTON:	78,294 (30.3%)
PEROT:	73,481 (28.4%)

Perot won a very impressive 28.4 percent in Alaska, running a close third in this overwhelmingly Republican state and helping to reduce Bush's support to only 39.5 percent. Alaska, the Frontier State, was Perot's second-strongest state.

Perot carried three of the state's forty election districts, winning 40 percent in District 28, a rural area north of Anchorage. This archconservative area had been a Libertarian party stronghold. Ed Clark, the Libertarian standard-bearer, ran second to Ronald Reagan in this area in 1980. Perot also carried District 9 in Anchorage and District 7 along the coast south of Kenai, where George Wallace won his highest support (21 percent) in 1968. (Election district numbers change frequently in this state, and direct comparisons, even with 1988, are difficult.)

Perot received solid support everywhere except in the liberal stronghold of Juneau, the state capital and university center, which went heavily for Clinton, and in Wade Hampton (District 38), the poorest and most heavily Native American region. Perot won 31.3 percent in Fairbanks, 28.3 percent in Greater Anchorage, but less than 20 percent in Juneau.

In the three poorest, most heavily Native American areas (districts 36, 38, 39), Perot won 20.7 percent, just slightly above his national average. These bailiwicks of old Alaska have a high church membership (61 percent compared to 32 percent statewide) but a per capita income of only 55.8 percent of the state average. Its people are only 60.7 percent as likely to be college educated as Alaskans in general. These areas have three times as many people living below the poverty level as those in the state as a whole, and 76.5 percent are Native Americans compared to 16 percent in the state. Not unexpectedly, only 72.6 percent of registered voters showed up on election day compared to 82.1 percent statewide.

What makes Native Alaska unusual is the degree of social traditional-ism and conservatism still existing, which probably explains why Bush won 40 percent, to Clinton's 37 percent, and Perot 21 percent. In the Na-tive American counties in the lower forty-eight, Bush did very poorly.

ARIZONA

1992 Presidential Election Results	
ELECTORAL VOTES:	8 (Bush)
TOTAL VOTE:	1,486,975
BUSH:	572,086 (38.5%)
CLINTON:	543,050 (36.5%)
PEROT:	353,741 (23.8%)

Arizona shows a slight reversal of the patterns found in most of the country. Perot received his best results in Phoenix, where 59 percent of the state votes are cast. The large Phoenix area (Maricopa County) gave 25 percent of its ballots to Perot compared to the 24 percent that Perot received in the rural counties. His poorest showing was 19 percent in Tucson, which is a lib-eral stronghold, but this matched his national average. All four of his county strongholds—Mohave, La Paz, Gila, and Yavapai—are below the state av-erage in income and education. In comparison to other rural areas of the state, however, the Perot counties are about average or even slightly above aver-age in per capita income. His Arizona vote of nearly 24 percent was one of his most impressive showings in the country and nearly cost Bush the state.

One interesting county where Perot did well was Coconino, where Flagstaff is the largest city. This small-town county in the northern part of the state had been a Republican stronghold for forty years until Bill Clinton won it decisively by twelve percentage points. The last Democrat to win Co-conino County was Harry Truman in 1948. Coconino is also Arizona's best-educated county, again showing the connection between high education and support for Clinton. The University of Northern Arizona is located here. Although the Phoenix area may have more colleges and students, they com-prise a smaller percentage of the total population and the total vote.

ARKANSAS

1992 Presidential Election Results	
ELECTORAL VOTES:	6 (Clinton)
TOTAL VOTE:	950,653
BUSH:	337,324 (35.5%)
CLINTON:	505,823 (53.2%)
PEROT:	99,132 (10.4%)

Perot's Arkansas vote was only slightly over 10 percent, one of his poorest national figures. In Arkansas, however, he managed to win up to 21 percent in Marion County, which is one of the Ozark counties in the northern part of the state bordering Missouri. Neighboring Baxter County gave Perot 19 percent.

Perot's Arkansas vote came by and large in Republican-leaning counties in the northern part of the state. Clinton beat Bush by only about six percentage points in high Perot counties, a reflection of their Republican orientation. (They favored Reagan and Bush three times before.) In fact, two of Perot's best counties, Sebastian and Crawford, in the northwest part of the state, still went for Bush in 1992. Perot also cut into the old Republican mountain county of Newton, a rather isolated area, which this time went for Clinton. Perot's Arkansas vote was relatively middle class. His counties were near the statewide-average per capita income, though well below the average educational level.

Another unusual factor is that five of Perot's top-eleven counties bordered Texas or Oklahoma, evidencing the spillover effect—since Perot was strong in those states, counties which bordered them may have been influenced by this effect.

CALIFORNIA

1992 Presidential Election Results	
ELECTORAL VOTES:	54 (Clinton)
TOTAL VOTE:	11,131,721
BUSH:	3,630,574 (32.6%)
CLINTON:	5,121,325 (46.0%)
PEROT:	2,296,006 (20.6%)

In the great state of California where more than 11 million presidential ballots were cast, almost 2.3 million or 21 percent went for Ross Perot. His strongholds were isolated rural areas which had been Republican since World War II and which still gave Bush the edge over Clinton. Five of Perot's top-ten counties border Nevada and two of them, Alpine and Mono, are among the most Republican counties in the country. Thanks to Perot, Bush fell to 35 percent of the vote in these two counties, Perot taking almost 30 percent. Perot also won a large vote in Modoc, Lassen, and Sierra counties in this area. Nearby, in Amador and Calaveras counties, Perot polled more than one-fourth of the votes. In the northern part of the state, Tehama and Del Norte counties were also among his strongholds. (Del Norte borders Oregon.) He also carried nearby Trinity County, a small, very independent county which swings between parties. It gave George Wallace his highest California percentage in 1968, though it still went for Hubert Humphrey that year. Reagan and Bush won here three times before the county was carried by Perot. Perot's strongholds in California were well below the state average in per capita income and education.

Perot did, however, win substantial votes everywhere in southern California and even in some of the San Francisco suburbs. He won a very significant 27 percent in Ventura County, a middle-class Los Angeles suburb. The Perot vote helped Clinton carry the county, the first Democrat since Lyndon Johnson to do so. Perot's 26 percent in San Diego also helped Clinton become the first Democrat since Franklin Roosevelt in 1944 to win that large southern California county. Conservative Orange County gave Perot a solid 24 percent, though Bush still carried the county by twelve points. Bush's percentage in almost every southern California county was lower than Barry Goldwater's. Riverside County, a strongly Republican southern

California county with an old Yankee Protestant heritage, went Democratic for the first time since 1936. Perot took almost a quarter of the vote here. Perot won 20 percent to 23 percent support in San Bernardino and Santa Barbara counties, and also cut into the high-tech area in Santa Clara County—the so-called Silicon Valley. Clinton was a decisive winner in Santa Clara County. Perot took 20 percent in Sacramento. Only in parts of the Central Valley, Oakland, San Francisco, Los Angeles, and in the liberal, high-income San Francisco suburb of Marin County did Perot fail to equal his national level of support. His poorest showing was in liberal San Francisco, where he only won 9 percent of the vote, while Clinton won a landslide of 72 percent. George Bush's 32.6 percent voter support in California was the worst Republican showing since Alf Landon's in 1936.

In vote-rich Los Angeles County, which casts more votes than forty-two states, Assembly District 36 in the San Fernando Valley was both George Bush's best and Ross Perot's strongest (26 percent) area. Naturally, it was Bill Clinton's poorest. Perot also did well in districts 38, 53, 54, and 59, most of which went for Clinton.

COLORADO

1992 Presidential Election Results	
ELECTORAL VOTES:	8 (Clinton)
TOTAL VOTE:	1,569,180
BUSH:	562,850 (35.9%)
CLINTON:	629,681 (40.1%)
PEROT:	366,010 (23.3%)

Colorado was one of Ross Perot's best states. He topped 23 percent in that state and exceeded his national average in fifty-seven of the state's sixty-three counties. He even carried San Juan and Moffat counties, the latter being in the northwest corner of the state, while the former is in the southwest. Most of Perot's top-ten counties were rural areas in the northwest. Perot clearly damaged Bush in Colorado. The ten counties with the highest Perot vote split almost three ways with Clinton actually slightly ahead,

Perot second, and Bush in third place in normally Republican counties. Perot's strongest counties were somewhat below average in income but were well educated.

Colorado is unusual in having five counties—Pitkin, Gunnison, Summit, San Miguel, and Eagle—that are among the top-twenty-five counties of the United States containing the largest percentage of college-educated adults. The intellectual voters had easily gone Republican in the 1980s, but in 1992 Clinton won 42 percent and Perot 31 percent, leaving George Bush with a poor, third-place, 27 percent showing. These are among the few counties in the nation where Perot scored well among the very well educated.

Perot's top-ten counties, including two of the five previously mentioned counties with college-educated population, were also a good deal more liberal than the rest of the state on certain very contentious social issues. One of the more significant findings buried in the 1992 data is that Perot voters are moderate to liberal on social issues. The ten Perot counties voted 51 percent in favor of gay rights in the bitter 1992 Colorado referendum, a voter response which was more than 4 percent more liberal than the rest of the state and 20 percent more supportive of gay rights than rural Colorado in general.* The Perot counties also voted 71 percent against vouchers for private and parochial schools, and they supported public funding of abortion in a 1986 referendum.

Perot did well in the high-income Republican stronghold of Douglas County, where he came in second to Bush by winning 28 percent of the vote. This is one of those middle-aged, affluent, suburban or exurban counties where the Republicans piled up huge majorities in the 1980s. Perot cut Bush's support down to only 46 percent in Douglas County. Perot also did well in a number of Denver suburbs, winning 26 percent in Jefferson and Adams counties and 24 percent in Arapahoe County. Perot ran a very strong race in several small-town counties, too (Weld and Larimer), where he took a quarter of the vote.

He did less well in the liberal college town of Boulder where he won 22 percent, though that still exceeds his national average and was close to Bush's showing. Conservative Colorado Springs, which has a large military

---

*Those opposed to equal treatment of gay citizens successfully campaigned for Amendment 2 which eliminated gay rights statutes statewide. The referendum decision has been declared unconstitutional.

and a growing evangelical Christian vote, gave Perot a little over 20 percent while still giving Bush a majority. Moderately Hispanic Pueblo and Denver gave Perot 17 percent. They remained Clinton strongholds. Perot's poorest Colorado showing came in four counties that are heavily Hispanic Catholic. These counties in the southern part of the state bordering New Mexico have an old Hispanic culture going back centuries and remain Democratic strongholds. Perot's support ranged from 11 percent to 16 percent here.

Perot's extraordinary ability to appeal to different kinds of voters can be seen clearly in rural Colorado, which breaks down rather neatly into four worlds: secular liberal, secular conservative, evangelical, and Hispanic Catholic.

Perot won 31.3 percent of the votes cast in the secular liberal counties, where he ran second to Clinton. These counties have a highly educated population of average to above-average income and a low church membership. There are almost twice as many college-educated adults as there are church members, which would boggle the mind in the South, where there are probably six or seven times as many church members as college-educated adults. Not surprisingly, these counties supported gay rights by opposing Amendment 2 by 58 percent to 42 percent, while the rest of rural Colorado voted two to one in favor of the amendment.

Perot also won 28.6 percent of the votes in the secular conservative counties, where he ran second to Bush. These counties have a low church membership, about half the state average, and about the same as the secular liberal counties. The secular conservative counties, however, opposed gay rights 64 percent to 36 percent and are Republican. Less of the populace here is well-educated than in the liberal counties, and the per capita income is 30 percent lower. These are areas of conservative populism.

In strongly religious areas of rural Colorado, Perot did less well, though his 24.5 percent in the evangelical counties in the eastern part of the state, which border Nebraska, was one of his better state results among conservative Protestants. These evangelical counties were the most opposed to gay rights (68 percent against) of any region of the state, and they gave Bush a fourteen-percentage-point edge over Clinton. Income here is well below the state average and the residents are only half as likely to be college educated as are all Coloradans. These counties have five times as many church members as college graduates.

The Hispanic Catholic counties bordering New Mexico are known for a kind of lyrical and quite ancient Hispanic culture. Still an isolated and very poor region, with low levels of formal education and heavily Catholic and Democratic, it was Clinton's strongest region and Perot's weakest (15.1 percent). These counties voted 64 to 36 percent against gay rights.

CONNECTICUT

1992 Presidential Election Results	
ELECTORAL VOTES:	8 (Clinton)
TOTAL VOTE:	1,616,332
BUSH:	578,313 (35.8%)
CLINTON:	682,318 (42.2%)
PEROT:	348,771 (21.6%)

Perot's support in Connecticut was quite wide. He received almost 22 percent of the state vote and was relatively stronger in rural areas than in cities and towns, where he won just under 20 percent. His best county showing was in Windham County, which is substantially French Catholic, and he also did well in New London, Tolland, and Litchfield counties. He did least well in the Democratic cities of New Haven and Hartford, and in Republican Fairfield County.

Perot's strongest town and city showings were in Naugatuck, Bristol, New Milford, Norwich, and in Democratic towns like Torrington, Groton, and Enfield. His Connecticut support came mainly from middle- to lower-middle income voters who earned on average 13 percent less than the state per capita income.

Perot did not have a particularly strong appeal to wealthy Connecticuters. In the state's four highest-income towns (Darien, Greenwich, Ridgefield, and Westport) he polled less than 15 percent, a good deal less than his 22 percent statewide. Unlike Massachusetts, Connecticut's upper class remained Republican, with Bush beating Clinton 48 percent to 38 percent. Even in high-income areas, however, Perot's vote came from Bush's former supporters.

By and large, Perot damaged Bush in Democratic towns in Connecticut by taking votes from the Republican minorities in towns like Groton, Norwich, East Haven, and Glastonbury. However, in a few towns, such as Naugatuck, Bristol, East Hartford, and Ansonia, Perot took almost as many votes from the Democrats as he had from the Republicans. One of the more bizarre showings in the state was in Ansonia, where Dukakis had been a narrow winner in 1988; in 1992 Bush achieved a narrow victory.

Another interesting factor was that Perot did well in socially conservative swing areas. There were nine towns in Connecticut that went for George Bush in 1988 but voted for the moderate Democratic challenger Joe Liberman, who defeated liberal Republican Senator Lowell Weicker in the U.S. Senate race. In eight of these nine towns Perot topped his statewide average vote percentage. Perot seems to have had considerable appeal for independent-minded middle-income voters who perhaps prefer moderate-to-conservative Democrats in state races.

DELAWARE

1992 Presidential Election Results	
ELECTORAL VOTES:	3 (Clinton)
TOTAL VOTE:	289,735
BUSH:	102,313 (35.3%)
CLINTON:	126,054 (43.5%)
PEROT:	59,213 (20.4%)

Tiny Delaware, forty-ninth in land area and forty-sixth in population, has only three counties: New Castle, including Wilmington and its suburbs, where more than two-thirds of the vote is cast, and the rural counties of Kent and Sussex, which are largely white, Southern-oriented, and Methodist, especially in Sussex. Rural Delaware resembles Maryland's Eastern Shore, which it adjoins in the Delmarva Peninsula, culturally and politically. (The Delmarva Peninsula contains Delaware and the eastern shores of Maryland and Virginia.)

Perot did better in rural Delaware (24 percent in Sussex and 22 percent in Kent) than in the greater Wilmington area (19 percent), and his statewide vote exceeded his national average. Sussex and Kent counties have a lower per capita income and percentage of college-educated adults than the Wilmington area; Bush narrowly carried both in spite of the large Perot vote. Clinton, however, easily won New Castle County by a margin of twenty-five thousand votes and thus carried the state. The city of Wilmington has a large African-American population, making the state the ninth most African-American state. It also has a significant Italian-American vote.

Most of the state's population growth from 1980 to 1990 occurred outside of Wilmington, including its little capital of Dover, where the population rose 17 percent. The state ranks first in percentage of students attending private schools and in the number of corporations and foundations per population.

FLORIDA

1992 Presidential Election Results	
ELECTORAL VOTES:	25 (Bush)
TOTAL VOTE:	5,314,392
BUSH:	2,173,310 (40.9%)
CLINTON:	2,072,698 (39.0%)
PEROT:	1,053,067 (19.8%)

Florida and Texas were the only southern states where Perot topped his national average. In Florida, he won almost 20 percent of the votes, capturing more than one million ballots. Perot's Florida strongholds were a curious mixture geographically. Three counties—Santa Rosa, Okaloosa, and Walton—are in the panhandle just east of Pensacola. North Florida's Wakulla, Taylor, and Gilchrist counties are all rural, Deep South, and white. Citrus County, north of Tampa, is a fast-growing retirement area with many middle-income migrants from the Midwest. Indian River, St. Lucie, and Okeechobee counties are on the Florida Gold Coast between Cape Canaveral and Palm Beach. Perot's best county in Florida, in fact, was St. Lucie, where he won 29 percent of the vote. This part of southeast Florida tends to be somewhat more WASPish, less Catholic, less Jewish, and less Hispanic than the Palm Beach, Fort Lauderdale, and Miami areas, which all went heavily for Bill Clinton. Perot's second-best county in Florida was Monroe, where he took almost 29 percent. Monroe County encompasses Key West, an area of strong individualistic heritage, moderately prosperous, and socially liberal, with an important gay vote. Monroe County went for Clinton after having gone for Reagan and Bush three times before, but Perot's strong showing is noticeable.

In general Perot's Florida support was somewhat below middle class. His counties averaged only about 83 percent of the state per capita income, and residents in Perot counties were only 73 percent as likely to be college educated as the state population. Indian River and Monroe counties were the two Perot strongholds where voters were likely to be above the state average in income and in education.

Perot ran second to Bush in Walton, Indian River, Okaloosa, and Santa Rosa counties. The panhandle counties in particular have become conservative and Republican since the 1970s. This part of the state, which was once heavily Deep South Democratic, has not gone for a Democrat since John Kennedy in 1960. Even Jimmy Carter, who grew up not a hundred miles from this area, failed to carry these counties in 1976. They are heavily white, southern, relatively conservative in religion, and filled with military retirees. Reagan and Bush both were able to exceed 80 percent in this part of Florida, so Perot's vote in this region of the state was clearly conservative.

Perot's higher relative appeal to conservatives than liberals in Florida is also shown by the fact that in the top George Wallace counties of the state Perot won 24 percent, again above his statewide average. Perot topped his state average in fifty-six of Florida's sixty-seven counties. He did not do so in Miami, Fort Lauderdale, Jacksonville, and Palm Beach, which have many minority voters and strong political organizations of the major parties.

Perot did quite well in the ten counties (Charlotte, Highlands, Pasco, Sarasota, Citrus, Hernando, Lake, Martin, Indian River, and Manatee) that have the highest concentration of voters over age sixty-five. He won 24.1 percent; Clinton, 35 percent; and Bush, 40.9 percent. Perot's vote came exclusively from 1988 Bush voters, who gave the then vice president 64.5 percent of their ballots. Perot's candidacy also generated much enthusiasm in these ten counties, where voter turnout increased 26.4 percent between 1988 and 1992. Two of these gray-power counties were on Perot's top ten in Florida.

This showing points up an apparent contradiction with exit-polling data, which claimed that Perot did much better among younger than among older or retired voters. It may be, however, that Perot's strength among the elderly was concentrated in areas where many senior citizens live in communities of like-minded people. This is also true in the fifteen counties outside of Florida that have the highest senior-citizen vote (including Llano County, Texas, which has the highest percentage of residents over age sixty-five in the nation). Perot won 22.3 percent (Clinton, 38.2 percent, and Bush, 39.5 percent). In both sets of counties Perot exceeded his national average. In Florida and elsewhere, the Clinton vote remained at the Dukakis level, while the Bush vote plummeted.

GEORGIA

1992 Presidential Election Results	
ELECTORAL VOTES:	13 (Clinton)
TOTAL VOTE:	2,321,125
BUSH:	995,252 (42.9%)
CLINTON:	1,008,966 (43.5%)
PEROT:	309,657 (13.3%)

Georgia was not one of Perot's better states. Although he won only 13 percent of the vote in this large and fast-growing state, his support had some interesting geographical and political aspects. His best showing (26 percent) was in rural Echols County on the Florida border, nearly George Wallace's best county in the state in 1968. Another interesting connection with Wallace was seen in Miller County, which is closer to the Alabama line. Wallace had his second-best showing here and Perot his third-best. In a state of 162 counties, it is probably meaningful that two small, rather isolated areas ranked at the very top of the list for two presidential candidates. Another belt of Perot strongholds comprises three highly individualistic areas north of Atlanta, Lumpkin, Dawson, and Forsyth counties. Forsyth was a county wracked by racial conflict during the 1980s, and is an all-white area with a good deal of hostility toward blacks. Forsyth gave Bush a higher percentage of the vote in 1988 than it had given Reagan in 1984, and though it still presented Bush with a majority in 1992, it gave Perot 20 percent. Neighboring Dawson County has always had something of a quirky streak. It was the only county in the nation to vote for Thomas Dewey in 1948 and then switch to Adlai Stevenson in 1952. It frequently votes for losers, though, and backed Bush in 1992; Perot won 20 percent. Perot also did well in Houston County, south of Macon, which is dominated by the Warner-Robbins Air Force Base. Perot won a very strong 19 percent here. Some of his other counties—Brantley, Jeff Davis, Candler, and Heard—are rural counties scattered about the state. In general there was not much pattern in Georgia's Perot vote. He did reasonably well in the counties that might be considered exurbs of Atlanta. In Republican, high-growth Fayette County, for example, he received 18 percent.

The Perot counties in Georgia have in common a lower-than-average per capita income and a much lower educational attainment. With the exceptions of Forsyth and Houston, the other eight Perot counties are well below the state average in per capita income, and the educational level was lower in proportion to the state than in any of the other fifty states. Voters in the Perot counties were only half as likely to be college educated as the rest of Georgians.

HAWAII

1992 Presidential Election Results	
ELECTORAL VOTES:	4 (Clinton)
TOTAL VOTE:	372,842
BUSH:	136,822 (36.7%)
CLINTON:	179,310 (48.1%)
PEROT:	53,003 (14.2%)

Perot won about 18 percent of the vote in Maui and Hawaii counties, which are two of the smaller counties in the state. More than 70 percent of the state vote is cast in Honolulu. Overall, Perot's support in Hawaii was 14 percent, one of his lower showings, but he seems to have hurt both Clinton and Bush almost equally on a statewide basis. His two strongest counties, Maui and Hawaii, are about 12 percent below the state average in per capita income and 25 percent below in education. Hawaii County, in particular, is quite heavily Catholic though the state also has a large Buddhist community, and Perot did well nationwide among many non-Protestant religious groups.

IDAHO

1992 Presidential Election Results	
ELECTORAL VOTES:	4 (Bush)
TOTAL VOTE:	482,142
BUSH:	202,645 (42.0%)
CLINTON:	137,013 (28.4%)
PEROT:	130,395 (27.0%)

Idaho was one of Perot's best states—he won 27 percent of the vote and came close to edging out Bill Clinton for second place. In Perot's top-ten counties in the state he won 33.4 percent, beating both Bush and Clinton. Even though he didn't carry any of the counties, he came in second in most of them. Perot's Idaho counties show his ability to win votes across the spectrum. He did well in all parts of the state—the panhandle, some of the interior, and some of the eastern part of the state. His best counties tended to be middle class or a little bit below, but he also did very well in the wealthiest and also the best-educated county in the state, Blaine County. Perot won 35 percent here and ran second to Clinton. Blaine County, Idaho, is very similar to many of the counties in Colorado where high education and high income combined to produce a very anti-Bush vote in 1992. Bush plunged from more than 55 percent to only 28 percent in Blaine County. Some of Perot's other counties, Valley and Teton, are also well educated, but are below average in income.

One interesting cultural phenomenon in Idaho is the clash between the state's largest religious group, the Mormons, and those of other or no religious traditions. Idaho Mormons are strongest in the southeastern part of the state and are fiercely conservative. They gave a majority to Barry Goldwater in 1964 and 75 percent to Bush over Dukakis in 1988. The non-Mormon counties, which include many Catholics in the northern panhandle, and university students and academics in some counties, gave Bush only 52 percent. Dukakis did twice as well among non-Mormons in Idaho and in Utah as he did among Mormons. In 1992, Perot did well among both Mormon and non-Mormon counties.

Idaho has ten counties with Mormon majorities. In two of those counties, Franklin and Madison, Mormons constitute more than 90 percent of the population, and politics tends toward the extreme right wing. In 1972 independent presidential candidate John Schmitz, an extreme rightist, outpolled George McGovern in Franklin and Madison counties, even though Nixon carried them. The state has fourteen counties where fewer than 10 percent are Mormons. The voting cultures of the Mormons and non-Mormons in Idaho are quite dissimilar and often hostile toward each other.

As mentioned, Perot did well among both sets of counties, winning almost 29 percent in the high non-Mormon counties and 26.5 percent in the Mormon counties. This ability to transcend cultural divides has been one of the characteristics of the Perot vote throughout the country. Whether it's the French versus the English in Maine; the Lutherans versus the Catholics in Minnesota, Iowa, Wisconsin, and North Dakota; or the Mormons versus the non-Mormons in Utah and Idaho, Perot has done well among traditionally hostile groups.

Perot ran second to Bush among Idaho's Mormons, and Bush dropped from 75 percent to only 49 percent in the Mormon counties. Clinton won 17 percent while 7 percent voted for extreme right-wing candidates, primarily Bo Gritz of the Populist party. These Mormon counties have always had a tendency toward the extreme right. The ten Mormon counties gave 14 percent to John Schmitz against Nixon and McGovern in 1972 and 13 percent to George Wallace against Nixon and Humphrey in 1968. This time they gave 7 percent to Gritz. The non-Mormon counties gave only 1 percent to the far-right parties. Clinton edged out Bush about 37 percent to 33 percent in the non-Mormon counties and Perot won 29 percent.

ILLINOIS

1992 Presidential Election Results	
ELECTORAL VOTES:	22 (Clinton)
TOTAL VOTE:	5,050,157
BUSH:	1,734,096 (34.3%)
CLINTON:	2,453,350 (48.6%)
PEROT:	840,515 (16.6%)

Illinois, which had been Republican since 1968, gave a smashing victory to Bill Clinton in 1992. The state moved from mainstream Republican to become one of Clinton's top-ten states, though Clinton still failed to win a majority. Therefore, the Perot vote had less of an impact. Perot won only about one out of six votes in Illinois, or 16.6 percent, below his national average.

Perot's top-ten counties, where he won almost 24 percent of the vote, are scattered among several regions. Five of Perot's strongest counties are Republican strongholds in the northern part of the state. Several are Chicago exurbs, but most are more rural than exurban. Perot did very well in DeKalb, Grundy, Kendall, McHenry, and Ogle counties. These five areas had been Republican strongholds for generations and had backed virtually every Republican candidate in modern times. DeKalb County, seat of the University of Northern Illinois, bolted to Clinton and was one of seven longtime Republican counties in Illinois that went for Clinton. Perot may have helped the process in DeKalb County since it was also one of his strongholds. Some of the other Perot counties were small and rural and scattered in different parts of the state: Putnam, Cumberland, Effingham (which has many German-American voters), Jersey, and Monroe. Jersey and Monroe are exurbs of St. Louis, and Monroe County in particular gave Dukakis its support in 1988.

The Perot counties (those in which he received his highest voter support) were somewhat below the average per capita income, but in Kendall, McHenry, and Grundy Counties, the per capita income was above the state average. The educational level of Perot's counties was well below the state average. Residents of these counties were a good deal less likely to be college educated than all Illinois voters, except in DeKalb and McHenry counties. McHenry, in fact, was probably the one upscale county in which Perot did quite well. In the city of Chicago with its 1.1 million votes, Perot won only 9 percent, but his vote in the city was centered in six white, ethnic, Catholic wards in the northwest and southwest parts of the city, where he averaged 18 percent of the vote. When the city's first black Democratic mayor, Harold Washington, was running for mayor, he won only 5 percent of the votes in these wards. They have been the most Republican wards in the city, but five of the six went for Clinton in 1992, at least partially because of the Perot vote. Perot's vote came entirely from Republicans, not only in this part of Chicago, but throughout the city in general. Bush managed to carry only Ward 41 in the city's far northwest corner, the most Republican ward in recent decades, but it was also Perot's second-strongest ward. Bush dropped twenty-three points in these Republican wards where Clinton gained four and Perot topped more than 18 percent.

Perot won about 11 percent in the liberal Lake Front wards, which are filled with highly educated, highly skilled, well-to-do professionals, and an above-average Protestant and Jewish vote. His vote here also came from 1988 Bush voters. Perot won 9 percent in the four Hispanic wards in Chicago, but here he seems to have taken votes from the Democrats, because Clinton dropped six points behind Dukakis, and Bush dropped only three points. For some reason Perot took more Hispanic Democratic votes than he took Republican Hispanic votes. Perot won only 2 percent in black areas. One unusual fact was that the Perot strongholds in the northwest area were the only parts of the city where the vote was down in 1992 compared to 1988, which may be due to a declining population rather than to lack of interest in the election.

Perot's Chicago vote, while not exceptionally high, is typical of his strength among certain communities in almost all northern cities. Perot's top ward was the forty-fifth. Here is how David K. Fremon describes this area in his delightful *Chicago Politics Ward by Ward*:

> Chicago's Bungalow Belt is like the South's Bible Belt—as much a state of mind as of geography. The Bungalow Belt refers to Northwest and Southwest Side working-class residential neighborhoods, with street after street of similar houses whose home owners are white ethnics of eastern and southern European background. . . . Bungalow Belt residents

generally are Catholic; tuition for parochial schools is a major expense for many families. If they are Protestant, most likely they belong to a conservative or even fundamentalist denomination. Baptists thrive there; Episcopalians and Unitarians do not. Concerns here mirror Middle America. Crime is a major worry. Taxes are a sore point to those who feel the poor pay nothing and the rich escape through loopholes.*

Perot did well in the consistently Republican forty-first ward in the far northwest, which Freeman describes as "a collection of disparate and geographically separated suburbs." Both of the above wards are significantly Polish-American.

Perot received a strong vote in the twenty-third ward in the far southwest, which is also a Polish-American area of single-family homes, geographically and politically isolated from the rest of the city. The thirteenth ward next-door includes Midway Airport and is a "diverse and relatively prosperous area," which includes factories, railroad yards, and food industry plants, as well as a Museum of Lithuanian Culture.

Perot also received strong support in the northwestern thirty-eighth ward, which is Polish, German, and Italian, and contains a high percentage of elderly voters.

INDIANA

1992 Presidential Election Results	
ELECTORAL VOTES:	12 (Bush)
TOTAL VOTE:	2,305,871
BUSH:	989,375 (42.9%)
CLINTON:	848,420 (36.8%)
PEROT:	455,934 (19.8%)

Indiana was one of the states where Perot did relatively well everywhere but exceptionally well nowhere. He won about 20 percent of the state vote, a bit above his national average and, in his highest counties, won a

---

*Bloomington: Indiana University Press, 1988, p. 147.

little more than one-fourth of the vote. His best counties, scattered through-out the state, mainly in the central and northern parts, tended to be a bit below per capita income and a good deal below the educational attainment average for the state. They were all Republican, too. Perot's ten-strongest counties went for Bush in both 1988 and 1992, but Perot managed to come in second in heavily Republican Morgan County. By breaking into Morgan and Steuben counties Perot cracked two of the most Republican strong-holds in the nation. (Steuben County, incidentally, is a winter resort area and is sometimes called the Switzerland of Indiana.)

Of his major counties in the state, only one, Howard, had an above-average per capita income, and only one other, Brown, had a higher-than-average percentage of college-educated citizens. Brown County, in partic-ular, is full of artists and antique dealers.* Brown County is not the only one with an arts-and-crafts image in which Perot did well. Throughout the nation both he and Clinton scored well among the individualists attracted to this type of endeavor. Brown County is also very secular; fewer than 20 percent of residents are members of any church.

Nineteen counties across central Indiana were strongholds of the Ku Klux Klan during the 1920s, when that group exercised immense power over Indiana's state and local government and terrorized blacks, Catholics, Jews, and immigrants. These counties were considered pretty much in the mainstream of Indiana politics, and many historians and scholars have noted how seemingly banal and "mainstreet" was the domination of Indi-ana politics by the Klan. These counties voted much like the rest of Indi-ana, though lingering anti-Catholicism helped Nixon run five percentage points stronger here than statewide in 1960 when John F. Kennedy was his opponent. Four years before, Eisenhower had received the same vote per-centage in these counties as he did statewide.

In common with many other subregions of America, those counties which tended to be unsympathetic to civil rights leaned toward Reagan and Bush in the 1980s. These Indiana Klan counties gave Bush 67.7 percent of their ballots in 1988, which was almost eight percentage points better than statewide. Bush was stronger than Eisenhower in these old Klan areas.

In 1992 Perot received 22.3 percent in these counties, somewhat better

---

*Bill and Phyllis Thomas, *Indiana Off the Beaten Path* (Chester, Conn.: Globe Pequot Press, 1989), pp. 103–108.

than statewide. Bush declined to 49.5 percent and Clinton received 28.2 percent. Perot's percentage may have been higher than expected because his Indiana supporters are rural white Protestants of middle to lower-middle income groups whose members gravitated toward the Perot candidacy nationwide.

IOWA

1992 Presidential Election Results	
ELECTORAL VOTES:	7 (Clinton)
TOTAL VOTE:	1,354,607
BUSH:	504,891 (37.3%)
CLINTON:	586,353 (43.3%)
PEROT:	253,468 (18.7%)

Perot received 18.7 percent of the vote in the Hawkeye State, which is very close to his national average. His best counties were scattered in several parts of the state. Four of his top five were in the southwestern corner, in rural farm country, south of Council Bluffs. Another group was in the northeastern part of the state, somewhat north of Cedar Rapids. One county, Monona, is in the far west. These small-town and rural counties have been politically divided in recent years. Once they were Republican but, owing to the economic decline of the state during the 1980s, they have become Democratic. The Perot counties split exactly fifty-fifty during the Dukakis-Bush election, and they split again in 1992, this time exactly 37 percent to 37 percent between Bush and Clinton, with Perot winning 26 percent. Iowa was an unusual state in that it was the only state in the Union where Clinton did not run as well against Bush as Dukakis had four years before.

It may be that the economy bottomed out in Iowa in 1988 and was beginning to come back slightly in 1992, or that the attacks on Clinton's draft record and his personal life had some effect in the "morality belt," which is often said to characterize much of Iowa, the Dakotas, Minnesota, and Wisconsin. For whatever reason, thirteen counties in the state went for Dukakis in 1988 but switched to Bush in 1992. Dutch and German voters were frequently found in these antitrend counties, but the Perot vote was also a factor. In the strong Perot counties, however, there was no particular sympathy for Bush. In these counties, Bush's support dropped slightly more than Clinton's, which means that these counties were somewhat more anti-Bush than the rest of the state.

Another difference in the Perot counties of Iowa is that they are quite religious, in contrast to Perot counties elsewhere in the country, where church membership is generally much lower than the state percentage. In Iowa about 65 percent of the population in the Perot counties are church members compared to 60 percent statewide. Methodists and Lutherans predominate in all but one county. The Perot counties of Iowa are thus typical of the mainstream, rural, small-town Midwest.

Another clue to the Iowa Perot showing is relatively low income and low education. The Iowa Perot counties have only 77 percent of the statewide per capita income and only a 70 percent likelihood of being college educated in comparison to the rest of the state. None of the counties is particularly prosperous and well-educated.

One of the relatively strong Perot counties was Winneshiek, which includes the Norwegian Lutheran town of Decorah, a town with a notable ethnic museum and a Lutheran college. Winneshiek County, which went for Clinton, also includes a large Czech Catholic community in the town of Spillville, as well as the Laura Ingalls Wilder museum. Its interesting ethnic mix also reveals Perot's ability to draw from strikingly different ethnic communities.

KANSAS

1992 Presidential Election Results	
ELECTORAL VOTES:	6 (Bush)
TOTAL VOTE:	1,157,335
BUSH:	449,951 (38.9%)
CLINTON:	390,434 (33.7%)
PEROT:	312,358 (27.0%)

Kansas was one of Perot's success stories: he received 27 percent of the vote and did well virtually everywhere. In fifty counties his vote exceeded

30 percent and he topped his national average in every single county, carrying three counties and tying George Bush in another. In a dozen counties he won almost 35 percent of the vote. Typically, the high Perot counties were rural and below average in income and educational level. (Residents were only 63 percent as likely to be college educated as were all Kansans.) These counties tended to be more in the eastern part of the state than elsewhere, though four of them were in the southern part.

One interesting factor in Kansas is that six of the twelve best Perot counties were longtime Republican strongholds and had backed every GOP presidential candidate since Dewey in 1948 (and often before that). In 1992 one of those counties, Jefferson, was carried by Perot, the only one of the nation's staunch postwar Republican counties that went for Perot, though he did well in dozens of others. (Twenty of the staunch Republican counties defected to Clinton.)

Interestingly, Perot's fourth-best county in the state was Russell County, home of Sen. Robert Dole, the current Republican majority leader of the Senate. Perot came within thirty-nine votes of defeating Bush in this Republican banner county.

Perot's counties displayed a higher church membership than the state average. Sixty-one percent of the population in the Perot counties are church members compared to 54 percent statewide. There was a mild Methodist factor, too. The Perot counties were a good deal more likely to be Methodist than the rest of the state (18 percent compared to 11 percent), but there was also a good Catholic population of 15.5 percent in the Perot counties. In three of his counties—Barton, Rooks, and Anderson—the Catholic population was greater than one-fourth.

Perot did well not only in rural areas, where he won 29 percent, but also in the state's four largest metropolitan counties, where he captured 25 percent of the votes.

KENTUCKY

1992 Presidential Election Results	
ELECTORAL VOTES:	8 (Clinton)
TOTAL VOTE:	1,492,900
BUSH:	617,178 (41.3%)
CLINTON:	665,104 (44.6%)
PEROT:	203,944 (13.7%)

Perot's Kentucky support—13.7 percent—was well below the national average. In only six counties did he top his national average. His top-ten counties were in the northern part of the state in the Cincinnati area, though most are rural. Boone County, where he captured 20 percent, is a Republican-oriented suburb of Cincinnati. The Perot counties leaned slightly toward the Republicans, though they were far less Republican than the areas dominated by Civil War voting patterns, which still shape much of Kentucky's voting behavior.

Perot's counties were somewhat below the state's per capita income but in comparison to other states they were very middle class. His top counties have about 95 percent of the average Kentucky income, and Anderson, Boone, and Scott are above average. In education, though, residents of the Perot counties were only 70 percent as likely to have a college education as all Kentuckians; however, in Boone and Scott counties they are above average in educational achievement. This actually means, of course, that the counties are relatively poorly educated when compared to the nation since Kentucky ranks near the bottom in the percentage of its adults who have a college education.

Perot's problems in Kentucky can best be seen by his two worst counties. He received only a little over 7 percent in staunchly Republican Jackson County, where Bush won 75 percent, and in Knott County, where Clinton won 75 percent. Perot was simply unable to break into the old tradition-bound party system, which makes Kentucky a very stable state politically and one that is generally unfavorable to minor-party candidates.

LOUISIANA

1992 Presidential Election Results	
ELECTORAL VOTES:	9 (Clinton)
TOTAL VOTE:	1,790,017
BUSH:	733,386 (41.0%)
CLINTON:	815,971 (45.6%)
PEROT:	211,478 (11.8%)

Louisiana was also not one of Perot's best states. He won about 12 percent of the state vote and exceeded his national average only in Cameron Parish (counties are called parishes in Louisiana). Cameron Parish is in the southern part of the state and is one of the Catholic Cajun parishes. Although its per capita income is above the state average, its educational level is one of the lowest. Only about half as many people in Cameron Parish are college educated compared to all Louisianans.

Perot's best parishes were an interesting mix. Five are predominantly Catholic parishes in southern Louisiana (Ascension, Cameron, Jeff Davis, Plaquemines, and Terrebonne). One parish, Calcasieu, is something of a mixture of Catholics and Baptists, with a small Catholic edge. Calcasieu includes the good-sized town of Lake Charles. Most of the other Perot parishes were rural. Several white Baptist parishes were also high in Perot support—Beauregard, Livingston (which was a strong George Wallace parish in 1968), Vernon, and West Carroll. West Carroll is the state's poorest parish and was also one of Perot's best. The income levels of Perot's parishes are about 79 percent of the state's average per capita income, and only about 64 percent of their residents are as likely to be college educated as those in the rest of the state.

Perot demonstrated an ability to draw from both French Catholics and white Baptists. His top-ten parishes were 31 percent Catholic and 26 percent white Baptist. About 13 percent were members of other Protestant churches. The church-membership index for the Perot parishes was about the same as the rest of Louisiana.

There was also a slight tendency for Perot to do relatively well in the parishes where George Wallace did best in 1968. These parishes gave Perot 14 percent, which is certainly not near his national average but was

Table 25

Income, Education, and Louisiana Politics: 1991–1992

Parishes Favoring	Per capita Income	College Educated	Number of Parishes
Bush–Edwards	+ 7.6	+11.5	10
Clinton–Edwards	+ 5.8	– 5.0	35
Bush–Duke	–18.6	–34.5	9
Clinton–Duke	–26.5	–42.4	10
Bush	– 4.8	–10.3	19
Clinton	– 1.4	–13.3	45
Perot	–10.6	–36.0	0
Edwards	+ 6.2	– 1.3	45
Duke	–22.8	–38.7	19

Note: + and – refers to average income and education of the state. For example, the Bush-Edwards parishes have an income that is 7.6 percent higher than the state average.

a little better than his statewide percentage. Wallace strongholds, incidentally, still went for Bush, 45 percent to 41 percent over Clinton, as they did throughout most of the South.

In Louisiana, Bill Clinton cut into the rural white conservative vote that had favored Republican and controversial candidate David Duke for governor the previous year. Surprisingly, Clinton won ten of the parishes Duke carried while Bush carried nine. Income was the primary factor. The poor, rural parishes went for Clinton. The higher-income ones, Livingston and St. Bernard, which are distant suburbs of Baton Rouge and New Orleans respectively, went for Bush. Bush also carried the two parishes where Duke won his highest vote percentage (West Carroll and LaSalle). Bush won three of the four parishes where Duke's vote exceeded 60 percent.

Another interesting factor was a vote decline for president in many of these Duke bastions. More people turned out to vote for governor than for president, especially in Caldwell Parish, where the presidential vote declined 18 percent. It is likely that many Duke supporters skipped the presidential race altogether. Perot exceeded his statewide vote in fifteen of the nineteen Duke parishes but was not really a factor in any of them.

The real factor was economic and social deprivation. The parishes carried by Clinton and Duke have the lowest income and lowest level of

Table 26

Perot Vote in Parishes Carried by David Duke for Governor in 1991

Parish	Carried by	% for Perot
Beauregard	Bush	16.8
Caldwell	Clinton	13.9
Catahoula	Clinton	14.1
Concordia	Clinton	14.4
Franklin	Clinton	13.6
Grant	Bush	14.9
Jackson	Clinton	11.7
LaSalle	Bush	14.8
Livingston	Bush	15.8
Morehouse	Clinton	12.8
Ouachita	Bush	11.7
Richland	Bush	11.8
Sabine	Clinton	13.0
St. Bernard	Bush	13.1
Union	Bush	12.0
Vernon	Clinton	15.7
Washington	Clinton	12.3
W. Carroll	Bush	15.1
Winn	Clinton	11.2
Statewide		11.8

education in the state, even lower than the areas carried by both Republicans Bush and Duke. The parishes carried by Bush and by the Democrat Edwin Edwards were the upscale ones. The primary factor in Duke's support was low education, followed by low income. In the presidential race Perot's base of support came in parishes that were more disadvantaged than Bush's or Clinton's. (See Tables 25 and 26.)

MAINE

1992 Presidential Election Results	
ELECTORAL VOTES:	4 (Clinton)
TOTAL VOTE:	679,499
BUSH:	206,504 (30.4%)
CLINTON:	263,420 (38.8%)
PEROT:	206,820 (30.4%)

Maine proved to be a true success story for Perot. He had his best show-ing in this state, winning 30.4 percent of the vote, second to Bill Clinton. Perot edged out then President Bush even though Bush makes his summer home in Kennebunkport. Perot did well virtually everywhere, but carried only three counties: Somerset, Piscataquis, and Waldo. All sixteen coun-ties in Maine had gone for Bush in 1988; none of them did so in 1992.

The counties that Perot carried were disasters for Bush. Bush declined from 57 percent to 27 percent in these counties, losing over half of his 1988 vote. Clinton also declined eight points; Dukakis had won 43 percent but Clin-ton received only 35 percent support. Perot won these counties with 38 per-cent of the vote. The residents here had a per capita income that was 81 per-cent of the state average, and 72 percent were as likely to be college educated.

On the township level Perot did not do quite as well, winning only Fairfield and Lisbon, and even in the towns where he did best he was edged out by Clinton. Town residents, however, tend to be a bit more Democra-tic and have a higher income. Perot's top-ten towns are basically middle class, where the income is about average compared to the statewide in-come. For example, he won almost 33 percent in low-income places like Belfast, Rockland, Fairfield, Limestone, and Lincoln, but he won only 15 percent in the high-income towns (Cape Elizabeth, Falmouth, Cumberland, Yarmouth). Thus, Perot's support in Maine was decidedly lower to lower-middle income. But he did even better in lower-income towns than in middle-income ones. Clinton did best in middle-income towns, and Bush carried the higher-income communities but ran poorly elsewhere in Maine.

Perot did some serious damage to Bush in virtually every Maine county. The 1988 vote had gone strongly for Bush over Dukakis. Both Eng-lish and French areas favored Bush, a reversal of the 1960 pattern, when

Table 27

The Maine Miracle

County	Number of Precincts Carried by Perot	Perot above 40%
Androscoggin	9	3
Aroostook	4	3
Cumberland	1	0
Franklin	6	1
Hancock	18	11
Kennebec	11	0
Knox	4	0
Lincoln	2	0
Oxford	12	5
Penobscot	32	13
Piscataquis	12	7
Sagadahoc	2	0
Somerset	25	16
Waldo	17	7
Washington	16	5
York	4	0
Total	175	71

Kennedy ran well among those of French Catholic descent and poorly among those of English Protestant ancestry. Perot skirted the old English versus French cultural divide in the state of Maine, by doing well in both types of counties.

Perot also caused Clinton some trouble in a few working-class towns, particularly those with many French Catholic voters. While he still harmed Bush statewide, in towns like Millinocket, Rumford, and Jay, Perot took almost as many votes from the Democrats as he had from the Republicans.

Maine is a highly individualistic state. Down Easters pride themselves on being independent and have frequently surprised political analysts. They have never surprised the pundits more than in 1992. Perot had support everywhere in the state. In every one of the sixteen counties he managed to carry at least some precincts, which is an extraordinary showing for a candidate who had never before sought national office .

Looking at precincts from the state of Maine reveals (see Table 27) the extent of the Perot support, both in breadth and depth. Perot carried at least one precinct in every county. He carried 175 precincts, and in seventy-one

Table 28
Perot's Top Ten Towns in Maine

Town	County	% Perot
Perkins*	Franklin	71.4
Benedicta*	Aroostook	63.8
The Forks	Somerset	57.5
Byron	Oxford	56.2
Dennistown	Somerset	55.6
Osborn	Hancock	55.6
Great Pond	Hancock	52.9
Pleasant Ridge	Somerset	51.7
Moose River	Somerset	51.2
Highland	Somerset	51.1

*Unincorporated township

Table 29
Income, Size of Community and Presidential Vote in Maine

	% Perot	% Clinton	% Bush
Towns and Cities	27.4	41.6	30.6
Rural & Small Town Areas	33.9	35.5	30.1
State	30.4	38.8	30.4
In Towns & Cities			
High Income	20.2	38.0	41.8
Middle Income	28.3	45.1	26.6
Low Income	32.8	38.2	29.0
All Towns	27.4	41.6	30.6

of them he exceeded 40 percent of the total vote. Clinton ran second to Perot in fifty-six of those seventy-one precincts, leaving the incumbent U.S. president in a poor third place. Of these seventy-one high-Perot precincts, Bush received less than 20 percent of the vote in fifteen of them. In the village of Byron in Oxford County, Bush polled seven of the seventy-two votes cast, compared to forty-one for Perot and twenty-four for Clinton.

Bush's handling of the economy clearly led to his third-place finish in Maine. He received just 10 percent of the vote in the state's lowest-income town, Van Buren, while Clinton won 67 percent and Perot 23 percent. In the thirty-four towns where Clinton won a majority of the three-way vote, Perot came in second in twenty-eight of them.

Most of Perot's great victories came in small, isolated towns, which were truly off the beaten path. (Several were in unincorporated townships or plantations.) The largest town was Fairfield in Somerset County, where the total vote was a little over 3,500; here Perot exceeded 40 percent.

As Tables 28 and 29 show, size of locality and income level were major predictors of the Perot vote Down East. Perot was a strong second in the rural parts of the state, and ran third in the towns and cities. Bush ran third in rural Maine, a disastrous outcome for a Republican candidate.

MARYLAND

1992 Presidential Election Results	
ELECTORAL VOTES:	10 (Clinton)
TOTAL VOTE:	1,985,046
BUSH:	707,094 (35.6%)
CLINTON:	988,571 (49.8%)
PEROT:	281,414 (14.2%)

Perot did not do exceptionally well in Maryland, winning only 14 percent of the state vote. The state went for Clinton in a virtual landslide, Clinton winning heavily in cities and in most of the large suburban counties. Clinton carried Baltimore County and Howard County, the first time a Democrat had done so since 1964.

Perot's strongest counties were Republican-oriented exurbs and rural areas. His best county was Cecil, where he pulled 22 percent. Cecil is an upper eastern shore county with a rather ill-defined character—not quite suburban, not quite rural. It has low church membership and somewhat below-average per capita income. Perot also did well in Harford County and in Carroll County, both Republican-oriented exurbs near Baltimore. Carroll County is a Republican stronghold and still has a large agricultural and rural vote. In Anne Arundel County, where he went to school at Annapolis, and where at one time in the campaign it was predicted that he would win, Perot garnered 19 percent of the vote. He also did well in such eastern shore counties as Caroline, Queen Anne's, and Worcester, and in the southern Maryland county of Calvert, which is somewhat more Protestant than the other parts of southern Maryland and is fast becoming a kind of exurb of the Greater Washington area.

Perot's counties are below average in income and education, having a per capita income of only 86 percent of the state average and a college educational attainment of only 65 percent of the rest of the state. Perot's top-eight Maryland counties all went for Bush, but only by a ten-percentage-point margin over Clinton compared to Bush's thirty-one-point margin over Dukakis. Perot's voters clearly had gone for Bush in 1988.

Precinct data from Maryland also confirm the general contours of the county data. Perot's vote was strongest in middle-income to lower-income areas. Even in suburbs like Baltimore, Prince George's, and Montgomery counties, his vote was higher as one moved further away from population centers. Perot's best precincts were in northern Baltimore County, in Republican rural areas stretching to the Pennsylvania border, where he took a quarter of the vote, all at Bush's expense. Perot ran second to Bush in conservative areas like Taneytown, in Carroll County. In Montgomery County Perot's best showings were in conservative, rural Protestant areas like Damascus. The same was true in the city of Baltimore where his strongest support came in lower-middle-income Protestant working-class areas. Many voters in this area originally came from Appalachia. A few rather conservative Catholic lower-middle-income areas also gave him strong support. Perot won 25 percent to 30 percent of the vote in a number of rural precincts scattered throughout the state where voters are mostly white and Republican-leaning.

Unlike Perot voters in Massachusetts, Colorado, and other states, Perot's Maryland voters tend to be not only Republican but rather conservative on social issues. The Perot precincts uniformly voted against gun control in the 1988 referendum, which was approved statewide. In a bitterly contested 1992 abortion rights referendum, the Perot precincts tended to be in the low fifties in terms of their support. They supported abortion rights generally but by a lower margin than statewide, which was 62 percent. In a number of counties such as Anne Arundel and Baltimore, the strongest Perot precincts were less likely to support abortion rights than the Clinton or Bush precincts. This may have been a factor of class, however, since many Bush precincts contained upper-income voters, who tend to favor abortion rights. Clinton precincts were also generally liberal, Jewish, black, or well-educated enclaves. Perot's middle-income supporters were somewhat less supportive of abortion rights.

MASSACHUSETTS

1992 Presidential Election Results	
ELECTORAL VOTES:	12 (Clinton)
TOTAL VOTE:	2,773,700
BUSH:	805,049 (29.0%)
CLINTON:	1,318,662 (47.5%)
PEROT:	630,731 (22.7%)

Perot did exceedingly well in the state of Massachusetts, winning almost 23 percent of the statewide vote. This liberal stronghold did not seem to be prime territory for Perot, but he surprised everyone. His best counties were Plymouth, Franklin, Bristol, and Barnstable. Most are middle income, rural, or Cape Cod–oriented resort areas. But generally speaking, his Massachusetts counties are somewhat below average for the state in income and education, though not nearly as downscale as his counties in many states. Cape Cod, for example, is relatively prosperous, and Perot took a quarter of the vote there.

Perot's strongest support in Massachusetts, particularly in towns, came in the areas that people outside the state have never heard about. When people think of Massachusetts, they are inclined to think of Amherst, Cambridge, Boston's Beacon Hill, Marblehead, or Wellesley. These were not Perot areas. His greatest support came in the town of Dracut, where he won 35 percent, losing to Bill Clinton by only one percentage point. His next-best towns were Billorica, Tewksbury, North Attleboro, and Plymouth. These are the decidedly unfashionable parts of Massachusetts.

Perot received the most votes in both low-income and middle-income areas, but particularly in those falling between the middle- and lower-income levels. The highest-income towns were Bill Clinton's strongest towns. In places like Newton, Lexington, Wellesley, Needham, Brookline, Marblehead, and Winchester, Clinton piled up 59 percent to Bush's 27

Table 30
The Massachusetts Dozen
The 12 Towns Carried by Perot*

Town	County	% Perot	% Clinton	% Bush
Wales	Hampden	45.2	32.7	22.1
Russell	Hampden	39.9	34.0	26.1
Berkeley	Bristol	39.1	35.6	25.3
Peru	Berkshire	38.6	37.3	24.1
Savoy	Berkshire	38.1	34.2	27.7
Rochester	Plymouth	37.5	32.7	29.8
Tolland	Hampden	36.4	29.4	34.2
Erving	Franklin	36.4	34.7	28.9
Chesterfield	Hampshire	36.3	35.5	28.2
Tyngsboro	Middlesex	35.3	35.1	29.6
Middleborough	Plymouth	34.4	33.9	31.7
New Braintree	Worcester	34.3	32.5	33.2
ALL		36.3	34.2	29.5

*Perot also received 41.5 percent in the village of Washington in Berkshire County but ran second to Clinton.

Previous Votes

| 1988 | Bush | 60.0% | Dukakis | 40.0% |
| 1984 | Reagan | 65.2% | Mondale | 34.8% |

1986 Abortion Rights Referendum

% For	% Against
58.2	41.8

1986 Private and Parochial School Tax Aid Referendum

% For	% Against
23.4	76.6

Party Registration

Independent	57.4%
Democrat	25.6%
Republican	17.0%

Table 31
Massachusetts
Income, Town Size, and 1992 Presidential Vote

Large to Medium Towns	% Clinton	% Bush	% Perot
High Income	58.7	27.1	14.2
Middle Income	50.4	28.2	21.4
Low Income	54.8	23.2	22.0
Small Towns			
High Income	44.4	36.3	19.3
Middle Income	41.6	32.3	26.1
Low Income	45.6	26.9	27.5

Table 32
Abortion and Presidential Politics
Massachusetts

	% Pro-Choice Vote 1986 Referendum	1992 Election		
		% Clinton	% Bush	% Perot
High Pro-choice	79.0	65.2	20.8	14.0
High Anti-choice	45.2	48.1	27.2	24.7
Protestant Republican Pro-choice	71.0	40.5	37.7	21.8
High Reagan	60.7	34.6	37.6	27.8

percent and Perot's 14 percent. These high-income, well-educated areas are unquestionably liberal. Even in wealthy small towns, which have far more white Protestant residents, Clinton also won 44 percent to 36 percent over Bush, with Perot winning 19 percent. So Perot did not do particularly well in high-income areas. In lower-income towns like Chelsea, Fall River, Lawrence, New Bedford, Springfield, Fitchburg, Holyoke, and Taunton, Clinton won 55 percent, Bush 23 percent, and Perot 22 percent.

Perot's voters in Massachusetts displayed sharp differences in their previous preferences. Perot hurt Clinton in some working-class towns like Lawrence and Holyoke, but his vote in upper-income areas came solely from Republicans. For example, in upper-income towns where Perot did well, only 12 percent of Perot's vote had gone for Dukakis in 1988. But in lower-income towns 39 percent of Perot's vote had favored the state's governor in 1988.

Looking at the election from a slightly different perspective reveals an even more distinctive pattern of Perot support. (See Table 30.) Perot carried twelve small towns and precincts in eight counties—again in places unheard of outside the state. His best showing was the town of Wales in Hampden County, where he won 45 percent, but he also defeated his Democratic and Republican opponents in towns like Peru and Tolland and Chesterfield. In the towns where Perot won, Clinton came in second and Bush fell to third. Two factors stand out about the towns that Perot carried. The voters in these areas are decidedly independent. Massachusetts has long had a tradition of many people registering Independent rather than Democratic or Republican. In fact, in rough terms about as many people in Massachusetts are registered Independents as Democrats, with Republicans running a poor third. In the Perot towns over 57 percent of voters are registered Independent, compared to 26 percent who are Democrats and 17 percent who are Republicans.

A second significant characteristic is that Perot voters are moderate to liberal on social issues. In a 1986 referendum on abortion, 58 percent of voters in the Perot towns supported the freedom-of-choice position. At the same time a referendum to change the state's constitution to allow public tax support for parochial and private schools received very little support in the Perot areas. Fully 77 percent of voters in these towns opposed tax aid to private and church schools. These towns also gave 65 percent to Reagan in 1984 and almost 60 percent to Bush in 1988. They rejected their own state's governor in 1988.

This portrait of the Massachusetts Perot voter indicates an individualistic, socially liberal, economically moderate voter who has felt ignored by both parties. The Perot voter is clearly a type of forgotten voter, well below average in income and education and quite disenchanted with both national parties.

Perot ran a strong race across rural Massachusetts. In addition to the dozen towns he carried, he exceeded 30 percent of the vote in sixty towns. In these towns, Perot tied Clinton for first place in two, came second in thirty-eight, and ran third in twenty. The anti-Bush trend was obvious— Clinton carried forty-seven of these precincts and Bush only eleven.

Perot did exceptionally well in ten Democratic towns in Berkshire County, where he ran second to Clinton and forced the Democratic standard-bearer to win pluralities rather than majorities. George Bush did so poorly in many of these precincts that he received less than 20 percent of the vote in Clarksburg, Washington and Windsor.

The abortion issue may have had some impact on the presidential vote. Clinton swept the precincts that were most supportive of abortion rights in the 1986 referendum, winning 65 percent to Bush's 21 percent and Perot's 14 percent. These were mostly upper- or upper-middle-income, well-educated areas, or college towns and academic precincts. In the strongest antichoice precincts, largely blue collar, lower-middle-income areas, which averaged 55 percent against abortion rights, Clinton easily outperformed Bush 48 percent to 27 percent, and Perot won a rather large 25 percent. This does not invalidate the general finding that Perot's strongholds favored abortion rights, but it does suggest the class-based nature of the abortion struggle. The lower-middle-income segment of the population, where Perot did best, is the least supportive of abortion rights. Some voters may have chosen Perot because he was more moderate on the issue than Clinton but had a more appealing economic program. Perot did well in an opposite segment of the electorate: the Protestant, Republican, small-town dwellers who favored choice on abortion. Perot won 22 percent of these voters. Significantly, they shifted to Clinton over Bush by three percentage points. Clinton thus gained statewide among prochoice voters, but did not lose much among the antichoicers. (See Tables 31 and 32.)

Perot did extraordinarily well in those precincts where President Ronald Reagan had won by a landslide in 1984. Perot took almost 28 percent in the strongest Reagan areas, while Clinton came within three points of overtaking Bush. In some Massachusetts towns, Bush in 1992 received *less than half of the vote* received by Reagan in 1984, which indicates a considerable disaffection. (Also note that Reagan's strongest areas of support favored abortion rights 61 percent to 39 percent, despite Reagan's rhetoric and successive Republican platforms.)

MICHIGAN

1992 Presidential Election Results	
ELECTORAL VOTES:	18 (Clinton)
TOTAL VOTE:	4,274,673
BUSH:	1,554,940 (36.4%)
CLINTON:	1,871,182 (43.8%)
PEROT:	824,813 (19.3%)

In Michigan Perot won 19 percent, which was somewhat above his national average. He exceeded his national average in all but ten of the state's counties. His vote was decidedly rural. The counties where he did not do particularly well included Detroit, Ann Arbor, Grand Rapids, the Dutch areas in Ottawa County, and the upper-income Detroit suburb of Oakland County. But everywhere else he topped his national average.

His top-ten counties were scattered throughout the state. Five were rural counties in the north around Traverse City. Three were rural counties north of Detroit, including the small town of Port Huron, and a couple were rural counties along the Indiana border.

Perot's counties had been decidedly Republican in the past and most of his vote came at the expense of Bush. The per capita income and the education level of the Perot counties were about 80 percent of statewide, indicating some but not a serious level of socioeconomic disadvantage.

One interesting factor about the Perot counties in Michigan is that the residents display a much lower level of religious identification than the state as a whole. Only about 40 percent of the citizens in Perot's top-ten counties are members of churches, compared to a little over 50 percent statewide. There are also about as many Catholics as Protestants in the Perot counties. A number of counties throughout Michigan might best be called enclaves of "cultural Protestants," where fewer than 40 percent of the population is a member of any church but where the dwindling number of churchgoers tend to be mainline Protestants. Perot did well in all of them. This is a salient pattern not only in Michigan, but in parts of New England, Ohio, and elsewhere. The close identification of the Republican party with religious piety, with institutional religion, and with the religious right, may have cost George Bush many votes among traditional Republicans who are not actively involved in churches. Throughout Michigan's cultural Protestant counties Perot tended to average about 25 percent of the vote. These are historically mainline Protestant counties, where religious practice and attendance have been declining over several decades. The sharp Republican decline in 1992 may very well have been a factor related to the Republican party's attempt to define itself in religious terms.

This view is also strengthened by the fact that Perot did quite well in only one of the state's ten heaviest Catholic counties and only one of the fourteen heaviest Protestant counties. The Perot vote was highest in relatively unchurched or moderately secular areas.

MINNESOTA

1992 Presidential Election Results	
ELECTORAL VOTES:	10 (Clinton)
TOTAL VOTE:	2,347,948
BUSH:	747,841 (31.9%)
CLINTON:	1,020,997 (43.5%)
PEROT:	562,506 (24.0%)

Perot's message played very well in the state of Minnesota, winning him 24 percent of the vote statewide and surpassing his national average in all but four of the state's eighty-seven counties. Perot's best counties are located mainly in the suburbs and rural areas near the twin cities of Minneapolis–St. Paul. He was very competitive in many of these counties, topping 30 percent of the vote in seven of them. His best county was Sibley, a historically Republican German Lutheran county. Perot did so well here that George Bush slipped to third place. The last Democrat to win Sibley County was Franklin Roosevelt in 1936. Bill Clinton emerged the victor by a mere fourteen votes over Perot, and Bush had the worst Republican showing since Hoover. Sibley is a farm county with incomes about one-third below the state average. Only 8 percent of its voters have a college education compared to 17 percent throughout Minnesota.

But Perot scored high among many different ethnic groups in the state.

He did well in predominantly Swedish Lutheran Chisago County, where he also ran second to Clinton. His support was largely from small communities and rural areas in terms of its greatest intensity, but he did best in the Minneapolis–St. Paul suburbs, where he won 26.5 percent of the vote. He won a little over 26 percent in rural Minnesota and about 21 percent in the cities of Minneapolis, St. Paul, and Duluth. Perot's counties tended to be below average in income. They had only 83 percent of the per capita income of the state, and educational levels were even lower. In Perot strongholds the percentage of college-educated voters was only 62 percent of the state average.

In cultural terms, Perot was able to win strong support from the state's two largest cultural groups, its Lutherans and Catholics, who have traditionally tended to pull against each other. Perot won 27 percent in German Catholic areas and 26 percent in Scandinavian Lutheran enclaves. In many previous election campaigns going back to 1928, these voters have frequently moved in opposite directions. In this election both were narrowly for Clinton, particularly voters of Scandinavian descent, but Perot was competitive. Scandinavian Lutherans, who are somewhat more Democratic, went for Clinton by five percentage points.

Minnesota's 1990 senatorial and gubernatorial elections were among its most interesting. Both challengers were elected. The incumbent Democratic Governor Rudy Perpich, a colorful populist and a Catholic of Croatian ancestry, was defeated in his bid for reelection. Sen. Rudy Boschwitz, a Republican Senator who happens to be Jewish, was defeated by Paul Wellstone, a very liberal college professor, who is also Jewish. The elections were close in both instances, with Perpich winning 48 percent in the governor's race and Wellstone 51 percent in the contest for the U.S. Senate. But Minnesotans crossed party lines in this unusual election. Twenty-eight counties voted for the more conservative Democrat Perpich but not for the more liberal Democrat Wellstone. Eight counties, primarily in the Minneapolis–St. Paul area, voted for Wellstone and not Perpich. Perot's support was extraordinarily similar in both sets of counties. He won 25.2 percent in the counties that went for Wellstone but not Perpich, and 25.1 percent in the counties that liked Gov. Perpich but did not vote for Mr. Wellstone. Perot's extraordinary ability to cross conservative and liberal lines was one of the keys to his unusually good vote in Minnesota.

MISSISSIPPI

1992 Presidential Election Results	
ELECTORAL VOTES:	7 (Bush)
TOTAL VOTE:	981,793
BUSH:	487,792 (49.7%)
CLINTON:	400,258 (40.8%)
PEROT:	85,626 (8.7%)

Mississippi was Perot's weakest state. He received fewer than 9 percent of the vote here. It was George Bush's strongest state, the only state in the union where Bush's vote was slightly higher than the combined Clinton-Perot vote. Perot did, however, win a substantial vote in a number of counties along the Gulf Coast and the adjoining area of south Mississippi. His best county was Hancock County, where he won 17 percent. This is also the state's most Catholic county, where more than one-fourth of the population is Catholic and many people are of French descent. Perot also did well in neighboring Harrison County, which includes cities like Biloxi and Gulfport. It, too, has a substantial Catholic population by Mississippi standards (about 17 percent). Nearby Jackson, Pearl River, and Greene counties are similar. Perot did well in George County, where he won 14 percent of the vote. In that unusual county almost 15 percent of the voters went for other right-wing splinter parties. George County was George Wallace's second highest county in the entire United States, giving the Alabama governor 91.5 percent of its vote in 1968. Perot also did relatively well in Adams County, which includes the graceful old antebellum town of Natchez. Natchez is also 8 percent Catholic.

So Perot's Mississippi vote was primarily centered in the part of the state that is somewhat less dominated by racial politics and populated by people who had moved to the state since World War II. The unusually high Catholic population is also worth noting even though the Perot counties, like the rest of Mississippi, are still predominantly Baptist. The Perot counties are also modestly prosperous. They have about the same per capita income as the state though their educational level is only 83 percent of the state average.

Mississippi is a state where race and religious, social, and cultural conservatism still dominate the political process. This can be seen in the seven counties that gave the highest voter support to George Bush. What these counties have in common is a high percentage of white Southern Baptists (over 44 percent), a relatively low black population, and a strong heritage of political conservatism. Nearly eight out of ten voters had supported George Wallace in 1968. It is in counties like these that the Republican party has taken on such a strong religiously and politically conservative cast. Thus, it is not surprising that the chairman of the Republican National Committee, Haley Barbour, hails from the Magnolia State.

With the exception of Rankin, a fast-growing, relatively prosperous Jackson suburb, these counties are not particularly well off. The Bush counties were about average in per capita income and below average in college education. In two of the counties, Neshoba and Clarke, fewer than half the voters had even completed high school. (Neshoba County, incidentally, was the site of the murder of three civil rights workers in the 1960s.)

MISSOURI

1992 Presidential Election Results	
ELECTORAL VOTES:	11 (Clinton)
TOTAL VOTE:	2,391,565
BUSH:	811,159 (33.9%)
CLINTON:	1,053,873 (44.1%)
PEROT:	518,741 (21.7%)

Missouri was one of Perot's strongest states. He won almost 22 percent, scoring well throughout most of the state. But his strongest counties were near Kansas City—nine of his top-ten counties were in rural regions north and south of Kansas City. In these areas he topped 30 percent of the vote and was a very significant factor. There was a strong swing against Bush in these counties. Eight of the ten had gone for Bush in 1988. In 1992, nine of the ten went for Clinton, and Perot was quite competitive, running second in three of the counties.

As is true in most parts of the country, Perot's strongest counties in Missouri are in areas of economic difficulty or decline. They average about 87 percent of the state's per capita income and their educational attainment level is about 72 percent of the state level. Only one county, Platte, can be called prosperous or upscale. It is above average in both education and income. Cass County is above in income and Johnson County is above in education.

One Perot stronghold was exurban Franklin County in the St. Louis area, where he also captured more than 30 percent of the vote. His highest support in Missouri has a somewhat different cultural pattern from that of many Perot counties in other states. The religious makeup of Missouri's Perot voters consists of a higher percentage of Baptists, Methodists, and Disciples of Christ than the percentage of these groups in the state as a whole. Sixty-four percent of residents in the Perot strongholds are church members compared to 57 percent statewide. Twenty-six percent are white Southern Baptists and 7 percent are Catholics. Statewide, Catholics and Baptists are about even (about 20 percent), with a slight Catholic edge. Franklin County, in the St. Louis orbit, is about one-fourth Catholic, but the other Perot strongholds tend to be significantly more Baptist. Davies County has a large Baptist community and also a large number of Amish, who generally do not vote. One of Bush's worst showings was in Davies County. He dropped from first place to third here, with Clinton winning and Perot coming in second. Platte County, which has the second-highest income in the state and is well educated, had a below-average church membership. So Perot seems to have drawn significant numbers of voters from many religious groups in the state, but there was a more positive showing among Baptists, who are important in Missouri, and who tend to be combative outsiders rather than the dominant group that they are in the old-line southern states.

At the other end of Missouri, Perot was least successful in the southeastern boot region, the Deep South-oriented counties where George Wallace had done well in 1968. Missouri was an exception to the pattern evident throughout much of the West and North, where Perot posted gains in counties that leaned toward Wallace. Support for Wallace in Missouri was in declining, culturally southern counties of the Old South like Dunklin, Pemiscot, and New Madrid. These were Perot's weakest counties, and they all went for Clinton in 1992. Perot also had a poor showing in St. Louis City; throughout the country there was a general lack of support for Perot in multicultural or strong minority-oriented areas. But in St. Charles County, a middle-income suburb northwest of St. Louis, Perot did well. He won at least 20 percent in most of the St. Louis suburbs and 23 percent or so in Jackson County (Kansas City).

The two largest sociocultural groups in the state are German-Americans and "Old Stock Native Americans," who claimed no ethnic ancestry in the Census Bureau surveys conducted in 1980 and 1990. In the ten counties of Missouri with the largest German-American population, Perot won 25.7 percent of the vote compared to the 19.5 percent he received in the Old Stock counties. Missouri's Germans have long been Republican-oriented, which is why Bush edged Clinton by 3.5 percentage points. But the president's vote declined by twenty-four points from 1988, and his defectors went to Perot.

The Old Stock voters, many of whose ancestors came to the state from Kentucky, Tennessee, and Virginia, and thus were once regular Democrats, favored Clinton by seven points. Among this group of voters, Bush declined about eighteen points from 1988, and his defectors also went to Perot.

When Republicans carry both of these ethnic groups by large margins, they win the Show-Me State easily. When they do not, the Democratic orientation of other groups ensures a Democratic victory, as in 1992.

Most German and Old Stock voters reside in rural areas or in the exurbs of St. Louis—all of which were economically hard hit during the late 1980s. Perot's strong support among German Americans represented the small-town, middle-income, isolationist voters, who perhaps resented Bush's almost total concern with foreign-policy issues and his disinterest in domestic problems. Bush's support among Missouri's Germans was near rock bottom despite his cozy relationship with and strong support from radio personality Rush Limbaugh, a Missouri German from Cape Girardeau. Another extraordinary happening was Clinton's victory in German-oriented Warren County, which last supported a Democrat in 1860! Perot's large vote (28 percent) made it possible, but Clinton certainly deserves a nod of praise. It is a long-distance run between Stephen Douglas and Bill Clinton, which speaks volumes about George Bush's image among Missouri Germans. Bush's support level in staunchly German Gasconade County, which has supported every Republican since Lincoln, was only

42.6 percent, the lowest vote ever given to a presidential candidate of Lincoln's party. Clinton won 31 percent and Perot 26.5 percent.

MONTANA

1992 Presidential Election Results	
ELECTORAL VOTES:	3 (Clinton)
TOTAL VOTE:	410,611
BUSH:	144,207 (35.1%)
CLINTON:	154,507 (37.6%)
PEROT:	107,225 (26.1%)

Montana was another of Perot's success stories. He won 26 percent there, taking enough votes from Bush to give Clinton the state. Clinton was the first Democrat to win in Montana since Lyndon Johnson more than twenty years earlier. Perot topped his national average in every single county. His top-ten counties gave him a 33 percent average vote, and he ran second to Bush in most of them. Two of the Perot counties were longtime Republican strongholds—Garfield and Petroleum counties, both of which are among the poorest counties in the state. Petroleum County, even though it is rural and isolated (as are most of the Perot counties), has an above-average number of college-educated voters. One factor these Perot counties have in common is a very small population, and even with the enthusiasm for Perot the total vote increased here only 6 percent over the 1988 turnout.

Seven of the ten counties where Perot had his best showing are in the east-central area of Montana. Perot's popularity among Republicans caused Garfield and Madison counties to give Bush only a plurality rather than a majority of their vote. The turnout for Bush even among Republicans here was the poorest since the Depression days. In Garfield County the Democrats did not do well. Clinton won only 15 percent, his poorest showing in the entire state. Perot also took some Democratic votes in these strong counties, because Clinton dropped almost eleven points behind Michael Dukakis's 1988 vote. It appears that about one-third of the Perot vote in his Montana strongholds had gone for Dukakis.

Perhaps the main factor was the relative economic deprivation of the Perot counties. Their per capita income was only 69 percent of the state average, and residents of the top Perot counties were only 73 percent as likely to have a college education.

NEBRASKA

1992 Presidential Election Results	
ELECTORAL VOTES:	5 (Bush)
TOTAL VOTE:	737,546
BUSH:	343,678 (46.6%)
CLINTON:	216,864 (29.4%)
PEROT:	174,104 (23.6%)

In Nebraska Perot did very well, winning almost 24 percent of the vote and surpassing his national average in every county except tiny McPherson County. In his top-ten counties, rural, farming regions, Perot took 32 percent of the vote. His strongest showing was in Republican areas, and he ran second to Bush in nine of his top-ten counties. His highest percentage was 37 percent in the state's smallest county, Arthur County, where most people are engaged in farming. In this unusual county Bill Clinton received only 7 percent of the vote, his lowest percentage in the country. Seven of Perot's top-ten counties had gone for every Republican candidate since World War II, and, in fact, supported Bush in 1992. Perot also did well in German Catholic Cedar County, his second-best county vote, where he received more than one-third of the vote. Here Clinton ran twenty points behind the percentage Dukakis had received in 1988, while Bush dropped only about thirteen points, compared to his 1988 showing. Another rural Catholic stronghold, Howard County, also gave Clinton a third-place finish, and here Perot apparently took more from the Democrats than he did from the Republicans. The progressive and isolationist tendencies of German Catholics in the Midwest help to explain why Perot did so well.

Perot did less well in Omaha, the state capital, where he won only 19 percent; and in the state's most liberal county, Lancaster, which includes the

University of Nebraska, he won 21 percent; here Clinton almost defeated Bush. Perot did not do quite as well in Sarpy County, a suburb of Omaha, which is also the headquarters of the Strategic Air Command. He received 23 percent of the vote in that county, but Bush still won a majority.

The ten counties where Perot won his highest percentage are quite economically distressed, having a per capita income of only 61 percent of the state's average; their educational level is only 63 percent of the state's average. Red Willow, a middle-income county in the heart of Willa Cather country (which derives some income from tourism associated with fans of the novelist), is the only exception. Arthur County, for example, in staunchly Republican farm country where Perot did so well, is one of the nation's poorest counties.

While Nebraska, like most states, saw many Republican voters defect to Perot, about 40 percent of the Perot vote in his strongest counties had gone for Dukakis in 1988—which raises interesting questions. In several of the state's Czech Catholic counties (Colfax, Butler) Perot ran second to Bush as the Democratic vote declined more than expected. Many rural Catholic Democrats may have found the Democratic ticket too liberal on social and cultural issues.

NEVADA

1992 Presidential Election Results	
ELECTORAL VOTES:	4 (Clinton)
TOTAL VOTE:	506,318
BUSH:	175,828 (34.7%)
CLINTON:	189,148 (37.4%)
PEROT:	132,580 (26.2%)

Perot's 26 percent of the vote in Nevada represents one of his strongest showings in an area of the country that responded well to his message. The Perot vote probably contributed to Clinton's victory in the state. Clinton was the first Democrat since Johnson to win this traditionally Republican state. Perot's best counties were all in rural Nevada, where he won almost

30 percent, coming in second to Bush. He carried Storey County, where the culturally tolerant, highly individualistic, and fabled old town of Virginia City is found. He won 27 percent in Reno and 25 percent in Las Vegas. Clinton carried the state because of a 27,000-vote majority in Las Vegas, where nearly 60 percent of the state's voters are located. Bush won a narrow victory in Reno, where about 23 percent of the state vote is cast. Bush and Perot received their best totals in the same areas and essentially vied for the same constituency. Nevada is one of those states where virtually the entire Perot vote had gone for Bush in 1988. Perot's counties were a bit below average in per capita income and in education, not as poor as in many states, but still about 12 percent below the average per capita income and college education.

The most upscale Perot area was Douglas County, which is among the top-fifty highest-income counties in the nation, is well above average in education, and is one of the state's historic Republican strongholds. Here Perot came in second with 32 percent, his most impressive showing in a high-income area.

Nevada can be characterized as an economically conservative but culturally liberal state. It has the lowest church membership of any state in the Union, which may have contributed to the Perot voter appeal. In many indices of demography, Nevada is the direct opposite of its neighbor Utah.

NEW HAMPSHIRE

1992 Presidential Election Results	
ELECTORAL VOTES:	5 (Clinton)
TOTAL VOTE:	537,943
BUSH:	202,484 (37.6%)
CLINTON:	209,040 (38.9%)
PEROT:	121,337 (22.6%)

Perot's New Hampshire vote of 22.6 percent showed his ability to win support across the board. His best county was the state's most Republican, most conservative county, Carroll, which had been the only New England county to stick with Barry Goldwater in 1964. Perot's four best counties were a mixed bag in regard to per capita income and education level; they included the highest-income county in the state, Rockingham, as well as the lowest-income county, Coos.

Perot's top-ten cities scored somewhat above the state average in per capita income and included upper-income cities like Windham and lower-income cities like Raymond. In college towns like Hanover (Dartmouth College) and Durham (University of New Hampshire) he did not do as well. He was also a bit below his state average in Concord, the state's liberal Republican capital, and in the largely Catholic, conservative city of Manchester.

Bill Clinton won heavily in Concord and in liberal towns like Portsmouth, but he also won an upset victory in Manchester. New Hampshire was one of the most anti-Bush states in the Union in 1992. It had been his second best state in 1988, but he lost it in 1992, which is surely one of the largest shifts of an electorate against an incumbent president in modern history.

Perot's ability to win across economic lines can also be seen in New Hampshire's seven highest-income cities, where he won 23 percent, and in a comparable number of low-income cities where he won 22 percent.

Perot's two strongest counties, Carroll and Rockingham, were the two fastest-growing counties in population during the past decade.

NEW JERSEY

1992 Presidential Election Results	
ELECTORAL VOTES:	15 (Clinton)
TOTAL VOTE:	3,343,594
BUSH:	1,356,865 (40.6%)
CLINTON:	1,436,206 (43.0%)
PEROT:	521,829 (15.6%)

In New Jersey Perot won a little less than 16 percent of the vote, which ranks below his national average. The state went for Clinton by about a two-percentage-point margin over Bush. Clinton's victory was the first for a Democrat since 1964.

Perot's vote demonstrates some distinct patterns. His strongest region, where he won 26 percent, was Salem County in southern New Jersey. This is the least Catholic county and the third poorest, and it has a rather southern conservative flavor. Bush still beat Clinton narrowly here, though the county had strongly supported Jimmy Carter in 1976. Clinton's inability to win Salem County, even though he won the rest of the state, shows his inability to win in southern-oriented, conservative counties whether they be in the Old South or in the North. Perot did well in the resort areas, such as Cape May and Ocean counties, which were among his top ten, and in all three of the northwestern counties of the state—Hunterdon, Sussex, and Warren. Warren and Hunterdon, in fact, were his second- and third-best counties. Perot made one of his few major campaign appearances in Flemington in Hunterdon County in the closing days of the campaign. This part of the state has changed. Historically, it was German, Dutch, Protestant, and Democrat. But in 1920 the voters became Republicans, and this is one of the few regions of the country where nineteenth-century Democrats did not vote for Franklin Roosevelt. These counties have voted Republican since 1920 with the exception of 1964, when Barry Goldwater lost to Lyndon Johnson. And while Bush won these counties, Perot did well in all of them. Bush, in fact, was able to win a majority only in Sussex County and in high-income Morris County across the state. Perot's New Jersey popularity then was largely confined to small towns and to resort- and retirement-oriented communities.

Perot's counties averaged 89 percent of the state's per capita income and 79 percent of its college-education level, which suggests that he did better in middle- to lower-income areas, a pattern that stayed with him throughout the election. Another factor was religion. New Jersey is one of the most Catholic states in the Union, but Perot did somewhat better in less Catholic areas. For example, he did well in Cumberland County, the state's most Protestant and the poorest. His top New Jersey counties were 28 percent Catholic compared to the state total Catholic population of 41 percent. The Protestant percentage in Perot strongholds reflected the state average. Perot's top counties were somewhat more secular—only 47 percent of the residents were church members compared to 61 percent statewide. In New Jersey's multicultural, multiethnic cities, Perot had little support, winning only 8 percent in the Jersey City area and under 10 percent in Essex County and Newark. His vote was also low in places like Union and Passaic counties and in well-to-do Bergen County.

The northwest part of the state, comprising Hunterdon, Sussex, and Warren counties, has changed character, becoming a major retirement area. Many retirees are Catholic. This used to be a strongly Protestant area, but Catholics now outnumber Protestants in all three counties, particularly in Warren.

Perot's New Jersey supporters had voted Republican in previous years. In his strongest counties Perot's vote came entirely at Bush's expense. Perot also took some votes from Bush in prosperous areas, where voters may have done well during the 1980s but feared for the future. He received 18 percent of the vote in the four counties that experienced large increases in per capita income between 1979 and 1989 (Hunterdon, Sussex, Somerset, Morris). Not unexpectedly, Bush still prevailed with 50 percent to Clinton's 32 percent in these counties. In 1988 Bush won with 68 percent of the electorate.

NEW MEXICO

1992 Presidential Election Results	
ELECTORAL VOTES:	5 (Clinton)
TOTAL VOTE:	569,986
BUSH:	212,824 (37.3%)
CLINTON:	261,617 (45.9%)
PEROT:	91,895 (16.1%)

In New Mexico Perot attracted only 16 percent of the vote, his lowest percentage in any state west of the Mississippi River. New Mexico, which had been Republican since 1968, went for Bill Clinton by an almost 50,000-vote majority. Clinton beat Bush by nearly nine percentage points, so the New Mexico story pertains more to Clinton than to Perot, though Perot's percentage of the vote was still higher than Clinton's majority over Bush.

Perot's support in New Mexico was largely Republican and disproportionately Protestant. His strongest county was Lincoln, site of a nineteenth-century war and the most Republican county in the state since World War

II. Perot's 24 percent of the vote here, however, cut Bush down to a mere plurality. Perot's other strong counties are mostly Republican and have a percentage of Baptists and Methodists that is higher than the state average.

Culturally, New Mexico is a state sharply divided into Hispanic Catholics, particularly in the northern part of the state, and mostly Baptist and Methodist Anglos who reside in the "little Dixie" section at the eastern end of the state. These voters have frequently voted in opposition to each other, particularly when Catholic candidates like John Kennedy and Al Smith were on the ballot in presidential races. Religion even affected some of the statewide voting returns.

New Mexico is historically a Catholic and Hispanic state, whose Hispanic population traces its ancestry to the pre-nineteenth-century Spanish era rather than twentieth-century Mexican migrations. The northern New Mexico counties are populated by people who list their ancestry as "Hispanic" or "Other Spanish" on census forms. These voters are still staunchly Catholic and increasingly Democratic. This is one part of the country where Democrats are actually stronger today than they were a generation ago, and Bill Clinton swept to majority victories in places like Taos, Santa Fe, Rio Arriba, Guadalupe, and nearby counties. The state has a declining Catholic population but is still about 31 percent Catholic, compared to 14 percent who are Baptist or Methodist and about 14 percent who belong to other Protestant churches.

The Perot counties were far less Catholic than the statewide percentage (23.7 percent) and far more Baptist or Methodist (23.5 percent). Perot did well in Lea County, a heavily Baptist area in the southeastern part of the state bordering Texas. None of Perot's top-ten counties was majority Catholic, though he did well in substantially Catholic Otero and Luna counties.

Perot's worst showings in New Mexico were in eight heavily Hispanic Catholic or American Indian counties in the northern part of the state. He received fewer than one out of seven votes (14.3 percent) here and less than 10 percent in several of these counties. Clinton won a majority in all of them. Perot also posted a poor showing in McKinley County, which is overwhelmingly Native American and voted two to one for Clinton. One Clinton landslide came in Santa Fe, which is far less Catholic than it used to be, owing to the migration of many liberal white professionals from the East. Santa Fe gave Clinton a three-to-one victory over Bush, while Perot won 13 percent.

About 35 percent of New Mexico's vote is cast in Albuquerque (Bernalillo County). Clinton was the first Democrat since Lyndon Johnson to win here, and Perot won about 16 percent, the same as he did statewide.

One of Perot's better counties, where he won 22 percent, was the anomalous Los Alamos County. This county is the exception that proves the rule. It is the single best-educated county in the country in terms of percentage of adults who are college educated, but it remains Republican. Bush narrowly defeated Clinton here by four percentage points. The reason is the unusual structure of the population. The people are well educated, but they are predominantly middle-aged, white, and Protestant, and they work for the federal government. They tend to be involved in scientific and engineering activities, which are likely to produce a more conservative voter than other types of professions. This is a high-tech center and Perot might have been expected to do well, as he did.

The geographic pattern of the Perot counties tends a bit more to the southern part of the state, running from the southeast in Lea County to the southwest in Hidalgo County. They also include the state's most northeasterly Union County.

NEW YORK

1992 Presidential Election Results	
ELECTORAL VOTES:	33 (Clinton)
TOTAL VOTE:	6,926,925
BUSH:	2,346,649 (33.9%)
CLINTON:	3,444,450 (49.7%)
PEROT:	1,090,721 (15.7%)

New York is almost two states in one as far as the Perot vote is concerned. He did exceptionally well in upstate areas, but in the rest of the state he had a poor showing. All told, he exceeded his national average in forty-nine of the state's sixty-three counties.

He topped 30 percent of the vote in Niagara County, his best county, and in Cattaraugus County, a Republican stronghold where Perot ran second to

Bush. His support was mainly centered in western New York State. In addition to the two counties just mentioned, he did very well in Erie County (Greater Buffalo) where he almost beat out Bush for second place. Orleans, Wyoming, and traditionally Republican Chautauqua gave Perot 29 percent. Clinton's victory in Chautauqua was only the second time in the past seventy-five years that a Democrat carried the county. In central New York State Perot did well in Oswego, Cayuga, Tioga, and Madison counties.

In most of upstate New York he was competitive and averaged almost three out of ten votes. In these counties he took about two votes from Bush for every one that he took from Clinton, though in his best county, Niagara, he took almost as much from the Democrats as from the Republicans. Perot damaged the Democrats in Niagara, Erie, Montgomery, and Monroe counties. Some of these counties have many working-class Catholic Democrats of Italian and Irish ancestry, and many of them voted for Perot. The same is also true of Rensselaer County, which includes the heavily blue-collar town of Troy.

But most of the rural upstate New York counties where Perot did well are traditionally Republican and nominally Protestant counties where he took most of his votes at the expense of Bush. He managed to run second in several Republican strongholds, including Wyoming County. Eight of the ten strongest Perot counties had gone for Bush in 1988.

The Perot counties had a per capita income 22 percent below that of the state, and their residents were 36 percent less likely to be college graduates. The Perot vote was clearly linked to economic deprivation in New York State.

In the rest of the state he received little support, particularly in New York City and its nearby suburbs. In the boroughs of New York City and the counties of Westchester, Nassau, Rockland, and Orange, Perot received a lower percentage of the vote than his national average. What votes he did receive in the New York area came solely at the expense of Bush. He also did relatively poorly in Albany; in Tompkins County, where Cornell University is located; and in French Catholic Clinton County along the Canadian border (which is unusual since he had a strong showing almost everywhere else among French Canadian Catholic voters). Perot also received just under his national vote in Monroe County (Rochester).

In New York City Perot was hardly a factor. He received only 6.7 percent of the 2.1 million votes cast in New York City. The few pockets of Perot strength, though, were clearly Republican, white, middle-class areas. Perot's best showing was in District 61 on Staten Island. This was also Bush's best assembly district in New York, the only one of the sixty-one assembly districts where Bush won a majority of the three-way vote. District 61 is mostly white, middle class, and Italian Catholic. Perot's second best showing was District 38 in Queens, which is mostly German and Irish Catholic. His third-best showing was District 60 in Staten Island, another middle-income Catholic Republican area. Perot's three best assembly districts were the only three districts that Bush carried in the city. Perot topped 10 percent in only seven of New York City's sixty-one districts, so his vote was essentially negligible, but drawn solely at the expense of the Republicans.

Perot's New York counties were decidedly more secular than the state as a whole. In the counties where he received his highest support only 51.3 percent of the population were church members, compared to 65.7 percent statewide. Only 29.6 percent were Roman Catholics, compared to 40.5 percent statewide. A number of Perot's strong counties in New York are part of what religious sociologists call the "burned over region." These counties in western and central New York State were scenes of tremendous revivals in the nineteenth century, and a high percentage of the population was swept up into conservative Protestant Christianity and its attendant enthusiasms, the abolitionist and prohibitionist movements. Since that time though, most of the converts and their descendants who were members of such mainline churches as Methodist, Presbyterian, and Lutheran have more or less drifted away and church membership is relatively low in this area. In fact there are more Catholic church members than Protestants in this part of the state, though about half the population declines church membership of any kind.

NORTH CAROLINA

1992 Presidential Election Results	
ELECTORAL VOTES:	14 (Bush)
TOTAL VOTE:	2,611,850
BUSH:	1,134,661 (43.4%)
CLINTON:	1,114,042 (42.7%)
PEROT:	357,864 (13.7%)

North Carolina was not one of Perot's better states. He received only 13.7 percent of the vote in the Tar Heel State. Along with Georgia, North Carolina was a closely contested state, going narrowly for Bush by only 20,000 votes out of 2.6 million cast.

Only in two counties, Dare and Currituck, did Perot exceed his national average. Both are in the Outer Banks region of North Carolina, the state's once isolated island and resort area now populated largely by migrants. This political swing area usually favors Republicans. Dare was one of the few counties to go for Bush in 1992 after having voted for Democrat Harvey Gantt for the Senate in 1990. It is racially more moderate than the rest of the state. The Methodists are strong in this part of North Carolina.

Perot also did well in Camden, Pamlico, and Onslow counties in the eastern part of the state. Onslow, where a majority of the work force is employed by the government, was his third-best county. His returns were good in some Republican-leaning central counties such as Davidson, Randolph, Rowan, and Moore. Rowan County in particular has a large number of German Lutherans in its population. One western Republican stronghold, Avery County, gave Perot a higher-than-average vote as well. Perot's best counties gave him about 18 percent, which robbed Bush of a majority; in 1988 Bush had won two-thirds of the vote in these counties. Perot counties were a bit below the state average in per capita income (8 percent below), but they were 27 percent below average in percentage of college-educated voters. Only in Dare and Moore counties were voters likely to be above average in these categories.

Perot did relatively well in what are sometimes called the "Jessecrat" counties of the state. He received 15 percent in these counties, compared to Bush's 52 percent, and Clinton's 33 percent. These counties, in the central region of the state, are traditional Democratic strongholds, with many German and English-descended white voters, but they vote Republican in presidential elections. They also vote for Jesse Helms in the U.S. Senate races and have helped him win four times in a row. These ten counties, for example, gave Helms a 90,000-vote majority over Gov. Hunt in 1984, which offset Hunt's 12,000-vote majority in the rest of the state. They gave Helms the same percentage in 1990 over black Democrat Harvey Gantt. These counties began to vote Republican in 1952 when Eisenhower led the GOP and have gone for every Republican candidate since then except Gerald Ford in 1976. The high Baptist population here managed to give Carter a narrow victory in these counties.

Perot captured 14 percent of the vote in the strongest George Wallace (1968) counties of the state, which was only slightly better than his statewide average. The Wallace counties, incidentally, favored Helms as expected in 1990, but favored Clinton by six points over Bush. The Wallace voters in North Carolina are somewhat more Democratic than those in the Deep South, where Wallace voters still favored Bush heavily in 1992. All in all, Perot was not a particularly strong factor in North Carolina, but the closeness of the Bush-Clinton race makes the seventh of the population that supported Perot still critical in 1996.

NORTH DAKOTA

1992 Presidential Election Results	
ELECTORAL VOTES:	3 (Bush)
TOTAL VOTE:	308,133
BUSH:	136,244 (44.2%)
CLINTON:	99,168 (32.2%)
PEROT:	71,084 (23.1%)

Perot won 23 percent in North Dakota, a very respectable showing. His vote was broad-based throughout the state and he topped his national average in all but three counties. Perot strongholds could be found in the western part of the state. In that region he exceeded 30 percent of the vote in a dozen counties and ran second to George Bush in eleven of those twelve counties. He averaged about one-third of the vote in this part of the state and came within nine votes of beating Bush in tiny Billings County. He damaged Bush more than Clinton in this part of the state. Bush dropped almost twenty-one percentage points in these dozen counties, compared to his 1988 showing. Included were two longtime Republican strongholds, Grant and Golden Valley counties, where Bush was pushed down to the 45 percent level by Perot's third of the vote.

The Perot counties were somewhat below average in income and education. His counties were 13 percent below the average per capita income and 32 percent below in percentage of residents who were college educated. Perot had considerable appeal to Republican voters: in six of the seven longtime Republican strongholds in the state Perot topped 25 percent of the vote.

The two leading cultural groups in North Dakota, which usually move in opposite directions to each other, are German Catholics and Scandinavian Lutherans. Perot did well among both, receiving 27 percent among German Catholics and 23 percent among Scandinavian Lutherans. Perot came very close to beating out Clinton for second place among German Catholics, who have been voting Republican since 1940. Scandinavian Lutherans, who are somewhat more Democratic in North Dakota (they liked Roosevelt, for example) gave Perot a very respectable vote, though both groups gave Bush the edge over Clinton.

Perot even managed to garner a 20 percent vote in the two American Indian counties. One is Rolette on the Canadian border and the other is Sioux on the South Dakota border. Both are predominantly Catholic and Native American. Clinton won both, but Perot's 20 percent in the American Indian counties came at the expense of the Democrats. About 70 percent of Perot's American Indian vote in North Dakota had gone for Dukakis in 1988. These counties are desperately poor and the economic factor may have pushed many voters to Perot.

Perot did not do as well in the more metropolitan areas of the state. His poorest showing was in Cass County, the county with the largest population and the biggest city in the state, Fargo. Bush was still able to win a majority in the capital of Bismark. Nonetheless, Perot's strong support cost Bush considerably. While Bush carried the state, he won only three counties with a majority.

OHIO

1992 Presidential Election Results	
ELECTORAL VOTES:	21 (Clinton)
TOTAL VOTE:	4,939,967
BUSH:	1,894,310 (38.3%)
CLINTON:	1,984,942 (40.2%)
PEROT:	1,036,426 (21.0%)

Perot won 21 percent of the Ohio vote, enough, many would say, to have shifted the state to Clinton, who beat Bush by two percentage points and a margin of 90,000 votes.

Ohio's Perot voters were found everywhere except in the large cities. His worst showing was in Cincinnati, where he received only 15 percent. He also received a below-average portion of the vote in the other big cities of Cleveland, Columbus, Dayton, and Toledo. But he had strong support throughout much of rural Ohio. His top-ten counties, where he averaged 28 percent, were scattered throughout the state. What they had in common generally was a rural and historically Republican political culture. They were about 13 percent below the state average in per capita income and 33 percent below in percentage of college-educated voters. Only in Medina County were voters a bit above average in both categories. Perot's top-ten counties also include Portage, the home of Kent State University. This is one of the few college-oriented counties where Perot performed well. The county went for Clinton comfortably, as did most university-influenced areas. But Perot almost beat Bush for second place. Perot did in fact run second to Bush and ahead of Clinton in Shelby and Williams counties in the far western part of the state.

Perot's strong counties also include two very poor rural counties, Carroll and Perry. These longtime Republican, rural, Protestant counties finally got the message: their Republican voters, of modest income, defected in large numbers in 1992, and Clinton carried both Carroll and Perry counties, while Perot received a large vote as well. These counties are also well below average church membership, so the secular factor may also have helped Perot.

Generally speaking, the residents of Perot's top-ten counties were less likely to be churchgoers than the rest of Ohioans; 45 percent of the population in these counties are church members as compared to 50 percent statewide. Only 15 percent were Catholic compared to 20 percent statewide, but that difference is not as great as in some states. Perot damaged Bush far more than he damaged Clinton in Ohio. In his strongest counties nearly 80 percent of the Perot vote had gone for Bush in 1988.

OKLAHOMA

1992 Presidential Election Results	
ELECTORAL VOTES:	8 (Bush)
TOTAL VOTE:	1,390,359
BUSH:	592,929 (42.6%)
CLINTON:	473,066 (34.0%)
PEROT:	319,878 (23.0%)

In the Sooner State Perot received some of his best results. He won 23 percent of the vote, and although Bush carried Oklahoma, his majority over Clinton was less than nine percentage points. Perot exceeded his national average of 19 percent in all but six counties and did exceedingly well throughout much of rural Oklahoma. He topped 30 percent of the vote in Kay County, a rather upscale area, where per capita income and educational attainment are a bit above the state average. Perot also did well in Woodward County, a longtime Republican stronghold, where he won 28 percent to Clinton's 24 percent, leaving Bush with only 47 percent. It was the worst Republican showing in the county since before World War II.

But Perot also cut into longtime Democratic strongholds like Love County, where he won 28 percent to Bush's 25 percent and Clinton's 46 percent. This county usually gives Democrats large majorities, so Clinton's 46 percent was a relatively poor showing. Thus Perot was able to cut into both parties' support. In his strongest counties, where Perot won almost 30 percent, the contest between Bush and Clinton was very close. In these same counties in 1988 about one-third of the Perot vote had gone to Dukakis and two-thirds to Bush. Perot won a respectable vote even in Oklahoma City and Tulsa, and there was hardly a region in the state where he did not do reasonably well. His counties were 9 percent below average in per capita income and 28 percent below average in educational attainment.

While the Perot counties were somewhat economically distressed, some prosperous areas also supported him. In upscale Washington County, for example, he won 24 percent to Clinton's 28 percent and Bush's 48 percent. Perot's impressive vote limited Bush to only nine counties where he won a majority, one of the poorest showings for a modern Republican candidate. Oklahoma voters had been among the strongest supporters of Harry Truman in 1948, but, since bolting to Eisenhower in 1952, they have gone for every Republican except Barry Goldwater in 1964, and even Goldwater ran about six points above his national average in Oklahoma. The state's religious conservatism is undoubtedly a factor in this swift rightward turn.

A number of Perot's strongest counties are in the southern region of the state bordering Texas, though a few are in the north and a couple in the central region. Those bordering Texas are historically Democratic, but are close to Perot's home base in Dallas.

OREGON

1992 Presidential Election Results	
ELECTORAL VOTES:	7 (Clinton)
TOTAL VOTE:	1,462,643
BUSH:	475,757 (32.5%)
CLINTON:	621,314 (42.5%)
PEROT:	354,091 (24.2%)

Oregon shows Perot's ability to attract votes all across the political spectrum. He won 24 percent in the state and took votes from both Democrats and Republicans in a variety of rural counties. While Bill Clinton won the state by ten percentage points, Dukakis had done almost as well in 1988. Perot topped his national average in every county, surpassing 30 percent in four counties and averaging about 30 percent in his top-ten counties.

Perot counties were scattered throughout the state. A number were in the conservative eastern part, including his best counties, Grant and Morrow, but he did well in Wallowa in the far northeastern corner and in Curry in the far southwestern corner. In the counties where he received his highest returns Perot took almost as many votes from Democrats as Republicans. About 44 percent of the Perot vote had gone for Dukakis in 1988. Still, he managed to hurt Bush just a little more.

His strongest counties tended to be somewhat economically disadvantaged, having a per capita income 15 percent below the state average and a college educational level of 33 percent below the state. In fact, not a single Perot county was above the state average in either education or income.

Perot received a good deal of support from the right. He did very well in Morrow (as mentioned above) and Baker counties in the eastern part of the state, where more than 10 percent had voted for George Wallace in 1968 and for John Schmitz in 1972. Perot also won a quarter of the vote in the state's two most Republican counties, Malheur and Josephine. Both have a substantial right-wing vote, going back to William Lemke in 1936. Candidates like Wallace and Schmitz have routinely drained off a good 10 percent of the vote in these counties. In Josephine County Perot received a fourth of the vote, reducing Bush's support to less than 39 percent. Josephine is also a very secular county and the Republican ties to the religious right may have cost it some votes here, since Bush's vote total was the lowest for a Republican since the early New Deal days. In Malheur County Bush managed to get just over half the vote, while Perot beat out Clinton 25 percent to 24 percent.

Perot cut into the Democratic vote in places like Coos, Columbia, and Clatsop counties, where he prevented Clinton from winning a majority in these normally Democratic strongholds. But Clinton won a decisive victory in the Portland area (Multnomah County), which he carried by a 92,000-vote majority. This sweep represented two-thirds of his state majority. Clinton also swept Lane County, where the University of Oregon was a major factor. He also carried Benton County, dominated by Oregon State University. In all of these counties Perot won a respectable 21 percent to 25 percent. Clinton and Perot damaged Bush in upscale Washington County, which has a per capita income well above average, and a percentage of college-educated voters almost 45 percent higher than the statewide figure. Clinton won in Washington County but Perot took a quarter of the vote.

Oregon is the most secular state in the Union in many respects. It has the highest percentage of voters (17 percent) who say they have no religious affiliation. Only about a third of all voters (32 percent) are members of any religious group and in the Perot counties only 28 percent are members.

PENNSYLVANIA

1992 Presidential Election Results	
ELECTORAL VOTES:	23 (Clinton)
TOTAL VOTE:	4,959,810
BUSH:	1,791,841 (36.1%)
CLINTON:	2,239,164 (45.1%)
PEROT:	902,667 (18.2%)

Pennsylvania is an ideal state for microscopic voter analysis because its demographics are very similar to the national average in income, education, and the diversity of its population. It has strong Catholic, Protestant, and Jewish communities, and every ethnic group in the United States has some representation in the Keystone State. Its population is stable, which makes it a political analyst's dream. Pennsylvania ranks first in the percentage of its resident population who were born in the state (80 percent), and in some rural counties 95 percent of residents are native-born Pennsylvanians. Its historic divisions between Catholic and Protestant, and between rich and poor, continue to affect voting behavior in the 1990s. While it is slightly more Democratic than the nation in presidential elections, it is not far from the national middle. Clinton carried the state by nine percentage points, compared to 5.6 nationally. The Perot vote was nearly a mirror of the national vote. Perot won 18.2 percent in Pennsylvania, compared to 18.9 percent nationwide. Because of the close similarity in voting patterns between Pennsylvania and the nation as a whole, it is worth looking at the returns from both the counties and the precincts.

The County Analysis

Perot's total vote exceeded his national average in the vast majority of the state's counties, once again showing his unusual appeal in rural America. His strongest counties, where he averaged about a quarter of the vote, are historically Republican, and he received most of his votes from 1988 Bush supporters. His best showing was in Elk County, the state's most Catholic and rural area, where he won 28 percent. Elk is an interesting place politically. Its large Catholic population goes back to the earliest days of the country, even to the Revolutionary period, when Prince Gallitzin,* the "Apostle to the Alleghenies," was active in the area. Most Elk County Catholics trace their heritage to Marylanders who emigrated to this region before the year 1800. Consequently, Catholics in this area are old-time white native Americans, who in the past have often resembled some of their rural Protestant brethren in voting behavior.

The county was Republican from the Civil War until Al Smith carried it in 1928, whereupon it moved toward the Democrats for a while during the New Deal. But in 1936, a solid chunk of Elk County Catholics followed the extreme right-wing movement led by Father Charles Coughlin.† In the town of Benziger, for example, almost three out of ten voters chose Union party candidate William Lemke, the extreme-right-wing, third-party candidate, rather than Roosevelt or Alf Landon in 1936. In the 1950s Elk County Catholics were far more Republican and conservative than their counterparts elsewhere in the state. They favored Eisenhower three to one in 1956, while nearly 60 percent of the rest of Pennsylvania Catholics voted for Adlai Stevenson. Even in 1960, Elk County Catholics gave John F. Kennedy only 57 percent of their ballots, far below his showing in the rest of the state and the nation. Since 1968 they have voted Republican, but in 1992 a solid chunk went for Perot and Clinton, with Clinton carrying the

---

*Demetrius Augustine Gallitzin (1770–1840) was a Catholic priest of noble Russian ancestry, whose missionary efforts in Cambria County, Pennsylvania, earned him this epithet. He founded the town of Loretto in 1799 and was vicar general for western Pennsylvania. Gallitzin, Pennsylvania, is named in his honor.

†Father Charles Coughlin (1891–1979) was a Catholic priest who became a national celebrity in the 1930s through regular radio broadcasts, which reached an audience of millions. He founded the National Union for Social Justice in 1935 and published the magazine *Social Justice* from 1936 to 1942. He supported both the Union party and the anti-Semitic, pro-Fascist Christian Front. In 1942 he was silenced by church authorities.

county by one percentage point. Perot carried two of the five precincts in the heavily Catholic community of Benziger, where he emerged with 32 percent of the vote.

Perot's second-best county was Warren, a Protestant Republican stronghold, which voted Democratic for only the second time in its history. Clinton won the county and Perot received a sizable 26 percent. In both Elk and Warren counties the Republican presidential vote fell to about 35 percent, one of the worst showings for the party in its history.

Perot also did well in Butler County, still the most Republican county in the western part of the state owing to its relative prosperity. But Bush squeaked ahead of Clinton there. Other Republican Protestant strongholds like McKean County and Bradford County were on Perot's top-ten list. Perot also did well in Carbon County, a working-class county in the eastern part of the state, and in Monroe County, which is primarily a Pocono Mountain resort area. Once again we find Perot doing unusually well in a resort and retirement area, where he took a quarter of the vote.

Perot scored well in Berks County, which includes the Democratic city of Reading and a large Pennsylvania Dutch agricultural area. He took a quarter of the vote here while Bush edged Clinton by five percentage points. Berks county is one of those Pennsylvania Dutch Democratic counties that began to move Republican in 1952 when Eisenhower was leading the party. It has stayed Republican in presidential voting for most of the past forty years. Before that time Berks had been a Democratic county and had even given the Socialist Party a large presidential vote in 1928 and 1932. But times change, owing to circumstances and to the increasing conservatism of small-town German Protestant voters. The Perot vote here is undoubtedly significant.

Just missing the top ten was Westmoreland County, where Perot won 24 percent. This was his eleventh-best county and here Perot damaged the Democrats as much as the Republicans. This Democratic stronghold, with large Catholic and Scottish-Irish populations, went for Clinton, but he received only 45 percent of the vote. This economically hard-hit area should have leaned toward Clinton in much higher numbers which shows Perot's ability to cut into some of the working-class, blue-collar, economically distressed regions of western Pennsylvania.

Perot did relatively well throughout the state except in Philadelphia,

Pittsburgh, Erie, Lancaster, Harrisburg, and some of the suburbs close to Philadelphia. Perot won a respectable one out of six votes in these areas, but this was below his showing in the rest of Pennsylvania.

With the exception of prosperous Berks County, the Perot counties were to a large extent hard pressed economically. Typically, they were about 12 percent below average in per capita income and about 29 percent less likely to have college-educated voters than the rest of the state.

Religion is a major factor in Pennsylvania politics, where the state is about evenly divided between Catholics and Protestants. The Perot counties were about 6 percent less Catholic than the rest of the state and about the same percentage Protestant. They were 5 percent less likely to be church members than the state as a whole.

In Pennsylvania's largest city, Philadelphia, Perot's 10.3 percent of the vote was confined largely to the white, middle-income, and largely Catholic northeast area, which tended to vote Republican during the 1980s. Perot exceeded 20 percent in wards 31, 41, 45, and 66, the Delaware River wards and the far northeast. He won 17 percent to 20 percent in a number of other wards in the same area. All ten of Perot's strongest wards had gone for Bush in 1988 but defected to Clinton in 1992, though Clinton won a clear majority in only two of them.

Although many Philadelphia Catholics voted for Perot, his support in the heaviest Italian Catholic areas of south Philadelphia was only 14 percent. This Catholic ethnic community went to Clinton by 53 percent, giving Bush only 33 percent after having favored him 54 percent to 46 percent in 1988.

Northeast Philadelphia is a middle-class swing area in which predictable voting patterns have not been established. Swing voters are individuals whose voting choices shifted from election to election and those who were often attracted to independent or outsider candidates tended to give Perot higher-than-average support. It includes some heavily Jewish neighborhoods, where Perot won 13.4 percent, Bush 23.7 percent, and Clinton 62.9 percent. The northeast had been one of the few white middle-class areas of the northern states to support Adlai Stevenson in 1952 and 1956. It also supported Kennedy in 1960, Johnson in 1964, Humphrey in 1968, and Carter in 1976, before defecting to Reagan and Bush in three successive elections. Clinton's solid win was a good omen for Democrats in the hard-pressed, white, inner-city neighborhoods, though Perot's near 20 percent support in some wards represents a significant level of voter support.

In the University of Pennsylvania area, Perot won only 8 percent. In liberal elite neighborhoods he captured only 7 percent, while he could muster only 3 percent in black areas. Perot's poorest twenty wards were all in African-American neighborhoods. Clinton, on the other hand, won landslides in the liberal, black, and student areas.

The Precinct Analysis

Perot carried thirteen political subdivisions, one each in ten counties and three in Warren County in the state's northwest. He won 37 percent of the vote in these precincts, while Clinton took 32.2 percent and Bush won 30.8 percent. Four years before, Bush had won 58.6 percent and carried eleven of the precincts, while Michael Dukakis received 41.4 percent of the vote and carried one precinct (one precinct was tied). This pattern prevailed nationwide. Most areas carried by Perot had gone for Bush in 1988, and the shift to Perot in 1992 pushed Bush into third place. Bush's support collapsed wherever Perot was exceptionally popular. In the Perot baker's dozen Bush's support declined twenty-eight points while the Democrats' share declined by only nine points.

All of Perot's precincts were in rural areas. Here are some examples.

He won fifteen out of eighteen votes in a tiny hamlet called Valley-Hi in Fulton County. Bush, who had won thirteen of fifteen votes in 1988, dropped to two while Clinton received only one vote. (Amazingly, in 1984 Reagan won only eight to seven over Mondale.) Obviously, this is not a typical precinct.

Perot won the tiny Carbon County town of Lausanne, which went for Mondale in 1984 but was evenly divided between Dukakis and Bush in 1988.

Perot carried Howe, a village in Forest County which had supported Dukakis in 1988. This unpredictable hamlet supported Goldwater in 1964 and all other Republican presidential candidates—except when George Bush was running! It was also one of only seven precincts statewide (out of thousands) that supported Democrat Bob Casey for governor in 1986 but turned against the enormously popular governor in 1990.

Three of Perot's victories occurred in rock-ribbed Republican towns—

Armenia, Perry, and Limestone—which have never supported a Democratic candidate for president.

Sugar Grove Township in Warren County is heavily Swedish-American, a place where many members of the Swedish Covenant Church settled many decades ago. Sugar Grove has been a Republican stronghold, and, earlier in the century, was something of a Prohibition party bailiwick. The Prohibitionists often ran second in presidential races. By 1992 the Republican candidate George Bush ran third in Sugar Grove.

There were 126 precincts in forty-four counties where Perot received 30 percent of the vote or more. Most of these areas consist of Protestant Republican small towns and hamlets. A few of the high-Perot precincts in Berks and Bucks counties exceeded a thousand votes, as did Summit and Benziger, substantially Catholic towns in Butler and Elk counties respectively. Two fast-growing towns in the Poconos, Jackson and Ross in Monroe County, had about fifteen hundred votes. The fact that Perot drew so strongly in precincts in two-thirds of the state's counties indicates the geographic breadth of his support. (There were also dozens of other precincts where Perot's support topped 29 percent.)

Perot drew disproportionately from certain voting groups, classified by place of residence, income, religion, ethnicity, and political heritage. He received very strong support from rural Protestant Republican voters. He had a 26 percent showing among rural Protestant Democrats, who are often of German or Southern U.S. ancestry. These voters had been the backbone of the "old" Democratic party from Andrew Jackson through Harry Truman. But in modern times they have drifted toward the Republican candidate in presidential races. Since 1960 only Lyndon Johnson won a majority of their votes. Anti-Catholicism reduced Kennedy to only 42 percent of the vote in 1960—down 8 percent from Stevenson's vote and 25 percent less than Democratic registration. These voters have apparently viewed the Democrats as too liberal and too interested in the needs and aspirations of blacks, gays, feminists, environmentalists, and other groups not traditionally popular in small-town areas. Even in 1976 the quintessential rural Protestant Democrat Jimmy Carter was unable to win more than 48 percent in areas that once routinely gave 75 percent of their presidential ballots to the party of Jackson, Bryan, and Wilson. Bush won 65 percent over Dukakis and still beat Clinton 42 percent to 32 percent, but Perot's showing is intriguing and may suggest the first break in the Republican lock on this pro-GOP trending constituency.

Perot received 25 percent support from staunch Republican rural areas, where Democrats have *never* won in presidential, gubernatorial, or U.S. senatorial races. He pulled his ballots solely from Bush, whose support reached 75 percent in 1988. Moderate Republican rural voters, who rejected Goldwater in 1964, gave Perot 24 percent, again at Bush's expense. Yankee Protestants, those small-town descendants of the Connecticut migration in the late eighteenth century, gave Perot 24 percent. These voters, who reside mostly in the northern tier counties bordering New York, have always supported GOP candidates at the top of the ticket—even more loyally than the Yankee Protestants in New England, who defected to Clinton and Johnson. Perot also took a quarter of the votes from another small swing group, the Republicans who supported Jimmy Carter in 1976. These small-town voters include many evangelicals who have opposed almost all Democratic presidential candidates except Johnson (who won in a typical landslide) and Carter in 1976. This time Bush eked out a 38 percent to 37 percent margin over Clinton, but 25 percent opted for the Perot alternative. These Carter Republicans also liked Bob Casey, the state's moderate (socially conservative, economically liberal) Democratic governor in both 1986 and 1990, so their Republican ties occasionally loosen.

Perot received a strong (23 percent) vote among rural evangelical Protestants, who had demonstrated the volatility of traditional swing voters until the late 1960s when they settled down and voted Republican, more for cultural reasons than economic ones. In the past these voters were strongly anti-Catholic, voting more than three to one for Herbert Hoover against New York Governor Al Smith, a Catholic, in 1928. (Yankee Protestants and middle-income Protestant townsfolk supported Hoover by more than 90 percent.) In 1960 rural evangelicals gave Kennedy only 33 percent support, even though 55 percent were registered Democrats and 45 percent had voted for Stevenson in 1956. Other than Johnson's victory, no Democrat has received the nod in these bastions of conservative religion. Even Carter could manage no more than 46 percent in 1976. Bush won almost two to one in 1988 and still defeated Clinton easily 47 percent to 30 percent. But the Perot vote suggests a willingness of some rural evangelicals to look elsewhere. Governor Casey was the only Catholic candidate to do well among these voters, which may indicate that conservative Protestants have learned to tolerate Catholic candidates if those candidates are conservative on cultural issues.

Perot did well (20 percent to 21 percent) among voters who resided in fast-growing towns in the Pocono resort areas and in the middle-class Philadelphia suburbs. He received 20.4 percent of the ballots in high-population growth areas in the twenty largest counties.

As we've seen, another type of voter attracted to the Perot candidacy was the swing voter. Perot topped 20 percent in those precincts where Dukakis had made his strongest gains in 1988, compared to Mondale's support in 1984, and in those precincts that switched from Mondale in 1984 to Bush in 1988. Perot won 21 percent in what had been the strongholds of George Wallace in the 1968 election. Among Reagan Democrats, those previously Democratic voters who had supported Reagan and Bush three times, Perot won 19 percent, though these voters were so exceptionally anti-Bush that Clinton won a plurality. But Perot also received 19 percent among middle-income, anti-Reagan voters in western Pennsylvania, where the collapse of the economy during Reagan's first term pushed these voters from the Republican party (which they supported in the 1960s and 1970s) to Mondale in 1984. They stayed Democratic for Clinton by twenty points, a very slight improvement over Dukakis. But Perot picked up some of the angry western-area voters who had been leaning toward the Democrats. Perot also won 19 percent to 20 percent among both Protestant and Catholic middle-class voters in the Pittsburgh area. And he won 21 percent among "tory workers," those lower-income towns where voters have always supported the Republicans for historic, traditional, cultural, or religious reasons. This time a major chunk of the lower-income, Republican electorate defected to Perot. Among German-Americans, the state's largest ethnic group, Perot received a bit over 20 percent, all at Bush's expense. Perot won 21 percent among Democratic-leaning, low-income, white Protestants and 19 percent among middle-income, Protestant town dwellers, who had been long-time Republicans.

Perot's support was a bit below average (17 percent) among Catholics, though it was stronger among rural Catholics than among urban and suburban ones in the Philadelphia and Pittsburgh areas. Normally Republican suburbs gave him 17 percent, and low-income, white, blue-collar voters gave him 16 percent. He received 15.5 percent from upper-income voters and only 14.7 percent from residents of college towns. His support in moderate Republican suburbs, liberal elite areas, and among Jews and African Americans was low. "New Deal converts," the industry-oriented voters who had switched from the Republican to the Democratic camp because of Franklin Roosevelt's economic reforms, were not much attracted to Perot; he won 13.7 percent of the vote in these communities.

In the large, sprawling, and politically pivotal Philadelphia suburbs, Perot's vote varied sharply according to income, religion, and culture. Perot was strongest in those areas settled by the "Pennsylvania Dutch," the German-American farmers who were once Democrats but became Republicans during the 1950s. Perot received 26.1 percent in this community, all at Bush's expense. Perot did better in Protestant suburbs (22.8 percent) than in Catholic (19.2 percent) or Jewish (8.1 percent) areas. He ran stronger among middle-income communities (20.6 percent) than among the lower-middle-income (18.5 percent) or the upper income (15.0 percent) areas. He was decidedly stronger in the heaviest Republican precincts (21.3 percent) than in Democratic strongholds (12.0 percent). Clinton also made solid gains among all types of Philadelphia suburbanites, thus reducing the Bush vote to a near-record low.

*   *   *

This brings us to a final topic. How much did Perot damage the two major parties, and did he do more harm to one than to the other? The previously mentioned voting data strongly suggest that the Republican incumbent George Bush was the primary victim of the disaffection expressed by Perot voters. A county-by-county analysis of the strongest Republican and Democratic precincts (based on the 1988 presidential vote) confirms this impression.

There are forty counties in which the divisions between very Republican and very Democratic precincts are sufficiently distinct to warrant drawing some general conclusions. *In thirty-four of those counties, Perot was stronger in the most Republican precincts.* Only in Bedford, Blair, Butler, Lebanon, McKean, and Northumberland counties did Perot do better among staunch Democrats. And even in four of these six counties (excepting Blair and Northumberland), Perot's vote tended to come from

1988 Republican voters living in Democratic strongholds—in other words, most likely, lower-income Republicans.

In eight counties (Beaver, Bradford, Chester, Dauphin, Delaware, Montgomery, Somerset, and Westmoreland) Perot was considerably stronger in the most Republican precincts as opposed to the Democratic ones.

Looking at the precincts in even finer detail reveals that *the entire Perot vote in GOP strongholds came from 1988 Bush voters.* In eighteen counties Bush's support declined more than 20 percentage points in the most Republican areas. Perot exceeded his statewide average vote among the staunch Republicans in thirty-four of the forty counties, winning 29 percent in Elk and 28 percent in Warren counties. He ran second among strong Republicans in Bradford and Schuylkill counties.

But among the Democrats Perot exceeded his statewide average in only seventeen of the forty counties, doing exceptionally well in Butler County (27 percent) and Elk County (26 percent). Perot ran second among strong Democrats in Fayette, Greene, and Washington counties.

In the strongest Democratic precincts of these forty counties, Perot seems to have won a majority of his vote from 1988 Dukakis supporters in twenty-three counties. One might assume that this would have diminished the Clinton vote considerably, until a revealing fact is noted, one that is often missed by political analysts—in the other seventeen counties, the Perot vote *in the most Democratic precincts* came mostly from Republicans. These were apparently very committed voters, people who continue to vote Republican while residing in largely blue-collar, Democratic strongholds. They apparently could not bring themselves to vote for the Democrat Clinton, and they were disillusioned by Bush. So they chose the alternative, Perot.

Thus, the overall loss to the Republicans from the Perot intervention was much greater than that suffered by the Democrats. In Berks County, for example, Bush's support plummeted twenty-four points in his strongest 1988 precincts, while the Democratic vote remained unchanged. In the highest Dukakis precincts, however, Clinton lost nine points and Bush eight. So the loss to Bush among Republicans was much more severe than the relatively minor losses incurred by Clinton. It is worth noting, in passing, that Perot's vote tended to reflect the orientation of the precinct. Almost all of his vote in Republican precincts came from Republicans, and a slight majority of his vote in Democratic precincts came from Democrats. (But it bears repeating that a significant percentage of the Perot vote in Democratic strongholds came from Republican voters.)

Finally, Clinton won a majority of the total vote among staunch Democrats in *thirty of the forty counties.* Bush won a majority of the total vote among staunch Republicans in only *seventeen of the forty counties.* In other words, if the anti-Bush vote had been combined, he would have been defeated in the most loyally Republican precincts in twenty-three counties.

Another factor that helped to enhance the Perot vote was turnout. The increase in voter turnout was greater in Republican strongholds than in Democratic strongholds in thirty-six of the forty counties (all except Bedford, Butler, Crawford, and Lycoming). This confirms the view among election analysts that Republicans are more likely to vote than Democrats. More citizens than usual voted in GOP bastions, and a sizable portion of them voted for Perot.

Comparisons can also be made among Republican, Democratic, and mixed or marginal precincts in the forty counties that have considerable political diversity. Here again, the Perot-Republican connection is strong. Perot received his highest vote in the most Republican precincts in twenty-four counties, in the mixed or marginal precincts in ten counties, and in Democratic strongholds in five counties. (In Northampton County Perot did best in Republican and mixed precincts.)

A comparison of voters at opposite poles of the political hemisphere also reveals that Bill Clinton was clearly seen as a new kind of Democrat, especially among Republican voters. The relative popularity of Clinton, coupled with the higher-than-average Republican vote for Perot, produced a modest realignment of the voters in 1992. Consider the following conclusions derived from data in the forty key counties:

- Clinton made significant gains over Dukakis's vote among staunch Republicans in all forty counties. In thirty-six of those counties, Clinton's gains exceeded his statewide average gains.
- Among staunch Democrats Clinton was weaker than Dukakis in twenty-three counties, and he exceeded his statewide gain in only five counties.
- In all forty counties, Clinton's gains were greater among Republicans

than among his fellow Democrats. Clearly, Clinton's crossover appeal to Republicans, especially in the Philadelphia suburbs was noticeable, though much of this "swing" factor was due to the large Perot vote among Republicans. In some counties the response of the strongly committed voters was quite amazing. In the high-income Philadelphia suburb of Chester County, for example, Clinton gained fifteen points among Republicans and only three points among Democrats. In Allegheny County (Pittsburgh) he gained ten points among the GOP faithful while losing almost three points among Democrats. In Schuylkill County, in the coal-mining region, he gained thirteen and a half points among Republicans and lost two and a half among Democrats.

RHODE ISLAND

1992 Presidential Election Results	
ELECTORAL VOTES:	4 (Clinton)
TOTAL VOTE:	453,477
BUSH:	131,601 (29.0%)
CLINTON:	213,299 (47.0%)
PEROT:	105,045 (23.2%)

Perot won a very impressive 23 percent in Rhode Island, a state that was also one of independent candidate John Anderson's strongest supporters in 1980. Perot took more votes from Republicans than from Democrats, particularly in upper-income areas, but in a couple of key towns—Woonsocket and Providence—he took a significant number of votes away from Democrats.

Perot's Rhode Island supporters came from various economic levels. His two best counties, Kent and Washington, have a per capita income of 5 percent above the state average and an educational level 23 percent above. If one focuses only on rural areas in the state, the Perot voters appear to have been somewhat more prosperous. But looking at the top-eight towns and cities, where Perot won 30 percent or more of the votes, reveals a different picture. These towns have a per capita income of 7.5 percent below the state average and they include the second poorest town of

Woonsocket. In addition, Rhode Island's largest city, Providence, where 56 percent of the state vote is cast, is also located in the poorest and least educated county. Perot was thus able to do well at both ends of the scale. He won 20 percent in Central Falls, the poorest town in the state and one in which he took relatively more votes from Clinton than from Bush. But he won almost 18 percent of the vote in Barrington, the state's wealthiest town, and his support there came solely from 1988 Bush supporters.

In many upper-middle-income parts of Rhode Island, such as West Greenwich and East Greenwich, Bush declined more than anywhere else in the state. But in the affluent Rhode Island towns Bush's losses were as much Clinton's gains as they were Perot's, a pattern noted throughout the country.

At least one city stands out as a real problem area for the Democrats. The French Catholic working-class town of Woonsocket gave Perot 30 percent of its votes, which was second to Clinton's percent of the vote. But the Democrats under Clinton declined twenty percentage points in Woonsocket, winning 43 percent compared to Dukakis's 63 percent. It appears that about two-thirds of Perot's Woonsocket support came from those who voted for Dukakis in 1988. It is obvious that this area had problems with the Democratic ticket or saw Perot as more likely to bring about the kind of economic changes that the people here desired.

Perot also took a significant number of Democratic votes in the cities of Providence, Foster, and Burrillville.

SOUTH CAROLINA

1992 Presidential Election Results	
ELECTORAL VOTES:	8 (Bush)
TOTAL VOTE:	1,202,527
BUSH:	577,507 (48.0%)
CLINTON:	479,514 (39.9%)
PEROT:	138,872 (11.5%)

South Carolina represents one of Perot's less successful showings. He won only 11.5 percent in the Palmetto State and failed to exceed his national average in any county. However, he did receive a consistent 15 percent or so in a number of counties, which fall into interesting patterns. His best two counties are at opposite ends of the state: Oconee and Horry. The former is in the Piedmont region in the northwest and was an old Wallace stronghold in 1968. It also went heavily for Jimmy Carter in 1976 and in 1980. This county and its neighbors, Anderson, Abbeville, and Pickens, were all Wallace-Carter strongholds that switched heavily to Reagan and Bush during the 1980s. The religious right has been effective in reducing Democratic strength in this region. Walter Mondale received fewer than half the vote that Jimmy Carter received in 1976, and all of these counties remained loyal to Bush in 1992, which represents a long-range gain for the Republican party. But Perot did well in this part of the state.

He also won a respectable vote share in a group of counties in the northern part of the state near the North Carolina border: Cherokee, York, Chester, and Lancaster. These counties are similar in that they are working class and were Democratic until they began to shift toward the Republicans in the 1980s.

Perot received a good vote in three counties along the coast, Horry, Berkley, and Beaufort. Horry County was Perot's second-best county. In both Oconee and Horry he took one out of six votes. Horry County is one of the fastest-growing counties in the state since it includes the resort and retirement communities around Myrtle Beach. It has been moving in a Democratic direction during the past two elections as a result of the liberal immigrants it has been attracting. Dukakis made a significant gain here in 1988, while gaining almost nothing in the rest of the state. Bush beat Clinton by about nine percentage points here. A similar pattern is occurring in Beaufort County, which includes Hilton Head and is the state's wealthiest county. This was Perot's third-best county, where he won 16 percent, and Bush beat Clinton by only ten percentage points. So some of the out of staters must be Democrats or liberals by South Carolina standards because the combined Clinton and Perot vote was greater than the Bush vote in these coastal counties. Berkley County is somewhat similar, a county north of Charleston, though Bush did a little better there.

The Perot counties in South Carolina were relatively middle class. Their per capita income almost equalled that of the state though their educational level was still 17 percent below the state average.

Perot did not do well in the larger cities of Charleston, Greenville, and Columbia. In Columbia he received only about 7 percent of the vote. Voters in Columbia are quite unfavorable to third-party candidates. George Wallace received one of his lowest support levels in the South in Columbia in 1968.

SOUTH DAKOTA

1992 Presidential Election Results	
ELECTORAL VOTES:	3 (Bush)
TOTAL VOTE:	336,254
BUSH:	136,718 (40.7%)
CLINTON:	124,888 (37.1%)
PEROT:	73,295 (21.8%)

Perot won about 22 percent of the vote in this state, a good showing though not quite as strong as in some of the other western states. The state was closely contested, with Bush edging out Clinton by fewer than four percentage points. In a number of the counties the race was close and the winning candidate received under 40 percent in a three-way race. Perot's counties were rural and scattered throughout the state. Three were Republican strongholds in the northwest—Butte, Lawrence, and Perkins. Lawrence, in particular, is a relatively prosperous county with above-average per capita income and educational level. Perot did so well in these counties that Bush fell well below a majority, to only 39 percent in Lawrence County. Perot clearly cut into the Republican vote in this part of the state. Across the state in the southeastern corner in Gregory and Yankton counties, Perot did well, winning around 27 percent. Bush barely edged out Clinton by only twenty-six votes in Yankton County.

Another five counties in the northeast—Day, Clark, Hamlin, Codington, and Deuel—also gave Perot support of around 30 percent. Two of these even went for Clinton. Hubert Humphrey grew up in the Codington area, which has always been something of a swing county.

Most of the South Dakota Perot counties were about 15 percent below the state average in per capita income and 21 percent below in education. Some of the them, like Deuel and Gregory, are quite poor. About two-thirds of the Perot vote in South Dakota had gone for Bush in 1988. As in other states, Perot did not do quite as well in the cities as in rural areas. He won only 18 percent in the county where the state's largest city, Sioux Falls, is located. But he did receive a comfortable 22 percent in normally Republican Pennington County, which includes Rapid City and a large Air Force base. Perot won a respectable 22 percent in Clay County, a very independent-minded area dominated by South Dakota State University. Clay County, like university counties everywhere, went heavily for Clinton.

TENNESSEE

1992 Presidential Election Results	
ELECTORAL VOTES:	11 (Clinton)
TOTAL VOTE:	1,982,638
BUSH:	841,300 (42.4%)
CLINTON:	933,521 (47.1%)
PEROT:	199,968 (10.1%)

Tennessee is very much a barometer state. Since 1928 it has backed every presidential winner except Nixon in 1960, when anti-Catholicism pushed the state into the Republican column, and Nixon's support was even stronger than Eisenhower's had been. Other than that one exception, Tennessee seems to shift with the national trend. It went for the Clinton-Gore ticket by five percentage points. Al Gore was clearly a factor in the Democratic victory in the Volunteer State.

Ross Perot won only 10 percent in Tennessee, one of his worst percentages of the election, and he failed to exceed his national average in even a single Tennessee county. But he did receive a higher than statewide average vote in certain areas. He won 15 percent, his best showing, in Moore County, a small, rural, Democratic county in the central part of the state dominated by the town of Lynchburg, where Jack Daniels whiskey is made. His second-best showing was in a medium-size county in the same part of the state, Weatherford, dominated by the town of Murfreesboro. Cheatham, another county near Nashville, also gave him about one out of seven votes. There may be a slight connection between Perot and George Wallace here: Moore County had been Wallace's third-best county in the state and Cheatham County his second-best. But this pattern is not conclusive, since Perot won only 12 percent in the Wallace counties, only slightly better than statewide. Most of Perot's best counties were in the central part of the state south of Nashville.

Historically, Tennessee has been characterized by three distinct political regions. Middle Tennessee—the central region from Nashville in the south and as far north as the Kentucky border—is the classic populist area of the country, which is probably why Perot did best in this area. It is also Democratic and frequently carries the state for the Democrats. As far back as Andrew Jackson's day, this area was the Democratic bastion in most elections in Tennessee.

West Tennessee, the area around Memphis and the Mississippi River counties, is known as the black-belt region; the civil-rights movement created a backlash here among white voters in the 1950s and 1960s, and hence this part of the state resembles the Deep South in voting patterns. Both Strom Thurmond (in 1948) and George Wallace (in 1968) had their best showings in west Tennessee, and Barry Goldwater also did well in 1964. Consequently, the racial politics of west Tennessee made Perot very unpopular here; whites voted for Bush and blacks for Clinton. In Memphis, for example, Perot won only 5 percent of the vote.

East Tennessee, on the other hand, is a Republican stronghold and has been since the majority of its population supported the Union during the Civil War. This highly unusual part of the South has remained Republican through thick and thin. Some of Alf Landon's strongest majorities against Franklin Roosevelt in the heart of the Depression in 1936 were in east Tennessee and east Kentucky, where people voted their Civil War loyalties. Perot did not do particularly well here except in Greene County, where he won 14 percent.

The Gore factor was certainly important. Tennessee has three counties, Macon, Pickett, and Lincoln, which had not voted for a Democrat in modern history until they voted for Clinton. Macon and Pickett are near Gore's home county (Smith). Pickett County last voted for Democrat Franklin Roosevelt in 1932, while Macon County last voted for a Democrat in 1880. Tiny

Union County in east Tennessee had never voted for a Democrat since 1868, which shows the ability of Clinton to cut into some of the small-town Republican vote. Perot also captured a respectable vote in these three counties, enough to keep the Clinton vote below 50 percent. But the fact that Clinton could carry counties that did not support Lyndon Johnson, Franklin Roosevelt, or Woodrow Wilson has to be regarded as significant. In fact, Clinton did considerably better than Democrats usually do in east Tennessee.

The Perot counties in Tennessee were close to the statewide average in per capita income. In Rutherford County the voters were above average in income and education. These counties were not necessarily the most economically distressed, though they were still below the median.

TEXAS

1992 Presidential Election Results	
ELECTORAL VOTES:	32 (Bush)
TOTAL VOTE:	6,154,018
BUSH:	2,496,071 (40.6%)
CLINTON:	2,281,815 (37.1%)
PEROT:	1,354,781 (22.0%)

Perot won 22 percent of the vote in his home state of Texas; i.e., more than 1.3 million ballots cast were in his favor. It was an impressive showing and his vote reveals certain distinct patterns. His ten best counties, where he averaged 34 percent and ran second to Bush, are mostly in the Dallas–Fort Worth area, his home base. He did especially well in large Denton and Collins counties and in Rockwell County, all three of which are upscale areas with an above-average per capita income and education. He also carried four of his ten best counties, including tiny Irion in central Texas and isolated Loving County along the New Mexico border.

Loving County is worth commenting on though it is not particularly typical of Perot's Texas counties as a whole. It is the smallest county in the state and has the highest per capita income in the entire nation, due to the fact that it consists mostly of wealthy ranchers. Its per capita income is more than three times the state average, yet only 4 percent of its adults are college graduates. Loving County gave Perot 45 percent of the vote, Bush 31, and Clinton 20. This tiny county thus gave Perot his highest vote percentage in the country. Loving County also went for George Wallace in 1968 with an almost identical vote.

The heaviest Wallace counties in east Texas gave Perot 22 percent, which was identical to his statewide vote. Wallace did not win a majority in any Texas county, as he did in most of the South, but he did carry a number of counties in the southern-oriented eastern part of the state, and he topped 40 percent of the vote in eleven counties. Those counties went for Clinton in 1992 by twelve percentage points over Bush.

But the real strength of the Perot ticket came from the Greater Dallas–Fort Worth area. In the counties of Dallas and Tarrant (Fort Worth), with their multicultural population base Perot won 26 percent and 28 percent respectively, his best showings among the larger Texas counties. Twenty of the twenty-three counties in Texas where Perot topped 30 percent of the vote were in this television market, and every county surrounding Dallas County and Tarrant County gave Perot a vote in excess of 30 percent. Only one other small county, San Saba, in central Texas, gave Perot such support.

Because most of Perot's strength was in the wealthy Dallas–Fort Worth area, the per capita income of his Texas supporters was 5 percent above average, though they were still 12 percent below the state average in educational attainment. In this part of the state Perot clearly hurt Bush. Compared to 1988 election results, Bush dropped twenty-six points, while the Democrats under Clinton dropped eight points.

Perot also won a quarter of the vote in Montgomery County, a suburb of Houston, and in Wichita County, which is not too far from Dallas–Fort Worth, bordering Oklahoma. The Perot vote was average in the rest of Texas's major counties and slightly below-average in Galveston, where many working-class white voters live and where Wallace had done well in 1968. Perot also received a below-average vote in San Antonio, El Paso, and Hidalgo counties, western areas that are heavily Hispanic. Perot also received only 14 percent of the vote in Lubbock County, a religiously conservative Republican stronghold in the northern part of the state, where there is constant conflict over religious activities in the public schools and where the religious right is active.

Perot's poorest showings in Texas were in the heavily Hispanic areas of south Texas bordering Mexico. Perot received 10 percent in this part of the state, and the votes he did get were more at the expense of Clinton than Bush. As in Chicago, Perot seems to have taken a somewhat higher percentage of Hispanic Democrats than Hispanic Republicans. And one county in this region, Maverick County, lived up to its reputation as one of the handful of counties in the entire country where Bush actually did slightly better in 1992 than in 1988. The Hispanic rural vote was 62.5 percent for Clinton, 27.5 percent for Bush, and 10 percent for Perot. Four years earlier it gave Dukakis 69 percent and Bush 31 percent.

Interestingly, Perot did very well in the ten counties that have experienced the highest population growth since 1980. He received 28.4 percent in these high-growth areas, edging out Clinton, who won 28.2 percent. Bush received 43.4 percent.

The Harris County (Houston) vote was largely Republican. Perot's support was concentrated in prosperous white areas in the southeast (Districts 129 and 144) and the northeast (Districts 130, 135, and 150). Perot topped 20 percent of the vote in nine districts, and eight of them went for Bush. In Perot's five strongest districts Bush won 52.9 percent, Clinton 23.6 percent, and Perot 23.5 percent. On the other hand, Clinton won majorities in the seven districts where Perot received under 14 percent of the vote.

The turnout of registered voters in the top-five Perot districts exceeded the turnout in Bush and Clinton strongholds. In the Perot areas, 84.7 percent of registered voters cast ballots, compared to 82.4 percent in Bush strongholds and only 61.8 percent in Clinton's best districts. Clinton's overall Houston vote was diminished by the low turnout in Hispanic and African-American districts.

One of the many rallies where Perot supporters turned out by the thousands. (© 1996 by Shelly Katz)

For the 20 million Americans who voted for Perot, he was the only candidate who represented their concerns. (© 1996 by Shelly Katz)

Perot seemed to enjoy the role of underdog, knowing that the "experts" had been wrong before. (© 1996 by Shelly Katz)

Perot's participation in the 1992 presidential debates helped to keep all three candidates focused on the issues. (© 1996 by Shelly Katz)

UTAH

1992 Presidential Election Results	
ELECTORAL VOTES:	5 (Bush)
TOTAL VOTE:	743,999
BUSH:	322,632 (43.4%)
CLINTON:	183,429 (24.7%)
PEROT:	203,400 (27.3%)

In Utah Perot won 27.3 percent of the vote, one of his highest national showings. It was the only state where he ran second to President Bush, leaving Democrat Bill Clinton in third place. Perot's vote was scattered throughout Utah, though much of it was concentrated in the Greater Salt Lake City area. In Salt Lake City proper, where 43 percent of the state vote is cast, Perot ran a close third with 29 percent.

Perot's best showing was in Summit County, to the east of Salt Lake, where he won nearly a third of the vote, leaving the county almost equally divided between the three candidates. Summit is the state's wealthiest county and its residents are very well educated. (His worst showing was in the state's poorest county, San Juan.) Perot also did well in several other counties where residents have above-average incomes: Weber, Davis, and Toole.

His support was concentrated fairly close to Salt Lake City, though he also did well in Grand and Uintah counties in the eastern part of the state. Grand County, in particular, a non-Mormon county, gave Perot about 30 percent of the vote, and Clinton carried the county.

Among the staunchest Republican counties in the state, Perot did quite well in Box Elder, where he took 29 percent and left Clinton with only 14 percent. This is a strong manufacturing county, where Perot's appeal was undoubtedly related to his criticism of America's national economic decline. In counties with significant Perot support, Bush dropped twenty-seven percentage points from his 1988 showing, while Clinton dropped eight percentage points behind Dukakis's level of support.

Taken as a whole, the Perot counties were slightly above average in per capita income, one of the very few states where that was the pattern. Their educational level, though, was still below average; the voters were about 56 percent as likely to be college educated as all Utahans.

The religious factor is certainly critical in this bastion of Mormonism. The pattern of Perot support is somewhat mixed. Perot's top counties were about 9 percent less likely to be Mormon than the rest of the state, but this was not a particularly strong difference. Looking at certain rural areas also reveals a mixed pattern. Perot won 23.3 percent in the heaviest Mormon rural areas, but he also won 21.6 percent in the three largely non-Mormon rural counties. Perot did best in Salt Lake County and some of the larger, religiously mixed counties.

Rural, Mormon Utah is a region of the country that leans to the right politically. These counties gave Bush 54.5 percent, Perot 23.3 percent, and Clinton only 14.7 percent. Nearly 7.5 percent voted for the extreme right-wing Populist-party candidate Bo Gritz, himself a Utah native. These counties have always had a vigorous far-right vote. They gave 9 percent to American Independent party candidate John Schmitz in the 1972 presidential election and 7 percent to George Wallace in 1968. They tend to prefer nonsouthern candidates of the far right, however. In fact, the right wing siphoned off almost 5 percent of Utah's vote, mainly to Bo Gritz or to the libertarians. Three southern Utah Republican strongholds, Washington, Millard, and Sanpete counties, gave Gritz 10 percent to 12 percent of the vote, as did Duchesne County in the northern part of the state. These were among his highest support levels.

Perot's best counties tended not to be so far to the right. His counties had supported Lyndon Johnson in 1964, while the heaviest Mormon counties had given an edge to Goldwater. Clinton's best support came in the non-Mormon counties, where he beat Bush 44 percent to 31 percent. These counties had also favored Dukakis by five percentage points over Bush four years before. In rural Utah, at least, Mormonism is highly identified with Republican voting. Generally, only non-Mormons vote Democratic. In the larger cities of the state this is less true. Bush captured a very impressive 57 percent of the vote in Utah County, where Mormonism's citadel of learning, Brigham Young University, is located. Perot, however, won a respectable 23 percent in this same county, and Bill Clinton won his lowest Utah vote, 13 percent, in the area around BYU.

★　　★　　★

VERMONT

1992 Presidential Election Results	
ELECTORAL VOTES:	3 (Clinton)
TOTAL VOTE:	289,701
BUSH:	88,122 (30.4%)
CLINTON:	133,592 (46.1%)
PEROT:	65,991 (22.8%)

Tiny Vermont is one of the most interesting states because, though small, it represents a number of national trends. Perot won almost 23 percent in Vermont, an extraordinary showing considering the state's general reluctance to support third-party candidates. There is some precedent, however, since Vermont was John Anderson's second-best state in 1980, and eight of Vermont's fourteen counties were among Anderson's top-fifty counties nationwide.

Perhaps the most significant thing about Vermont is that Bill Clinton won 46 percent of the vote here, carrying all fourteen counties. This is only the second time in the state's entire history that a Democrat carried every county. The other time was 1964, when Lyndon Johnson won Vermont. In 1992, George Bush received the lowest percentage of the vote ever given to a Republican candidate in the state's history. He won just 30.4 percent, even lower than Barry Goldwater's percentage in 1964. This extraordinary rejection of the Republican party may be related as much to cultural and religious issues as to economic factors. Vermont is probably the most religiously tolerant state in the Union. Since its beginning, it has had an absence of religious strife, even though one-third of the population is Catholic and conflicts between Catholics and Protestants are generally frequent in states with a high Catholic population. Its representatives in Congress have been the most likely of any state's (along with Connecticut) to oppose the religious right's positions on abortion, prayer in public schools, religious activities in public schools, and aid to private schools. It could very well be that the Republican party's ties to the religious right caused its collapse in Vermont in 1992.

Perot's best counties were in the so-called Northeast Kingdom—Orleans, Essex, and Caledonia counties—and in predominantly French

Catholic Franklin County, also in the northern part of the state. This is an area of rural-village individualism. Perot's best county, and the state's poorest, is Essex. The per capita income in Perot's counties is 18 percent below the state average, and the percentage of adults who are college educated is almost 43 percent lower than the state average.

But in the cities and towns, Perot seems to have gotten a different type of vote. His top-seven townships are basically middle class and have a per capita income equal to the state average. His fourth-best showing was in prosperous Essex township, where he took a quarter of the vote, solely at the expense of George Bush. His best town, Milton, is a high-population-growth area. Not only did Perot win 32 percent and run second to Clinton but the voter turnout increased 29 percent. A similar pattern occurred in Colchester.

Throughout the state Perot received his vote almost entirely from former Bush supporters. Many of the middle- to upper-middle-class, well educated towns showed very large Bush declines, a strong Clinton showing, and a respectable Perot vote. Only in Barre City and Winooski, blue-collar Catholic strongholds, did Perot also take some votes from the Democrats. In these areas probably 30 percent to 35 percent of the Perot vote had gone to Dukakis in 1988. Perot did less well in Montpelier, the state capital, and in liberal strongholds like Brattleboro, Burlington, and Middlebury. These are college towns where Clinton won a decisive victory.

As mentioned above, the Anderson factor bears some relation to Perot's support, but it may not have been quite as direct in Vermont as in some other New England states. Vermont was John Anderson's second-highest state. Anderson's best county in Vermont, Windham, in the southeast corner, was Perot's worst county in the state. Windham has been increasingly leaning toward the Democrats, which the Anderson vote signaled. This longtime Republican county voted for Dukakis in 1988, only the second time in its history that it went Democratic. It was Clinton's strongest Vermont county, giving him an outright majority of 53 percent of the vote.

VIRGINIA

1992 Presidential Election Results	
ELECTORAL VOTES:	13 (Bush)
TOTAL VOTE:	2,558,665
BUSH:	1,150,517 (45.0%)
CLINTON:	1,038,650 (40.6%)
PEROT:	348,639 (13.6%)

Perot won 13.6 percent in Virginia, one of his less impressive showings. He surpassed his national average in only two counties, Gloucester and Mathews, both in the Northern Neck area (a rural area near Chesapeake Bay), and in one city, Manassas Park. Perot's Virginia vote, such as it was, was concentrated in the outer suburbs of Washington, D.C., in Loudon, Prince William, Stafford, Clarke, and King George counties, where people probably work in the suburbs and live even further out. These are traditional Republican areas, and Perot took most of his Virginia vote from the Republicans. He also did well in the Northern Neck counties of New Kent, Mathews, and York, and in one of the Eastern Shore counties, Accomack, which borders Maryland. He did not do particularly well anywhere in the rest of the state—in the Shenandoah Valley, in the far southwest, the racially divided Southside, or in the Richmond area. But in the conservative, Republican Richmond suburb of Chesterfield County he took one out of six votes, and his support was above his state average in Frederick, Warren, and Fauquier counties, which are exurbs of Washington, D.C.

In the state's independent cities he was not a particularly strong factor except in the blue-collar town of Manassas Park, where he took 21 percent of the vote. This is a conservative white town, and Bill Clinton won only a third of the vote here compared to the 60 percent that Jimmy Carter had won in 1976. Perot also won a respectable vote in Manassas, a middle-class Washington suburb, and in Virginia Beach, where he took 17.5 percent of the vote, entirely at the expense of George Bush. Virginia Beach is the headquarters of TV evangelist Pat Robertson and has many military and out-of-state voters, as well as a higher-than-average Catholic population. Perot's vote was low in Richmond, Alexandria, Charlottesville, Norfolk, and most other parts of this very stable and mostly Republican state.

Perot's counties were near the state average in per capita income—only 6 percent below. In the Washington exurbs of Prince William and Stafford counties, the voters have above-average income and education, and in King George and York counties, where Perot also managed to do reasonably well, the educational level is somewhat higher.

In the southside counties that gave George Wallace his greatest support, the Perot vote was 13.5 percent, almost identical to his statewide showing. Bush beat Clinton 47 percent to 39 percent in these old segregationist strongholds.

WASHINGTON

1992 Presidential Election Results	
ELECTORAL VOTES:	11 (Clinton)
TOTAL VOTE:	2,288,230
BUSH:	731,234 (32.0%)
CLINTON:	993,037 (43.4%)
PEROT:	541,780 (23.7%)

In Washington State Perot won 23.7 percent, or nearly one out of every four votes. It was one of his best showings in the nation, and while he took more votes from Republicans than Democrats, he damaged the Democrats in a number of counties. His support came from all over the state. He did well in Mason, Island and Grays Harbor near Seattle, and in Wahkiakum, Skamania, and Klickitat counties, which border Oregon. He also did well in three counties in the northeastern part of the state bordering Canada: Ferry, Okanogan, and Pend Orielle.

Perot's best county was Wahkiakum, which has many Democratic voters of Scandinavian descent. Here he secured almost a third of the vote and came in second to Clinton. His second-best county was Ferry, a rural county where he took almost 30 percent and came within eleven votes of running second. Ferry is the state's poorest county. Another poor county, Pend Orielle, was also among Perot's top-ten counties. All ten were carried by Clinton, and even four years before, six of the top ten and 51 percent of the vote here had gone for Dukakis.

As the nationwide voting patterns for Perot suggest, his counties generally were somewhat economically distressed. Their per capita income was 18 percent below the state average and their educational attainment level was 31 percent below the state average.

Washington can be roughly broken down into three sections. About a third of the vote is cast in King County, which comprises Seattle and most of its suburbs. Another third comes from four other large counties, which include the cities of Vancouver, Tacoma, Spokane, and the middle-class Seattle suburb of Snohomish. Perot did particularly well in these counties, particularly Snohomish, where he won 29 percent. The last third of the vote comes from the rural areas of the state.

In terms of Perot support, his vote resembled Arizona or Texas more in many respects than other parts of the country. He did best (25.6 percent) in the four medium-sized counties, compared to 24.1 percent in the rural areas and 21.5 percent in Seattle. Of the three candidates Perot's support was the most evenly distributed over the three sections. Bush's support was stronger in smaller counties, while Clinton's vote increased markedly as one moved into the urban Seattle area. Clinton beat Bush, for example, by twenty-three percentage points in the Greater Seattle area, but defeated Bush by only three percentage points in rural areas. In the central city of Seattle Clinton swept Bush by a 65 percent to 18 percent margin, and Perot achieved only 15 percent, a result that resembles the San Francisco pattern more than the rest of Washington State.

The education factor helped Clinton in Washington as elsewhere. Whitman County, in the far eastern part of the state bordering Idaho, is dominated by Washington State University. It has one of the best-educated electorates in the nation, with over 35 percent of adults holding a college degree. The county has been Republican since 1940. But Bill Clinton beat George Bush by seven percentage points here for the most impressive Democratic victory since Roosevelt in 1936. Whitman, Yakima, and Garfield are the only three counties where Perot failed to reach his national percentage. Even in Whitman, though, Perot won a respectable 18 percent of the vote.

Perot's vote, then, came from various sources. He received disproportionate support from Democrats in the Evergreen State, though almost two-thirds of his Washington vote came from those who had supported Bush and Reagan.

One other interesting county worth mentioning is San Juan, which is basically a county of island residents north of Seattle and near the British Columbia border. San Juan is upscale; its residents are extremely well educated and have above-average incomes. Clinton beat Bush by more than twenty percentage points here, and Perot won about a quarter of the vote. Perot ran second to Clinton in two of the state's counties and came very close in others.

WEST VIRGINIA

1992 Presidential Election Results	
ELECTORAL VOTES:	5 (Clinton)
TOTAL VOTE:	683,762
BUSH:	241,974 (35.4%)
CLINTON:	331,001 (48.4%)
PEROT:	108,829 (15.9%)

West Virginia was not one of Perot's best states. He won just under 16 percent, though it was enough to deprive Bill Clinton of a majority of the total vote. Perot's vote in this state came from two distinct sectors.

One was the manufacturing–industrial base in the northern counties, which border Pennsylvania, Ohio, and Maryland. Perot did well and exceeded his national average in three of the four counties bordering both Pennsylvania and Ohio and in several other counties (Wetzel, Tyler, Pleasants, and Wood) along the Ohio border. Not far away, Preston County, which borders western Maryland, also gave Perot a good vote.

His second source of voter support came from Republican strongholds. Perot's best county, where he won 24 percent, was Tyler, a longtime Republican area, which has not supported a Democrat in more than a century. Perot and Clinton cut into Bush's strength here, and Clinton came within six votes of victory. Bush won less than 37 percent of the vote. Upshur County is another Republican stronghold; it has backed only one Democrat in the past century—Lyndon Johnson in 1964. Perot won an impressive 19 percent and Clinton came within four percentage points of beating Bush. Perot did not have much of an impact in the strongly Democratic coal-mining region or in the southern-oriented Panhandle counties, which border Virginia and Maryland.

Perot's West Virginia counties were relatively well off. His counties had a per capita income of almost 98 percent of the state average, which suggests a middle-class level of prosperity. Their educational level was 17 percent below the state average. Wood County, in particular, is an upscale county which supported Bush but where Perot won over 19 percent of the vote. His West Virginia vote came mainly from middle-class residents concerned about the national and state economies. His poorest showings were in old Democratic strongholds.

The Perot counties have a slightly higher church membership (45 percent) compared to the state's 41 percent average. But this is due to the high Catholic identity in Brooke, Hancock, and Marshall counties, the three northernmost areas that resemble Pennsylvania more than the rest of the state in their ethnic and religious identity.

WISCONSIN

1992 Presidential Election Results	
ELECTORAL VOTES:	11 (Clinton)
TOTAL VOTE:	2,531,114
BUSH:	930,855 (36.8%)
CLINTON:	1,041,066 (41.1%)
PEROT:	544,479 (21.5%)

Perot did well in Wisconsin, winning 21.5 percent of the vote in the old stronghold of Robert LaFollette. He exceeded his national average in all but four counties—Milwaukee, Madison, high-income Ozaukee County, and the Scandinavian Democratic stronghold of Douglas County, which includes the city of Superior. Perot's support came exclusively from rural counties, which are scattered all over the state from southwest Grant County to northeast Florence County. Beside their rural characters, they have several other things in common.

First, these counties are relatively poor and their educational level is below average. The per capita income averages 18 percent below the state average, and voters are only two-thirds as likely to have a college degree as those throughout the state. With the exception of St. Croix County, nine of Perot's top-ten counties are all below average in per capita income and education.

Second, voters in the Perot counties were sharply divided by the presidential race. Clinton carried six of the top-ten Perot counties and beat out Bush by one percentage point, while Perot averaged almost 30 percent in these counties. Four years before Bush had edged Dukakis 52 percent to 48 percent, so Bush lost more than Clinton did. Nevertheless, about 40 percent of the Perot vote in his best Wisconsin counties had gone for Dukakis in 1988. In strongly Republican Waushara in the central region of the state, Perot's solid 27 percent of the vote pushed Bush down to only 39 percent, one of the poorest Republican showings since the early Depression days in that county.

Perot had a strong appeal to both German Catholics and to Scandinavian Lutheran voters, a pattern we have seen in other states with similar ethnic populations. He won 25.4 percent in the top eight Lutheran counties, which are mostly Scandinavian. He also did well in the German Lutheran counties, where he received about the same vote. In eight heavily Catholic small-town counties he averaged 24.2 percent. These counties are heavily German. Most of rural Wisconsin was a closely divided battleground in this election. Bush edged out Clinton by one percentage point among German Catholics, who had been Republican since 1940. In heavy Scandinavian Lutheran counties Clinton won over Bush by less than two percentage points. But Perot's solid one-quarter of the vote cut across party, ethnic, and religious lines throughout Wisconsin.

Wisconsin is part of the "morality belt," where attacks on Clinton's draft record and personal life may have cut his vote down substantially. Clinton beat Bush by only four percentage points in the state, which was slightly better than the percentage Dukakis had received in the previous presidential election. Most of those gains came in Dane County, the liberal stronghold surrounding the University of Wisconsin and the state capital, and in Rock County, a historically Yankee Protestant county. In the real Scandinavian-German interior of Wisconsin, Clinton had to fight to hold the state, which is probably why President Bush made a last ditch effort on a whistle-stop train tour through the rural areas of Wisconsin. His enthusiastic reception there briefly enlivened the sagging Bush campaign. But Wisconsin's basic liberalism asserted itself and Clinton held the state, though not without a very strong and significant Perot vote.

The Bush vote in Wisconsin seems strongly related to income. The only two counties in which he won a majority of the three-way vote are the two highest-income counties—Ozaukee and Waukesha. Both counties are in the top-one-hundred counties of the United States in per capita income.

Another interesting county was Menominee, which is basically a large Indian reservation. Everyone who lives here is a Native American and 71 percent are Catholic. The county is a Democratic stronghold in which Clinton won 60 percent, Bush 21 percent, and Perot 19 percent. But Perot's 19 percent came more from the Democrats than from the Republicans, which means his votes were pulled from a staunchly Catholic electorate. Quite a departure from Perot's support among Catholics. Once again we find this unusual ability of Perot to cut across seemingly insuperable ethnic and cultural barriers.

WYOMING

1992 Presidential Election Results	
ELECTORAL VOTES:	3 (Bush)
TOTAL VOTE:	200,598
BUSH:	79,347 (39.6%)
CLINTON:	68,160 (34.0%)
PEROT:	51,263 (25.6%)

Former defense secretary Dick Cheney, in an interview in *Policy Review* magazine in the summer of 1993, confessed, "I'm still puzzled by the Perot vote. . . . But Mr. Perot was saying some things that were very appealing to people in Wyoming—my voters, my constituents." Mr. Cheney certainly should take notice because in his state Perot's nearly 26 percent of the vote came almost exclusively at the expense of the Republicans. Perot did well throughout this basically rural state, surpassing his national average in every county. The Perot-Republican connection comes through very clearly: the top-ten Perot counties, where he averaged 28.4 percent, were mostly Republican strongholds; six of the top-ten have been bastions of Republican strength since World War II. Perot also did well in Sublette County, where George Wallace posted good showings in 1968, and in the staunchly Mormon area of Uinta County.

Perot received considerable support in Natrona County, which is the second largest in population and includes the city of Casper, an upscale county, where the per capita income and educational level are higher than the statewide average. Clinton carried the county, a rarity for a Democrat, and Perot won 28 percent of the vote.

Perot also won 28 percent of the ballots in Teton County, one of the most Republican counties in the nation and Wyoming's second wealthiest county. What makes Teton so fascinating is that this steadfastly Republican area, where 33 percent of the adults have a college education, defected to Clinton. Teton has much in common with counties in Colorado and Idaho, which share similar high-education characteristics. George Bush plunged to 34 percent of the vote in Teton despite a Republican registration of 52 percent, and Republicans here defected to Clinton and to Perot in large numbers. Teton County is known for the celebrity-conscious town of Jackson Hole.

Perot's strongest Wyoming counties tended to be middle class. They were close to the state average in per capita income and education. Perot did well in both the wealthiest county (Campbell) and in the poorest county (Niobrara), and in highly educated counties (Sublette and Natrona) as well as in the least educated county (Hot Springs).

While Bush managed to carry Wyoming, as Republicans almost always do, he fell below 40 percent of the total vote. The Clinton-college connection shows up in Albany County, where Laramie is the county seat and the major employer is the University of Wyoming—Albany defected to Clinton. Although the county tends to vote Republican, its percentage declined to one of the lowest levels in history. In fact Albany turned out to be the most Democratic county in the state, which has never happened before. It became the second-least Republican county with George Bush at the head of the ticket. Clinton also won the old Democratic county of Sweetwater by thirteen percentage points, but Perot won a very respectable 26 percent and undoubtedly took some Democratic votes in Sweetwater County.

Part Four

Perot Voters and the
Future of American Politics

1

The Culture Wars and the 1992 Vote

Education and religion were major factors in shaping how voters responded to the issues and personalities of the 1992 presidential race.

Bill Clinton is only the second Democrat in history to win among college-educated voters, a high-status, influential, and historically conservative group (since education and income are almost directly correlated in terms of status and economic achievement). Clinton won 44 percent to 39 percent, and Perot 16 percent among all college-educated voters, and Clinton was comparatively stronger among women than men. Among voters with advanced degrees, Clinton won decisively—49 percent to Bush's 36 percent (15 percent for Perot)—a margin that may have exceeded Johnson's 1964 margin over Goldwater, the only other Democrat to win among this growing portion of the electorate. College-educated voters are religiously diverse and generally hold liberal positions on all of the cultural flashpoint issues—abortion, school prayer, public aid for nonpublic schools, gay rights, sex education, tolerance for alternative lifestyles, censorship of books and films, religious tolerance, and opposition to religious-based political appeals. The well-educated voters in every religious community tend to reject the belief that the Bible is literally true or inerrant and are opposed to the Religious Right's attempt to impose a narrow or unitary moral

175

vision on society. They were opposed to the religious intolerance displayed at the Republican convention in August 1992 and equally opposed to the sectarian slant of the position the GOP's platform took on numerous "family values." So were many voters who are not college graduates, but the defection from the Bush ticket by so many former supporters in the high-education, high-income echelons is a warning signal that Republican leaders will ignore to their peril. These issues also affected the highest-income voters—those making above $75,000 annually—who gave Bush only 48 percent of their support in 1992 compared to 68 percent in 1988.

Upscale voters may have reacted against Bush's "Know Nothing" campaign, his sneers at Clinton's Oxford education. (Bush did the same in 1988, lampooning Michael Dukakis's Harvard and Swarthmore education, as if Bush's prep school and Yale degrees were greatly different.) Bush's ignorance of history, for example, when he condemned the Democratic platform for omitting references to God, is evident, as most Republican and Democratic platforms before 1948 did not claim divine blessings for their political positions.

Republicans in Congress have been far more likely than Democrats to cut education and library spending and to attack the National Endowments for the Arts and Humanities and public television. The Republican platform's endorsement of a "common moral vision" in art and culture was considered inappropriate by many voters.

The cultural religious divide in this election looks at first blush quite simple: frequent church attendees versus casual attendees, and white Protestants versus everyone else. Here is what the Voter Research and Survey's exit-polling data show: Among the 40 percent of voters who attend church weekly—in whatever tradition—Bush won 47 percent , Clinton 38 percent, Perot 15 percent. Among the 60 percent who attend occasionally or not at all, Clinton won 47 percent, Bush 31 percent, Perot 22 percent. The difference was especially significant among Bush voters. Nearly half of weekly churchgoers supported Bush, while fewer than a third of the less observant did so.

The old Republican–white Protestant nexus remained partially intact, though, as we shall see, defections from moderate, liberal, mainline, and "cultural" Protestants reduced Bush's support level. White Protestants, who made up 49 percent of all voters in the election, favored Bush by 46 percent,

Clinton by 33 percent, Perot by 21 percent. All other voters (51 percent of the electorate) went for Clinton heavily, giving him 53 percent, Bush 30 percent, and Perot 17 percent. While the GOP has always received more support from white Protestants than from any other segment of the electorate, its support is now concentrated among more intensely involved, conservative Protestants of moderate income and education who reside in the South.

The intimations of a cultural war perceived at the GOP convention can be seen in how voters responded to major issues. The results show that the issues emphasized by the Republicans did not engage the concerns of the average voter. Indeed, the vast majority of voters were concerned about the economy, with the environment and education well behind: 43 percent of voters cited the economy as the paramount issue, and Clinton defeated Bush decisively among this group. Clinton also won a clear majority of the three-candidate slate among voters concerned about the environment, health care, jobs, and education. Bush won among voters concerned about taxes and foreign policy, and Perot tied Clinton among voters concerned about the budget deficit.

Where did that leave Bush? He won two-thirds of "family values" voters, but they were only 15 percent of all voters. (Of Bush's voters 27 percent cited family values as a factor in their votes, compared to only 8 percent of Clinton's and 9 percent of Perot's voters.) Bush defeated Clinton 54 percent to 38 percent among voters who cited abortion as a major concern, suggesting that antichoice activists are still more likely than prochoicers to let that issue affect their presidential vote. Still, only a third of voters listed abortion as a top priority. Bush won among the tiny segment of voters (12 percent) who raised the issue of marital fidelity. The Republicans emphasized issues that were of peripheral concern to most voters, and the repeatedly negative tone of the Bush campaign offended many. Fully 30 percent of voters said Bush's attacks on Clinton were "unfair," compared to 9 percent who thought Clinton's attacks were unfair. The electorate did not judge the Perot campaign to be negative.

Clues to the cultural war's voting impact are spread throughout the voter profiles that emerged from this election. Women went decisively for Clinton by eleven points, especially working women (12 percent margin) and single mothers (20 percent margin). Only homemakers gave Bush the edge. While Bush's support went up as voter income increased, he captured only 48 percent of those whose income exceeded $75,000. He garnered 23 percent among those whose family income was under $15,000. But this twenty-five-point difference pales when compared to religious differences, where fifty points separated Bush's support from top (evangelicals and fundamentalists) to bottom (Jews). Unmarried voters gave Clinton 49 percent, Bush 33 percent, and Perot 18 percent, while married voters split evenly. Even among the quarter of the electorate who said their family's financial situation had improved, only 62 percent voted for Bush. (In 1984 voters who felt that way gave 86 percent to Reagan.) Obviously, something other than economic self-interest was at work in this election. In all of the above categories, Clinton did well among culturally liberal and tolerant voters who rejected the Republican embrace of Religious Right extremism. In no area is that rejection more pronounced than in the educational attainments and religious convictions of the voters of this vast and diverse nation.

Voter profiles show that Clinton and Perot supporters were closer to each other on family morality issues than either was to Bush. Fully 28 percent of Bush's voters were white evangelicals and fundamentalists, compared to 14 percent of Perot's and 9 percent of Clinton's. Even among Bush's shrunken coalition, only a fourth singled out family-values issues as decisive. Many politically conservative areas that are *not* strongholds of religious conservatism gave Bush only a lukewarm plurality.

Let's look now at the religious voting patterns in 1992.

Clinton trounced Bush among Jews, black Protestants, Catholics, religious liberals, and religiously nonaffiliated voters. The Clinton-Gore ticket made sharp inroads among the historically Republican mainline Protestants in the West and North. The Bush-Quayle ticket prevailed among evangelical and fundamentalist white Protestants, especially in the Deep South, and among Mormons. One of the more intriguing patterns of this unusual election was Bush's victory among white Southern Baptists, the religious affiliation of both Governor Clinton and Senator Gore. Clinton did not do nearly as well among his fellow Baptists and among white Southerners generally as Jimmy Carter did in 1976. Clinton won only 40 percent compared to Carter's 58 percent in 1976.

The general contours of religious voting patterns can be seen in Clinton's triumph in all twelve of the nation's most heavily Catholic states—from New Mexico to Massachusetts—the first Democratic sweep of these states since Lyndon Johnson in 1964. Four years before, Catholics had been almost evenly divided. Clinton's emphasis on economic issues and social justice played well among Catholic voters; Bush's emphasis on family values and character did not. Clinton made a major policy address on family values and religious tolerance at the University of Notre Dame, while the Bush campaign played up several issues (aid to parochial schools, abortion) thought to be of specific importance to Catholic voters. Bush also made two campaign appearances at the side of Philadelphia's Cardinal Anthony Bevilacqua. But the strategy failed as Catholics voted 44 percent to 36 percent for Clinton, with 20 percent for Perot.

While Clinton's Catholic triumph represents a return home for Catholic voters, his margin was the same as Carter's in 1976 and a good deal less than that of Kennedy, Truman, and Humphrey. Hispanic voters, who are 70 percent Catholic, favored Clinton 62 percent to 24 percent, with about 14 percent for Perot. Hispanic support was extremely important in moving New Mexico to the Democratic column for the first time since 1964. Cajun Catholics in southern Louisiana helped carry that state for Clinton. The trend-setting French Catholics have gone for every winner since 1956 (except 1968). This time they gave Clinton 48 percent, Bush 39 percent, and Perot 13 percent.

Even in Cardinal Bevilacqua's bailiwick, Catholics went for Clinton. Delaware County, a significantly Catholic Philadelphia suburb, went Democratic for the first time since 1964, as did St. Louis County, Missouri; Baltimore County, Maryland; and Middlesex County, New Jersey, all of which have a high percentage of Catholic voters. Clinton even carried Manchester, New Hampshire. Clinton did well among all Catholic ethnic subgroups. Among Catholics of French descent in New England, Clinton came in a strong first, with Perot second, and Bush a poor third.

Mainline Protestants, a mainstay of the Republican party since 1856, were far less likely to support Bush than any previous Republican president. These voters, economic moderates but social-issue liberals, may have reacted against the extremism perceived at the Republican convention in August and the party's embrace of Religious Right platform positions. Clinton's victories in Vermont, Connecticut, Maine, New Hampshire, Ohio, Michigan, and Iowa—where many of these voters reside—were telltale signs of disapproval of recent trends in Republican politics.

Vermont, a state with many mainline and Catholic voters, went Democratic for only the second time in one hundred sixty years. The Green Mountain State, which may be the nation's most tolerant state, and whose Congressional representatives have steadfastly opposed Religious Right positions, gave Bush only 31 percent of its votes—lower than Barry Goldwater's 1964 showing and indeed the worst Republican showing in history.

Mainline Protestants, who almost always give 60 percent to 70 percent of their support to Republican presidential candidates, gave Bush just 38 percent nationwide. Clinton won slightly over 38 percent and Perot won 24 percent. "Yankee Protestants" all over New England deserted their party in droves as Clinton carried Cape Cod, Nantucket, Wellesley, and scores of similar communities.

Bush won decisively among the 17 percent of the electorate that called itself "white born-again Christian": he received 61 percent of these votes compared to Clinton's 23 percent and Perot's 15 percent. While Bush was down from the 81 percent he won four years previously, his strong showing among these voters saved a number of southern states and possibly Kansas for the GOP. Bush carried such religiously conservative cities as Greenville, South Carolina; Lubbock, Texas; and Bakersfield, California.

Bush's two strongest states were Mississippi and Alabama, the two most heavily Baptist states. In both states white Baptists and other Protestants, for a variety of racial, cultural, and religious reasons, have deserted Democratic presidential candidates, and even a Baptist governor of Arkansas could not bring them back. Bush's third strongest state was South Carolina, which has similar characteristics. The more religiously homogeneous regions of the Protestant South (North Carolina, parts of Florida, Georgia, Texas, and Louisiana) also favored the Bush-Quayle ticket.

In ninety-six heavily Southern Baptist counties in eleven southern states, Bush won 46 percent to Clinton's 40 percent and Perot's 14 percent. In suburban areas of the South, Bush appears to have won 55 percent of Baptists.

The Religion Factor

A total of 153 counties in twelve southern and border states supported Jimmy Carter in *both* 1976 and 1980, but opposed Bill Clinton in 1992.

These counties are in mostly rural areas with overwhelmingly white populations. The income level varies, and the educational level is below average.

The key factor is religion, though not necessarily church membership, which was only a slightly predictive factor. It is only 5 percent more likely that the populations of these counties are church members. The *significant factor is the Baptist percentage of the population,* specifically white Southern Baptists.

In Florida the anti-Clinton counties, which backed Carter twice and then Bush twice have three times as many Baptists as the state as a whole. In Texas it is twice as many. Even in the states where Baptists dominate the entire religious scene, the counties rejecting Clinton have a higher percentage of Baptists than the statewide average, especially in Louisiana and Kentucky. Only on Maryland's eastern shore, where Methodism has always been *the* evangelical church, is this not true. (One Tennessee county, Tipton, falls into this category but, as a growing exurb of Memphis, it is not representative of the state's Baptists. The Al Gore factor may have helped in the Volunteer State, since Clinton did better among Tennessee [and Arkansas] Baptists than he did elsewhere.)

The Southern Baptists may be the only segment of the population that responded favorably to the "family values" campaign of the GOP in 1992.

Perot was not much of a factor in these conservative Baptist counties, except in Texas and Kentucky. He had difficulty breaking into those electorates where religion, race, or historical memory were strong. (See Table 33.)

Bush also won 45 percent in heavily Mormon Utah, which had been his banner state with 67 percent in 1988. Independent Ross Perot cut into the Mormon vote here and ran second statewide. The heaviest Mormon counties in Utah and Idaho gave Bush 55 percent, Perot 27 percent, and Clinton 18 percent. Bush won his biggest margin in the county that includes Brigham Young University.

Bush can take comfort in the returns from one small evangelical subgroup, the fiercely conservative Dutch Reformed voters in rural Michigan and Iowa, who gave him 61 percent of their votes compared to 22 percent for Clinton and 17 percent for Perot.

Another predominantly midwestern religious group, the Lutherans, favored Clinton with 40 percent to Bush's 35 percent and Perot's 25 percent. Lutherans split almost evenly in 1988, so the high Perot support was something of a surprise in the 1992 election.

Table 33

The Religion Factor in the Anti-Clinton Vote

State	% Statewide		% In Anti-Clinton Counties		Ratio		Number of Anti-Clinton Counties
	Church Members	Baptists	Church Members	Baptists	Church Members	Baptists	
Alabama	71.0	32.9	72.8	42.9	1.025	1.304	12
Florida	43.8	9.1	49.3	27.5	1.126	3.022	13
Georgia	57.6	24.8	57.8	33.4	1.003	1.347	54
Kentucky	60.4	26.7	74.7	44.5	1.237	1.667	9
Louisiana	70.5	18.3	74.1	31.4	1.051	1.716	3
Maryland	48.3	3.6	54.0	3.0	1.118	.833	2
Mississippi	70.2	35.6	75.2	44.9	1.071	1.261	17
North Carolina	60.0	22.8	62.8	28.7	1.047	1.259	6
South Carolina	61.9	25.7	70.4	38.0	1.137	1.479	9
Tennessee	61.2	28.9	53.1	25.1	.868	.869	1
Texas	64.1	20.0	68.8	41.3	1.073	2.065	8
Virginia	47.9	13.0	48.2	15.3	1.006	1.177	9
All	59.4	24.0	62.7	36.9	1.055	1.536	143

Anger at the Republican party's capitulation to the Religious Right fueled Jewish defections to Clinton, who swept 78 percent of the Jewish vote, while Bush won 12 percent and Perot 10 percent. Bush had won at least 30 percent of the Jewish vote in the previous election. The Jewish landslide for Clinton helped to swing New York's Westchester, Rockland, and Nassau counties, Florida's Broward County, and Connecticut's Westport to the Democratic column. Jewish and mainline Protestant defections pushed Bucks and Montgomery counties in Pennsylvania to the Democrats for the first time since 1964.

Large, religiously pluralistic suburbs throughout the nation deserted the GOP. Clinton carried seventeen of the nation's twenty-six largest suburban counties. He did especially well in counties where a majority of voters are college educated and religiously diverse, e.g., Howard and Montgomery counties in Maryland, and Arlington and Alexandria counties in Virginia. Clinton may also have benefitted in San Diego, California, from voter anger at the Religious Right's takeover of the Republican party. This large population center, which remained loyal to Barry Goldwater in 1964, went for Clinton.

Finally, the 10 percent to 12 percent of the electorate who are religiously nonaffiliated or who adhere to religions outside the Judeo-Christ-

Table 34
Bastions of Cultural Liberalism

Location	% Clinton	% Bush	% Perot
*Brookline, MA	72	18	10
*Burlington, VT	62	22	16
*Cambridge, MA	75	14	10
*Chevy Chase/Bethesda, MD	61	30	8
*Lexington, MA	56	28	16
†Marin Co., CA	59	23	18
†Pitkin Co., CO	52	22	26
*Provincetown, MA	75	11	14
†San Francisco, CA	74	17	9
†Santa Cruz Co., CA	59	22	19
†Santa Fe, NM	64	23	13
*Takoma Park, MD	83	12	6

*Towns
†Counties

ian mainstream, rejected Bush as they had in 1988. These voters were instrumental in the Clinton sweeps of California, Washington, Oregon, Hawaii, and Nevada. Nevada, which has the lowest percentage of church members of any state, gave Clinton an upset victory. Religiously nonaffiliated voters gave Clinton 65 percent, Perot 20 percent, and Bush only 15 percent support.

Counties in Arizona, New Mexico, North Dakota, South Dakota, and Wisconsin where Native Americans form the majority of the population went for Clinton by a landslide of 62 percent, compared to 27 percent for Bush and 11 percent for Perot. The Republican vote has steadily declined in these areas since 1984. (Reagan won a majority in 1980.)

Clinton won a greater landslide than Lyndon Johnson in 1964 when his votes were tallied in San Francisco and its suburbs, especially in Marin County—all strongholds of religious diversity. Clinton won heavily in such religiously liberal areas as Pitkin County, Colorado, and Brookline, and Provincetown, Massachusetts. Clinton also won impressive majorities in almost every county where universities and colleges are the dominant cultural influence. Even in southern states carried by Bush, Clinton won two to one in religiously and culturally diverse towns like Chapel Hill, North Carolina; Charlottesville and Williamsburg, Virginia; and Gainesville, Florida.

Table 35
Liberal College Towns
(Usually Democratic)

Location	State	College	% Clinton	% Bush	% Perot
*Amherst	MA	Amherst	74	14	12
*Charlottesville	VA	Univ. of Virginia	59	32	9
†Dane	WI	Univ. of Wisconsin	55	30	15
*Hanover	NH	Dartmouth	63	26	11
†Johnson	IA	Univ. of Iowa	56	27	17
*Mansfield	CT	Univ. of Connecticut	59	22	19
†Orange	NC	Univ. of North Carolina	59	28	12
†Tompkins	NY	Cornell	55	28	17

*Towns
†Counties

Table 36
Moderate College Towns
(Usually Republican)

County	State	College	% Clinton	% Bush	% Perot
Albany	WY	Univ. of Wyoming	45	33	22
Boone	MO	Univ. of Missouri	46	33	21
Centre	PA	Penn State*	42	40	18
Champaign	IL	Univ. of Illinois	47	36	17
Douglas	KS	Univ. of Kansas	46	31	23
Ingham	MI	Michigan State	46	33	21
Latah	ID	Univ. of Idaho	45	33	22
Missoula	MT	Univ. of Montana	47	30	23
Monroe	IN	Indiana University	46	38	16
Washington	AR	Univ. of Arkansas	47	42	11

*In State College, where the university is located, the vote was: Clinton 53.2%; Bush 31.4%, and Perot 15.4%. Clinton carried Centre County because of the academic vote.

Table 37
College Swing Counties

County	State	College	% Clinton	% Bush	% Perot
Alachua	FL	Univ. of Florida	50	30	20
Athens	OH	Univ. of Ohio	52	28	20
Benton	OR	Oregon State	48	30	22
Boulder	CO	Univ. of Colorado	52	27	21
Clarke	GA	Univ. of Georgia	53	36	10
Clay	SD	South Dakota St.	47	31	22
Jackson	IL	Univ. of Southern Ill.	55	28	17
Story	IA	Iowa State	48	35	17
Washtenaw	MI	Univ. of Michigan	54	30	16

Table 38
Conservative Strongholds Outside the South
(Goldwater Majority 1964)

County	% Clinton	% Bush	% Perot
Du Page, IL	31	48	21
Johnson, KS	31	44	25
Maricopa, AZ	33	41	26
Orange, CA	32	44	24
San Diego, CA	38	35	27

Table 39
Religious Conservatives

County	% Clinton	% Bush	% Perot
Anderson, SC	33	52	15
Curry, NM	29	54	16
Greene, MO	39	44	17
Greenville, SC	31	57	12
Kern, CA	34	45	21
Lubbock, TX	27	59	14
Spartanburg, SC	35	52	13

2

The Bill Clinton Vote: Strengths and Weaknesses

A striking fact emerges from a comparison of the Democratic win in the 1992 presidential election with the last Democratic victory, that of Jimmy Carter in 1976. Although the popular vote results were not far apart (Clinton won by 5.6 percent and Carter by 2 percent), the state results showed how much America had changed in the intervening sixteen years.

Bill Clinton carried fifteen of the twenty-seven states that went for Republican Gerald Ford in 1976. All are in the West, Midwest, or Northeast regions of the country. And while Clinton still won seventeen of the twenty-three states carried by fellow Democrat Carter, six of the eleven southern states went for Carter in 1976 but for Bush in 1992. Thus in a short period of a decade and a half and with a "net swing"* to the Democrats of just 1.8 percent of the vote, twenty-one of the nation's fifty states switched sides. Obviously, a lot of political readjustment and reassessment has been going on. Much of it is due to economics, but some

---

*The "net swing" is a term used by statisticians especially when there is a multiparty or multi-candidate election. Clinton beat Bush by 5.6 percentage points, while Carter beat Ford by 2 percentage points. (You take 5.6 – 2.0 and divide by 2 to get the swing.) What this means is that the Democrats gained just under two voters out of a hundred between 1976 and 1992 when "switchers" to and from them are considered. As we have seen, though, a large number of people have switched sides during that time.

Table 40
Ten States That Supported Clinton and Dukakis

State	Straight-out Clinton vs Dukakis	"Swing" to Clinton
Hawaii	− 6.2	1.0
Iowa	−11.4	−2.1
Massachusetts	− 5.7	5.4
Minnesota	− 9.4	2.3
New York	− 1.9	5.9
Oregon	− 8.8	2.7
Rhode Island	− 8.6	3.2
Washington	− 6.6	5.0
West Virginia	− 3.8	4.2
Wisconsin	−10.3	.4
Nationwide	− 2.6	6.7

of it reflects concerns about the state of contemporary culture. It is these cultural issues, involving religion, education and values, that comprise the bulk of this chapter.

It should be acknowledged that Clinton's vote reveals both strengths and weaknesses. The strength of Clinton's voter appeal can be seen in the fact that he was the first Democrat since the Second World War to carry twenty-two solidly Republican counties in eleven states. Clinton won counties that supported Goldwater and Dewey, and eight of the counties had *never* supported Franklin Roosevelt. In two of those counties, DeKalb and Whiteside in Illinois, Clinton was the first Democrat in history to carry the county for president. In four counties (Hickory and Warren in Missouri and Johnson and Pope in Illinois), Clinton was the first Democrat to emerge victorious since Stephen Douglas in 1860, on the eve of the Civil War! The last time Union County, Tennessee, had backed a Democrat for president was the Reconstruction election of 1868. Interestingly, seven of these counties backed Franklin Roosevelt in 1932, but rejected the New Deal and returned to the GOP in 1936. This suggests that only very damaging economic times will move voters out of the Republican column in some rural areas.

These are impressive Clinton triumphs in long-time Republican bailiwicks, and they should not be ignored. Only in unusual elections like 1992 do so many counties break with long-established patterns.

Table 41
Twenty-two Swing States (Bush 1988, Clinton 1992)*

State	Clinton vs. Dukakis	Overall Swing
Arkansas	+11.0	16.0
California	− 1.6	8.5
Colorado	− 5.2	6.0
Connecticut	− 4.7	5.8
Delaware	0	10.3
Georgia	+ 4.0	10.5
Illinois	0	8.2
Kentucky	+ .7	7.5
Louisiana	+ 1.5	7.4
Maine	− 5.1	9.9
Maryland	+ 1.6	8.6
Michigan	− 1.9	7.7
Missouri	− 3.7	7.1
Montana	− 8.6	4.2
Nevada	− .5	11.9
New Hampshire	+ 2.6	13.7
New Jersey	+ .4	8.0
New Mexico	− 1.0	6.8
Ohio	− 3.9	6.4
Pennsylvania	− 3.3	5.7
Tennessee	+ 5.6	10.6
Vermont	− 1.5	9.6

*The swing to Clinton was greatest in these states. These are the "key" states which Clinton has to win in 1996.

Clinton's weaknesses occurred mainly in Democratic states which supported Dukakis, and where some Democrats defected to Perot. (See Table 40.)

Ross Perot deserves some of the credit for Clinton's success, perhaps indirectly, since Clinton did not win a majority in any of these twenty-two counties except Macon County, Tennessee, which borders Al Gore's home county. The Perot vote could still be quite a factor in 1996. (See Table 45.)

These Republican breakthroughs were not the only ones where Clinton did surprisingly well. He came within six votes of being the first Democrat in this century to carry Tyler County, West Virginia. He came within fifteen votes of winning Lincoln Parish, Louisiana, which last favored a Democrat in 1952. And he was the first Democrat since Truman to carry Coconino County, Arizona.

Table 42
Eighteen States That Supported Bush Twice*

State	Clinton vs. Dukakis	Overall Clinton Swing
Alabama	+ 1.0	6.3
Alaska	− 6.0	7.1
Arizona	− 2.2	9.7
Florida	+ .5	10.3
Idaho	− 7.6	6.3
Indiana	− 2.9	7.0
Kansas	− 8.9	4.0
Mississippi	+ 1.7	6.0
Nebraska	− 9.8	1.9
North Carolina	+ 1.0	7.8
North Dakota	−10.8	.5
Oklahoma	− 7.3	4.0
South Carolina	+ 2.3	7.9
South Dakota	− 9.4	1.4
Texas	− 6.2	4.6
Utah	− 7.3	7.8
Virginia	+ 1.4	8.1
Wyoming	− 4.0	8.5

*Clinton's gains varied in these Republican loyalist states but proved irrelevant at the end.

Clinton cut into Republican loyalties in areas where both economic and cultural voting patterns have diminished Republican support. Every county in Vermont went for Clinton: this is only the second time in history when such a Democratic sweep occurred in the Green Mountain State. (The other time was in 1964.) Similar results were seen in other parts of New England, upstate New York, Pennsylvania, and Michigan. It takes an earthquake to move many of the old Yankee Republican counties of the country away from their historic loyalties, but the Bush-Quayle administration apparently provoked widespread disillusion and disappointment among former supporters. All of these areas are strongholds of mainline Protestantism and are in the economically perturbed Rust Belt states. The twin issues of economics and cultural tolerance pushed the Republican vote to near-historic lows, and gave the Clinton-Gore ticket a major opportunity to realign the electorate in these areas. Clinton also carried about half of the nation's highest-income counties, particularly in strongholds of the liberal elite. (See Table 48.)

Table 43
Percentage of States Where:

State Victors	Clinton Improved on Dukakis Vote	Swing to Clinton Exceeded His National Average	Perot Exceeded His National Average*
Clinton-Dukakis	0	0	60.0
Bush '88-Clinton '92	40.0	77.3	54.5
Bush	33.3	50.0	72.2

*Note that Perot exceeded his national average in all three kinds of states, evidence of his widespread appeal.

Table 44

A Comparison of Highest Democratic Gains—1988 and 1992*

Top Ten Clinton Gains	Top Ten Dukakis Gains
1. Arkansas	1. Oklahoma
2. Tennessee	2. Hawaii
3. Georgia	3. Nebraska
4. New Hampshire	4. Colorado
5. South Carolina	5. Kansas
6. Mississippi	6. South Dakota
7. Maryland	7. Wyoming
8. Louisiana	8. Idaho
9. Virginia	9. North Dakota
10. Alabama & North Carolina (Tie)	10. Iowa

*Democratic presidential gains have been coming from different parts of the country, suggesting no permanent political directional pulls in this era of angry voters.

Table 45

Clinton's Republican Triumphs

State	County	Last Democratic Presidential Win	% Clinton	% Bush	% Perot
California	San Diego	1944	37.2	35.7	26.3
Florida	Palm Beach	1944	46.4	34.6	18.6
Illinois	Bureau	1932	42.2	38.2	19.3
Illinois	De Kalb	Never	40.1	37.0	22.4
Illinois	Johnson	1860	42.6	39.4	17.5
Illinois	McDonough	1932	41.8	38.0	19.9
Illinois	Pope	1860	44.1	39.4	16.2
Illinois	Warren	1932	43.3	39.4	17.0
Illinois	Whiteside	Never	45.4	37.4	16.9
Louisiana	Caddo	1944	46.5	41.6	11.5
Minnesota	Sibley	1936	33.7	32.2	33.5
Missouri	Benton	1932	43.9	34.5	21.3
Missouri	Hickory	1860	47.5	31.0	21.3
Missouri	Morgan	1932	37.4	36.3	26.1
Missouri	Warren	1860	37.1	34.1	28.5
South Dakota	Kingsbury	1932	40.3	35.4	23.7
Tennessee	Macon	1880	51.7	40.2	7.7
Tennessee	Pickett	1932	48.3	46.2	5.1
Tennessee	Union	1868	46.3	42.5	10.8
Virginia	Montgomery	1940	42.7	42.5	13.8
Washington	Whitman	1936	43.7	36.8	18.4
Wyoming	Teton	1940	37.2	34.0	27.9

Table 46

The Clinton-Johnson Connection

Thirty-nine Republican Counties Where the Only Victorious Democrats
Since 1920 were Johnson in 1964 and Clinton in 1992

State	County
Kansas	Douglas
Kentucky	Johnson, Ohio
Maine	Hancock, Knox, Lincoln
Massachusetts	Barnstable
Michigan	Benzie, Charlevoix, Iosco, Lenawee, Mecosta, Tuscola
New Hampshire	Cheshire, Grafton, Merrimack
New York	Cayuga, Chatauqua, Cortland, Nassau, Onondaga, Otsego, St. Lawrence, Seneca, Ulster, Westchester
Ohio	Carroll
Pennsylvania	Delaware, Forest, Montgomery, Warren
Vermont	Bennington, Caledonia, Lamoille, Orange, Orleans, Rutland, Washington, Windsor

Table 47

Other Historically Republican Counties That Supported Clinton

State	County	Only Two Previous Democratic Wins Since 1920
California	Riverside	1936, 1964
Illinois	Bond	1932, 1964
Michigan	Alcona	1932, 1964
Michigan	Alpena	1932, 1964
Michigan	Clare	1932, 1964
Michigan	Gladwin	1932, 1964
Michigan	Montcalm	1932, 1964
Michigan	Roscommon	1932, 1964
Michigan	Van Buren	1932, 1964
Michigan	Isabella	1932, 1964
Minnesota	Fillmore	1932, 1964
Missouri	Grundy	1932, 1964
Missouri	Harrison	1932, 1964
New York	Rensselear	1932, 1964
Missouri	Andrew	1932, 1964
Missouri	Lafayette	1932, 1964
Missouri	Montgomery	1932, 1964
Ohio	Ward	1932, 1964
West Virginia	Jackson	1932, 1964
Wisconsin	Richland	1932, 1964
Wisconsin	Marquette	1932, 1964

Table 48

1992 Vote in Highest Income Counties

County-State	% Bush	% Clinton	% Perot	County-State	% Bush	% Clinton	% Perot
Juneau, AK	30.4	50.5	17.7	Hennepin, MN	30.6	47.5	21.1
Contra Costa, CA	29.5	50.9	18.9	St. Louis, MO	35.2	44.1	20.4
Marin, CA	23.3	58.3	17.6	Douglas, NV	40.8	25.9	31.8
Orange, CA	43.9	31.6	23.9	Bergen, NJ	44.2	42.4	12.9
San Mateo, CA	27.2	54.0	18.3	Hunterton, NJ	46.6	28.6	23.6
Santa Clara, CA	28.4	49.2	21.4	Monmouth, NJ	44.2	38.2	17.1
Fairfield, CT	42.8	39.1	17.7	Morris, NJ	51.8	32.3	15.5
Arapahoe, CO	39.3	36.2	24.1	Somerset, NJ	46.4	35.5	17.4
Douglas, CO	46.4	24.9	28.3	Union, NJ	41.8	46.0	11.4
Pitkin, CO	22.6	51.1	25.5	Los Alamos, NM	40.6	36.6	22.0
Collier, FL	53.4	26.1	20.2	New York, NY	15.9	78.3	5.2
Palm Beach,FL	34.6	46.4	18.8	Rockland, NY	40.7	46.6	12.3
Cobb, GA	52.6	32.4	14.6	Westchester, NY	40.1	48.7	10.5
Fayette, GA	55.5	26.6	17.7	Nassau, NY	40.5	46.4	12.7
DuPage, IL	48.1	30.9	20.7	Montgomery, PA	39.5	42.9	16.9
Lake, IL	44.2	36.5	18.9	Loving, TX	32.3	20.8	46.9
Hamilton, IN	62.5	18.4	18.7	Midland, TX	58.4	22.2	19.1
Johnson, KS	43.8	30.6	25.2	Sherman, TX	62.2	19.1	18.7
Howard, MD	38.7	44.9	16.2	Alexandria, VA	31.7	58.4	9.4
Montgomery, MD	33.0	55.1	11.6	Arlington, VA	31.9	57.8	9.7
Middlesex, MA	28.1	49.9	21.3	Fairfax, VA	44.3	41.6	13.8
Nantucket, MA	27.5	48.3	23.5	Fairfax City, VA	44.7	40.1	14.8
Norfolk, MA	31.8	46.4	20.8	Falls Church, VA	35.4	53.0	11.1
Oakland, MI	43.6	38.6	17.1	Loudon, VA	46.4	34.8	17.8

3

The George Bush Vote: Strengths (Few) and Weaknesses (Many)

Where Bush Lost Ground

There is much evidence for the view that Bush's former friends and supporters were the most displeased with his presidential record and his campaign for reelection. Maine, as might be expected, showed the highest percentage of decline in support, followed closely by New Hampshire, which had been Bush's second-strongest state in 1988. Utah, Bush's strongest supporter in 1988, had the fourth-highest decline in support in 1992. No one would have predicted the extent of anti-Bush defections in New Hampshire and Utah, and in Nevada, which had the third-greatest decline in support for the beleaguered president.

Eight other states experienced declines of twenty percentage points or more in Bush support: staunchly Republican Arizona, Bill Clinton's Arkansas, Wyoming, Vermont, Delaware, Alaska, Idaho, and Florida. All of these states, which were anti-Bush in 1992, had supported him in 1988, and all of them except Vermont had given him support greater than his national showing when he ran against Governor Dukakis.

There were thus twelve states where Bush lost twenty or more per-

Table 49
Where Bush Lost Ground—1988 to 1992

State	% Decline	State	% Decline
Maine	24.9	New Jersey	15.6
New Hampshire	24.8	Maryland	15.5
Nevada	24.2	Tennessee	15.5
Utah	22.8	Texas	15.4
Arizona	21.5	Oklahoma	15.3
Arkansas	20.9	Rhode Island	14.9
Wyoming	20.9	Virginia	14.7
Vermont	20.7	New Mexico	14.6
Delaware	20.6	North Carolina	14.6
Alaska	20.1	Pennsylvania	14.6
Idaho	20.1	Kentucky	14.2
Florida	20.0	Oregon	14.1
California	18.5	Minnesota	14.0
Missouri	17.9	Nebraska	13.6
Colorado	17.2	New York	13.6
Michigan	17.2	South Carolina	13.5
Montana	17.0	Louisiana	13.3
Georgia	16.9	West Virginia	12.1
Indiana	16.9	South Dakota	12.1
Kansas	16.9	North Dakota	11.8
Ohio	16.7	Alabama	11.6
Washington	16.5	Wisconsin	11.0
Illinois	16.4	Mississippi	10.2
Massachusetts	16.4	Hawaii	8.1
Connecticut	16.2	Iowa	7.2

Nationally: 16.0 percent

centage points of support compared to only two states where he declined less than ten percentage points. (See Table 49.)

The ten states where Bush's decline was less severe fall into two categories. First are states like Iowa and Hawaii, where Bush was never popular and had less to lose. Iowa was Dukakis's second-strongest state in 1988, and Hawaii was the Massachusetts governor's third-strongest state. Two other Dukakis states, Wisconsin and West Virginia, had a much lower than average loss of support for Bush. Six other states with relatively small declines in Bush support were mostly conservative southern states—Mississippi, Alabama, Louisiana, and South Carolina—which Bush carried ex-

Table 50
The Changing Nature of the Republican Base
373 Counties in 35 States

State	Counties with a Bush Majority (1992)	1948–88 Old-line GOP Strongholds	State	Counties with a Bush Majority (1992)	1948–88 Old-line GOP Strongholds
AL	14	0	NM	2	0
CA	1	1	NY	1	0
CO	2	0	NC	14	9
FL	9	0	ND	3	2
GA	15	0	OH	9	3
ID	4	2	OK	9	5
IN	13	5	OR	1	1
IA	5	4	PA	8	3
KA	19	7	SC	10	0
KY	25	19	SD	11	7
LA	2	0	TN	14	11
MD	2	1	TX	51	1
MI	1	1	UT	11	9
MS	33	0	VA	32	9
MO	1	0	WV	2	1
MT	1	0	WI	2	0
NE	42	32	WY	2	2
NJ	2	0		373	135

cept for Louisiana (where the Cajun Catholic influence serves as a moderately liberal brake on archconservatism). The loyally Republican Dakotas were also less infected with the anti-Bush animus.

There were seventy congressional districts, out of 435, where Perot received 25 percent or more of the presidential vote. Perot's intervention clearly helped Clinton, who carried thirty-three of these districts. Dukakis had carried only ten of them. In 1992 thirty-seven of these districts had Republican members, while thirty-three were Democrats. The Republicans could be harmed more than the Democrats, especially when one considers that Bush's vote declined more in sixty-five of the seventy districts than it did nationwide. In nineteen of the high Perot districts, Bush's vote plummeted more than twenty-five percentage points from 1988 to 1992.

Perot's seventy strongest districts are filled with voters who routinely split their tickets. In eight of them, Republicans were elected to the House but Clinton was the presidential victor. In eleven of these districts, Bush was the presidential winner but a Democrat won the House seat. In 1994 voter discontent with Clinton gave the GOP 51 seats and the Democrats 19.

The Republican base vote in 1992 also changed dramatically as the party was reduced to Southern whites and religious and social conservatives. Only 36 percent of the Bush majority counties were in old-line traditional Republican areas. (See Table 50.)

The Ozarks

One subregion that exemplifies a hardy and individualistic strain of religious and social conservatism is the Ozark Mountains area of southwestern Missouri and northwestern Arkansas, roughly corresponding to the Third Congressional District in Arkansas and Missouri's Seventh Congressional District. This economically depressed but highly individualist area is typified by religious camp meetings, denominational rivalries and fundamentalist theology. There are virtually no Catholics, Jews, Episcopalians, and religious liberals here, which is why Al Smith and John Kennedy ran so poorly in 1928 and 1960. The most famous anti-Catholic magazine in U.S. history, a monthly called *The Menace,* was published in Aurora, Missouri, from 1911 to 1931. (At one time its circulation exceeded one million readers.) This is the land of television's "The Beverly Hillbillies," the "Christ of the Ozarks" monument in Eureka Springs, Passion plays, Bible colleges, and the headquarters of the fast-growing Assemblies of God denomination. The region's best interpreter, Vance Randolph, described the area where he lived and about which he wrote many books as "The most deliberately unprogressive people in the United States."*

The Ozarks area still has a low average household income ($21,808), a low per capita income ($10,953), is almost entirely white (96.5 percent), and nearly half of its residents live in rural areas. About five in eight residents reside in married-couple families and 37 percent have attended college. About one in six residents is over age sixty-five. Most residents are of Anglo-Saxon ancestry.

---

*Vance Randolph, *Ozark Superstitions* (New York: Columbia University Press, 1947), p. 3.

The population has grown considerably since the 1970s, and parts of the region are retirement meccas, which may eventually change the area's character somewhat. Service industries abound. Vigorous folk music and arts-and-crafts traditions also flavor the area.

A kind of ultraconservatism, or conservative populism, pervades the Ozarks. One of its congressmen, Republican Mel Hancock, was among the handful of members who voted against the Hate Crimes Act a few years ago. (He apparently saw nothing wrong with ignoring the verbal and physical abuse of people because of their race, religion, or ancestry.) In 1979 then-Congressman Gene Taylor vociferously opposed the Martin Luther King national holiday bill.

Despite low income, the Ozarks have leaned Republican since the 1960s, due in large part to cultural conservatism. Although Barry Goldwater lost in 1964, most Republicans since Eisenhower have won here. One exception came in 1976, when Jimmy Carter edged Gerald Ford by 51 percent to 49 percent. Carter was more adept at appealing to evangelical voters than any recent Democrat. Reagan won 70 percent in 1984 and Bush secured 64 percent in 1988.

In 1992 Bill Clinton lost the Ozarks 44 percent to 40 percent (16 percent voted for Perot), despite the fact that he was the well-known governor of about half the area. The Republicans won both Congressional seats, with 57 percent of the vote. Arkansas's Third District supported Tim Hutchinson, a Baptist preacher and Christian radio-station owner who is a graduate of Bob Jones University, a fiercely fundamentalist school in South Carolina.

Given this cultural scenario, it was not surprising that George Bush chose Branson, Missouri, a fast-growing mecca for country and western music, as the place to kick off his fall campaign. Bush went to Branson immediately after the Houston convention, where he received an enthusiastic welcome and was serenaded by Glen Campbell, Loretta Lynn, Boxcar Willie, Jim Stafford, and Missouri's gospel-singing Governor John Ashcroft.

Journalist Bruce Cook thought Bush picked the right place. "After all, these were his people. They stood foursquare for the 'family values' that had been extolled so fervently during the course of the convention. This is, as I had been told often, the buckle on the Bible Belt."* Bush easily won in Branson and surrounding Taney County on election day.†

If the Democrats have had a racial problem in the minds of many voters for the past quarter century, the Republicans now have a religious problem. It is now apparent that "born again Christians," mainly white evangelical or fundamentalist Protestants, are the most likely Republican presidential voters, just as blacks are the most reliably Democratic. Both groups have considerable influence on party policies and platforms. This cornering of the market could help assure election victories except for one unpleasant fact—many voters feel these groups exercise disproportionate pressure on their respective parties, and believe the parties have accommodated these interest groups too much.

Merely having certain segments of the electorate—even large and influential voting groups—in the party stable does not guarantee success if other voters feel ignored or slighted. For example, five Democrats (Humphrey, McGovern, Carter in 1980, Mondale, and Dukakis) won nearly 90 percent support among African-Americans but lost the presidency, usually by landslide margins, because of white defections. Bush was decisively defeated despite heavy support from white conservative evangelicals, who largely dictated the Republican platform's positions on critical family values issues like abortion, school prayer, vouchers for church-related schools, and censorship of artistic expression. Many voters of other religious traditions and persuasions found these 1992 GOP platform positions abhorrent at worst, irrelevant at best. A considerable portion of the voting public rejects the influence, goals, and agenda of the Religious Right and therefore refused to support the Bush-Quayle ticket because of these concerns. *More than half* of Bush's 1988 Jewish, religiously liberal, and religiously unaffiliated supporters deserted him in 1992. So did 40 percent of mainline, moderate, and nonevangelical Protestants and 28 percent of Catholics. So, too, did 20 percent of white evangelicals, which suggests that there is a vigorous liberal minority among the evangelical community.

In religious and ethnocultural terms, the Republican base narrowed considerably in 1992, and the religious factor was central to this regrouping.

---

*Bruce Cook, *The Town That Country Built* (New York: Avon Books, 1993), p. 246.

†Country music star Roy Clark echoes this sentiment in his autobiography *My Life* (New York: Simon & Schuster, 1994). Now a resident of Branson, he trumpeted the town as "America's capital of family values."

4

The NAFTA Vote

The House of Representatives' 234 to 200 approval of the North American Free Trade Agreement on November 17, 1993, reveals some of the sharpest, most startling divisions along geographical, cultural, and class lines ever recorded in recent political debates. NAFTA proponents argued that American workers would benefit from the hemisphere cooperation in free trade while opponents insisted that the proposal would harm American workers by causing job losses and environmental problems. When the dust from the acrimonious dispute cleared, the vote showed that an incumbent Democratic president lost 60 percent of his own party's members on a vote crucial to the success of his presidency, but won 75 percent of normally hostile Republicans. Furthermore, the most visible opponent of NAFTA, independent presidential candidate Ross Perot, was unable to convince a majority of members from districts where his support was highest to oppose the treaty.

Democrats voted 156 to 102 against NAFTA. Opposition was unanimous among Democrats in Connecticut, Wisconsin, Michigan, New Jersey, and Pennsylvania—all thirty-five of them. In New York sixteen of eighteen Democrats opposed NAFTA. Regionally, Democrats in the mid-Atlantic, Midwest, and New England regions opposed NAFTA while those in the

Table 51

The NAFTA Vote by Party and Region

Region	Democrat			Republicans			All		
	For	Against	% For	For	Against	% For	For	Against	% For
New England	4	10	28.6	6	2	75.0	10	13*	43.5
Mid-Atlantic	2	34	5.6	19	10	65.5	21	44	36.8
Border	9	12	42.9	6	6	50.0	15	18	45.5
South	47	30	61.0	35	13	72.9	82	43	65.6
Pacific Coast	23	21	52.3	19	6	76.0	42	27	60.9
Mountain	7	4	63.6	11	2	84.6	18	6	75.0
Midwest	10	45	18.2	36	4	90.0	46	49	48.4
Totals	102	156	39.5	132	43	75.4	234	200*	53.9

*Includes Independent Bernard Sanders of Vermont

South, the Pacific Coast, and mountain regions were favorable. Among Republicans the strongest support was registered in the Midwest, West, and South, with lower support in the border states. Including both parties, the NAFTA victory was crafted in the South and Far West—roughly the Sunbelt—where 65.1 percent of members voted yes, compared to only 42.6 percent support in the remainder of the nation—mainly the Rustbelt areas. Regional economic needs and expectations were determinative factors. The South can be credited with saving NAFTA. Representatives from states of the Old Confederacy voted 82 to 43 yes, a 39-vote margin (only Alabama and South Carolina voted against it).

But a map of state results would resemble a crazy quilt. (See Table 51.) All representatives from Arizona, Arkansas, Colorado, Delaware, Iowa, Nebraska, New Mexico, Tennessee, and Wyoming voted yes. But resolute opposition was found among all members in Alaska, Hawaii, Idaho, Maine, Montana, Nevada, North Dakota, South Dakota, Vermont, and West Virginia. In some states (Maryland and Massachusetts) both parties were split evenly. Neighboring states were divided. North Carolina voted yes 8 to 4, while South Carolina voted no 5 to 1. Wisconsin voted yes, thanks to Republicans, but Minnesota voted no. Tennessee voted yes, and Kentucky no. In Connecticut, Michigan, and Wisconsin all Democrats were against NAFTA and all Republicans favored it.

In a few states there was a kind of "normalcy," i.e., Democrats were more supportive of their president than Republicans. This was particularly

Table 52

Support for NAFTA by Congressional District Characteristics

Characteristic	% for NAFTA
High Bush vote	73.5
High Income	72.7
Conservative Democratic	71.4
High Perot vote	64.3
Hispanic-American majority	63.2
Rural	57.5
Low income	48.7
Freshmen Representatives	46.5
Marginal*	44.9
Urban	42.9
High Clinton vote	38.8
Pro-Labor Democratic	23.2
African-American majority	21.9
All	53.9

*Marginal districts are those in which the winner received less than 55% of the total vote cast.

true in Oklahoma, where all four Democrats voted yes, while the two Republicans split. Democrats were also more supportive than Republicans in Florida, Georgia, Kentucky, and South Carolina. But they were the only states where this occurred. Everywhere else, Republicans saved the day for NAFTA. The treaty agreement was approved by only 42.6 percent of members in the 256 districts carried by Bill Clinton, compared to 70.2 percent approval in the 178 districts carried by George Bush.

This pattern was accentuated somewhat by the strength of the presidential ticket. In the ninety-eight districts where Clinton won a *majority* of the total vote, only 38.8 percent supported NAFTA. In the thirty-four districts where Bush won a majority, 73.5 percent voted yes.

When the Perot vote is factored in, an unusual pattern emerges: the higher the Perot support in 1992, the greater the support for NAFTA—despite Perot's leadership in the anti-NAFTA campaign. In those 186 districts where Perot topped 20 percent of the vote, NAFTA received 58 percent support. In the seventy where Perot exceeded 25 percent of the total vote, NAFTA won 64.3 percent support. In the very high Perot districts, Republicans were less likely to be intimidated by fears of a backlash from

Table 53

Perot's 70 Strongest Congressional Districts

District	Presidential Winner	Party Holding the Seat	Voted on NAFTA	District	Presidential Winner	Party Holding the Seat	Voted on NAFTA
Maine 2	Clinton	Rep.‡	No	California 4	Bush	Rep.	Yes
Texas 26	Bush	Rep.	Yes	California 25	Bush	Rep.	Yes
Texas 3	Bush	Rep.	Yes	California 40	Bush	Rep.	Yes
Texas 4	Bush	Dem.	No	California 45	Bush	Rep.	Yes
Texas 6	Bush	Rep.	Yes	California 49	Clinton	Dem.†	No
California 52	Bush	Rep.	No	Colorado 3	Clinton	Rep.	Yes
Kansas 1	Bush	Rep.	Yes	Colorado 4	Bush	Rep.	Yes
Utah 2	Bush	Dem.†	Yes	Colorado 6	Bush	Rep.	Yes
Kansas 2	Bush	Dem.†	No	Florida 9	Bush	Rep.	No
Texas 12	Clinton	Dem.	Yes	Florida 15	Bush	Dem.†	Yes
Utah 1	Bush	Rep.	Yes	Florida 16	Bush	Rep.	Yes
Maine 1	Clinton	Dem.†	No	Kansas 3	Clinton	Rep.	Yes
Alaska AL	Bush	Rep.	No	Massachusetts 1	Clinton*	Dem.	No
Minnesota 2	Clinton	Dem.	No	Massachusetts 2	Clinton*	Dem.	No
Nevada 2	Bush	Rep.	No	Massachusetts 5	Clinton	Dem.	Yes
New York 30	Clinton*	Rep.	No	Massachusetts 6	Clinton*	Rep.	Yes
California 48	Bush	Rep.	Yes	Massachusetts 10	Clinton	Dem.	Yes
California 51	Bush	Rep.	Yes	Minnesota 1	Clinton	Dem.†	Yes
Connecticut 2	Clinton	Dem.	No	Missouri 4	Bush	Dem.	Yes
Idaho 1	Bush	Dem.†	No	Montana AL	Clinton	Dem.	No
Idaho 2	Bush	Rep.	No	New York 27	Bush	Rep.	Yes
Kansas 4	Bush	Dem.†	Yes	New York 31	Bush	Rep.	Yes
Minnesota 6	Clinton*	Rep.	Yes	Ohio 5	Bush	Rep.	Yes
Missouri 6	Clinton	Dem.	No	Oklahoma 4	Bush	Dem.†	Yes
Nebraska 3	Bush	Rep.	Yes	Oregon 4	Clinton*	Dem.	No
New York 29	Clinton*	Dem.	No	Oregon 5	Clinton*	Dem.†	Yes
Ohio 13	Clinton	Dem.	No	Washington 1	Clinton	Dem.†	Yes
Oregon 2	Bush	Rep.	Yes	Washington 3	Clinton*	Dem.†	Yes
Washington 2	Clinton	Dem.†	Yes	Washington 6	Clinton*	Dem.	Yes
Washington 8	Clinton	Rep.	Yes	Washington 9	Clinton	Dem.†	Yes
Arizona 3	Bush	Rep.	Yes	Wisconsin 6	Bush	Rep.	Yes
California 23	Clinton	Rep.	No	Wyoming AL	Bush	Rep.	Yes
Arizona 1	Bush	Dem.†	Yes	Texas 17	Bush	Dem.	Yes
Arizona 4	Bush	Rep.	Yes	Texas 24	Clinton	Dem.	Yes
California 2	Bush	Rep.	Yes	Utah 3	Bush	Dem.	No

*These 10 districts were the only ones of the 70 to support Dukakis in 1988.

Summary: Presidential Winner—37 Bush—33 Clinton

Party Holding Seat—Republicans 37—Democrats 33

NAFTA Vote—Yes 45—No 25

†Switched to the Republicans in 1994.

‡This always unpredictable district switched to the Democrats in 1994.

Perot backers in 1994. Republican members supported NAFTA 28 to 9 while Democrats did so by 17 to 16 in those congressional districts where Perot's vote exceeded 25 percent. Therefore, if Perot and his supporters want to punish pro-NAFTA representatives, they should set their sights at more Republicans than Democrats. They could start with Perot's own congressman, Republican Sam Johnson from Texas's Third district. (See Tables 52 and 53.)

Culture and Class

The vote revealed some interesting divisions along class, economic, ethnic, and racial lines. Members from districts where African-Americans are a majority of the population opposed NAFTA by 25 to 7, but members from Hispanic-majority districts favored it by 12 to 7. Even among Hispanic-area representatives, differences followed ancestry lines. All Cuban-American and Puerto Rican-American members opposed NAFTA, while most Mexican-American ones favored it. This may have resulted from geographical location and resentment at anti-Mexican statements that cropped up at anti-NAFTA rallies. Signs saying "Remember the Alamo. Defeat NAFTA" could not have helped in Mexican-American areas. Indeed, those states bordering Mexico voted 64 to 27 for NAFTA, a margin greater than its thirty-four-vote approval.

Representatives from urban areas opposed NAFTA 68 to 51, while majorities were favorable in suburbs and rural areas. This suggests that definitions of isolationism and protectionism have changed dramatically in light of the changing global economy. In previous decades the polyglot and multicultural cities were pro-internationalist, while rural America was isolationist and often xenophobic. Not so in the 1990s. Congressmen from the seventy-three districts where 50 percent or more of the population resides in rural areas supported NAFTA 42 to 31.

Thus, in a historic role reversal, 57.5 percent of rural House members supported NAFTA, while only 42.9 percent of the most urban-district members did so. The remaining districts, a mixture of suburbs and small towns, voted 58 percent in favor.

The primary isolationists of yesteryear—Republicans from rural areas—supported NAFTA 22 to 5. This 81.5 percent support was even higher than total Republican support. Rural Democrats were only 44.4 percent in favor. In Indiana, for example, the only two affirmative votes came from the two rural districts.

One-tenth of America's House districts can be considered prosperous. Their residents have per capita incomes exceeding $20,000. More than half of the forty-four are found in just three states: California, New York and New Jersey. These high-income districts are quite diverse. In California and New York, they are liberal and Democratic. The Democrats won eleven of the nineteen high-income districts in California and New York. In the twelve other states that have at least one high-income congressional district, the Democrats won only five of twenty-five seats in 1992.

The presidential vote was even more divided by geography. The bi-coastal appeal of Bill Clinton can be seen in the fact that he carried fifteen of the nineteen well-to-do California and New York districts. Outside of these two states he won only seven of twenty-five. There were seven high-income congressional districts that elected Republicans to the House but shifted to Clinton for president. Only one district (Virginia's Eleventh) elected a Democratic congressperson but favored Bush. Consequently, Clinton broke even, winning twenty-two of the forty-four high-income districts, while the Democrats won sixteen seats to the Republicans' twenty-eight in 1992.

This surely represents a net gain for the Democrats, since a generation ago virtually all high-income districts elected Republicans to Congress. These Democratic gains have come as cultural politics have moved to the fore among the well-educated and economically successful.

On NAFTA, representatives from high-income districts voted 32 to 12 (72.7 percent) for the treaty. Party differences were even stronger here than elsewhere, as Republican House members voted 26 to 2 (92.9 percent) in favor, while only six of sixteen Democrats (37.5 percent) supported the president.

In the thirty-nine districts with the lowest (below $10,000) per capita income, NAFTA lost 20 to 19. The five Republican representatives favored NAFTA 4 to 1, while the Democrats opposed it 19 to 15. These districts tend to be disproportionately Hispanic and African-American, though rural white areas in Arkansas, Oklahoma, Missouri, Kentucky, and West Virginia are also included. One district is the Mormon Utah Third and another is in the Cajun country of Louisiana.

Low-income districts shared one thing in common with high-income districts: They both liked Bill Clinton in 1992. Clinton carried all five of the districts that elected GOP congressional members, losing only two Democratic-held seats in Mississippi and Utah. Clinton carried thirty-seven of the thirty-nine poorest House districts, while the Democrats won thirty-four seats.

Left, Right, and Center: Did Philosophy Matter?

The way the debate was framed, it would appear that the anti-NAFTA coalition comprised the extreme left (Jesse Jackson and his Rainbow Coalition, Ralph Nader's consumer groups, Jerry Brown's social welfare advocates, some unions, and environmentalists) and the extreme right (Pat Buchanan and the America Firsters, the Lindberghs of the 1990s).* But the vote did not quite substantiate this appearance. True, many members from the liberal wing of the Democratic party opposed NAFTA, particularly those with large labor and African-American constituencies. But conservative Republicans were overwhelmingly supportive. And 75 percent of the tiny liberal Republican contingent voted yes, as did 71.4 percent of conservative Democrats.

Was this a classic isolationist versus internationalist vote? Hardly. Foreign-policy issues have in recent years become so complex that these old divisions no longer seem operative. The traditional base of isolationism has been the Midwest, especially the Republican party of that region. But GOP Midwesterners cast the highest pro-NAFTA vote (90 percent) of any subgroup. The only midwestern state where most Republicans voted no was Indiana. Elsewhere, support for NAFTA was almost unanimous. Midwestern Democrats, however, voted 45 to 10 (82 percent) against NAFTA. Evidently party perceptions have crisscrossed since the 1930s. Despite Democratic opposition, the Midwest was only slightly opposed to NAFTA. The new center of protectionism or isolationism is the Northeast, where members voted 57 to 31 against NAFTA and northeastern Democrats op-

---

*Buchanan has defined himself as an American nationalist who eschews entangling political and economic alliances abroad, much as Charles Lindbergh and the America First movement did during the 1930s.

posed it 44 to 6. So here we have a classic realignment since World War II: 88 percent of northeastern Democrats against NAFTA; 90 percent of midwestern Republicans in favor. There has rarely been so marked a realignment between parties and regions in U.S. political history.

Another strain of political thought that one might assume would oppose NAFTA is nativism, or conservative populism. Sentiments along these lines, which historically resemble the Buchanan position today, were largely confined to areas where the population was mostly white Protestant of Anglo-Saxon descent. Usually rural and possessing low incomes and low educational attainments, these areas had little cultural pluralism and very few Catholics, Jews, ethnic minorities, blacks, or religious liberals. The NAFTA vote shows a mixed pattern. The representatives of some states that reflect this orientation (Indiana, Kentucky, and West Virginia) voted 15 to 4 against NAFTA. But those of other states (Arkansas, Kansas, Oklahoma, and Tennessee) voted 21 to 2 in favor. (The home state loyalty of President Clinton's Arkansas and Vice President Gore's Tennessee was remarkable. All thirteen of their combined members supported NAFTA.) Both Republican members from the Ozarks region voted yes, as did the GOP loyalists from east Tennessee. So, a nativist bloc vote against NAFTA failed to materialize.

Other Influences

Members with less than impressive majorities in the last election appear to have feared voter backlash on NAFTA. Only 44 percent of the seventy-nine House members who represent marginal districts, i.e., where they received less than 55 percent of the vote, supported the treaty.

The freshman class opposed NAFTA 61 to 53, while the old timers supported it 181 to 139. This difference was pronounced in both parties, even more so among Republicans. One-third of freshman Republicans (sixteen of forty-eight) cast negative votes on NAFTA, compared to only one in five (twenty-seven of one hundred twenty-seven) of the nonfreshmen.

Even in Georgia, then Republican Whip Newt Gingrich could not hold his newly elected colleagues in line. Two of the three freshman Republicans voted no on NAFTA. Among Democrats only 32 percent of the freshman class supported NAFTA, compared to 42 percent of the nonfreshmen.

In states like Maryland, Georgia, Rhode Island, California, and New York, the freshman members were decidedly less likely to support NAFTA than the members with more seniority. If only the first-termers had voted, NAFTA would have been rejected. This is significant since the Congress elected in 1992 had the largest freshman class since 1948.

Labor

The influence of the labor-union movement was paramount in many Democratic districts. Fewer than one in five House members (eighteen of ninety-two) who received substantial union financial support in 1992 voted for NAFTA. Of the ninety-five House members who have supported AFL-CIO positions 90 percent or more of the time, only twenty-two supported NAFTA. All are Democrats.

The NAFTA vote appears not to have been as influential in the 1994 election as many analysts once thought, though the contours of that historic vote may shape future voting patterns on related issues.

5

Summary

In the past century there have been only four anti-incumbent voter rebellions of a magnitude exceeding a 15 percent vote swing. The first three inaugurated a period of party turnover that influenced national policy in many ways. The fourth—the 1992 election—is still having its effects as of this writing, and its full impact cannot yet be evaluated.

In 1920 voters had had enough of Democratic progressivism, social reform, and involvement in international conflicts. Woodrow Wilson's admirable idealism in foreign affairs and his New Freedom at home (which did not include African-Americans, who were treated shamefully by his administration) were succeeded by a crass, vulgar retreat into isolationism, Prohibition, xenophobia, and rampant political corruption overseen by a trio of weak Republican presidents (Harding, Coolidge, and Hoover).

This era of misrule led to the revolution of 1932, which swept Franklin Delano Roosevelt into the White House on an avalanche of anti-Republican voting. (Hoover's vote plummeted from 58.2 percent to 39.6 percent). The stock-market crash of 1929 and the deepening Depression were the proximate causes of this political shift, which made the Democrats the majority party in the national consciousness. Significant social and political change and an expanded concept of the federal government as guarantor

211

and protector of the general welfare were the primary characteristics of this new Democratic era, which lasted, except for a brief Eisenhower interregnum, until 1968.

In 1968 it all began to come apart. The Democrats seemed to have run out of energy and ideas; at least that's what 57 percent of the voters thought. Just four years after a great Democratic landslide, "the party of hope" and meaningful change dropped more than eighteen percentage points in a national election characterized by anger over the Vietnam War and disillusionment over violence and racial conflict at home.

For the next quarter of a century, except for a brief and atypical Democratic administration by a virtually unknown Georgia governor, a new Republican era presided over far-ranging economic and demographic change. This Republican era was anomalous in many respects. The presidential party rarely controlled Congress (in the Senate only six years of the twenty-four) and never really came close to becoming the majority party in registration or self-identification. (For a brief period of time, near Ronald Reagan's reelection of 1984, the GOP inched forward, especially among younger voters.) But voters stayed away from the polls in droves. In each national election from 1964 to 1988, a smaller percentage of voters cared enough to show up and register an opinion on the first Tuesday after the first Monday in November. By 1988 only half of the potential electorate made a choice for president. The actual number of votes cast declined for the first time since the wartime election of 1944, despite population growth.

Many political scientists interpreted the past two decades as an era of dealignment and disdain for a political process increasingly seen as unresponsive and out of control.

In 1992 the vanishing voters began to return to the political process. The incumbent president, George Bush, dropped sixteen percentage points. In some states his vote share plunged twenty or twenty-five points. Moreover, the presidential vote went up 14 percent, as 104 million voters went to the polls, compared to 91 million in 1988.

The 1992 election was thus a twin blow to the incumbent party: a massive loss of voter confidence accompanied by a turnout of millions of new voters. This *increase* in the total vote did not occur in 1932 or 1968, which makes the 1992 result even more intriguing and potentially far-reaching. The fact that most of the voter change from 1988 to 1992 went to a third-party candidate, rather than to the candidate who emerged victorious, is the real story of this extraordinary election. For, it is becoming increasingly apparent that the voters represented by Independent Ross Perot will heavily influence how the political drama of this decade will play out. These 20 million voters form a fascinating cadre of independent, unpredictable voters who see themselves unrepresented by the major parties.

Often lacking economic security and technological expertise, many Perot supporters are undoubtedly taking a wait-and-see attitude. If Perot runs again and articulates many of their concerns and grievances, they are likely to stick with him, possibly to be joined by new ranks of the disillusioned. But if Clinton's policies are seen as working, or even beginning to bear fruit, some Perot voters may be willing to give the young president a second chance. The battles over the deficit, jobs, the aftermath of the NAFTA treaty, health care, Medicare, and a host of other issues will surely chart the direction the political winds will take during the last decade of this century.

For the Republicans the likelihood of winning over the Perot voters is doubtful at this juncture. The party's negativism, the dismal economic record during the Bush years, and its ties to the Religious Right, symbolized by the harsh and extremist rhetoric at the Houston convention and, even more importantly, its platform, are stumbling blocks for the vast majority of Perot supporters. Perot voters share more in common with Clinton voters on many cultural and economic issues relating to religion and family life than they do with Bush voters.

Then, too, history is against the Republicans. In the three previous massive party turnovers, the rejected party did not return to office four years later. Of course, each election is unique. A rapidly deteriorating economy or an unpopular international crisis involving the nation could produce a rapid voter revolt. But the electorate in the past has not been inclined to second-guess itself. When voters are angry enough to oust an incumbent the way George Bush, Jimmy Carter, and Herbert Hoover were defeated, it is highly unlikely that the same voters will want the rejected party back in power just four years later.

There are several historical parallels that give little comfort to the GOP. In 1912 Woodrow Wilson won the same 43 percent as Bill Clinton. He was reelected in 1916 by winning a portion of Theodore Roosevelt's more liberal supporters. Richard Nixon won 43 percent in 1968 and was reelected by a landslide in 1972. Abraham Lincoln won only 40 percent in the 1860 four-way contest but was reelected in 1864. Those who assume that the 57 percent who voted against Bill Clinton will automatically do so in 1996 may be sadly mistaken.

The Perot phenomenon is greater than Perot himself. It is a movement over which he has only partial control. A lot will depend on what he *really* wants in 1996. He has to define his goals—at least to himself—and decide which course will best achieve those objectives. Should he establish a genuine third party and run candidates for Congress, and for state and local offices? That would be a bold undertaking since no other third-party movement in U.S. history has undertaken so elaborate a mechanism for permanence.

Should Perot run again? Here, history is somewhat against him since no previous *strong* third-party candidate ever ran for president twice. (Sometimes, history or fate may intervene. Robert LaFollette died a year after his presidential campaign and George Wallace barely survived an assassination attempt as he was trying to win the Democratic nomination in 1972.)

But Perot does not quite fit any historical pattern, as his voter support profile reveals. Win or lose, Ross Perot deserves praise for helping to elevate the 1992 campaign to a genuine and serious discussion of ideas (as does President Bill Clinton). He brought 6 million new voters to the polls and helped to set the tone for a positive economic agenda. His supporters seemed to want instantaneous change, a far-reaching, even radical change of direction, while Clinton's supporters opted for manageable, moderate change. George Bush's supporters, like those of Herbert Hoover in 1932, seemed to like things as they are. Many Perot supporters may find much to approve in President Clinton's economic proposals and in his plans to cut government waste and reduce the federal bureaucracy. They will want to see results, however, and in a relatively short period of time. The Perot voters may hold the key to the White House for several elections to come. They seem determined to play a vital role in the political process. They—and their candidate—appear poised to tip the balance of power. The two-party system as we know it may never be quite the same again.

Both the Republicans and Democrats have pluses and minuses in the way they have handled issues of concern to the Perot mainstream—keeping in mind that there is no "typical" Perot voter.

1. The Republicans have the advantage on some issues, particularly the reduction of government and the transferral of the locus of governmental decision-making from the federal to state and local levels of authority. This issue advantage is blurred somewhat by the fact that President Clinton has indicated support for this movement in a general way, and has in fact reduced the number of federal employees.

It is also clear that Perot voters do not wish to dismantle government, or to reduce the federal functions in all areas, as the conservative wing of the GOP seems intent on doing. Perot voters want *effective* government that attacks problems they see as serious and threatening to the future economic health of the United States and of their own lives. Economic protectionism, support for American jobs, and limitations on corporate empires and big business are generally widespread among Perotistas. The Republicans fail on this test, which is one reason so many 1988 Bush voters shifted to Perot in 1992. Also, Republican attempts to limit environmental protections, worker safety, and safe food and drug protections have not resonated favorably among Perot voters, many of whom are heirs to the Progressive-Populist heritage of strong governmental action on behalf of average citizens.

2. While Republicans talk a lot about budget deficit reduction, it is arguable that Clinton has moved in this direction—certainly more than his Republican predecessors.

3. Perot voters want campaign reforms and term limits, which neither party has delivered. The U.S. Supreme Court has struck a blow against the term-limits movement with a major negative ruling in 1995. This only fuels the movement for a constitutional amendment to mandate term limitations for federal officials. The Republicans may gain marginally on this issue, since more Republicans than Democrats supported the concept in congressional votes. But the failure of a Republican Congress to pass such an amendment may strike Perot voters as a weakness inherent in the party system, which they see as needing sweeping, comprehensive reforms.

Like populists in previous generations, Perot voters are impatient with constitutional impediments to changes they desire, and are hence more willing to risk constitutional changes. Many libertarian Republicans, as well as liberal Democrats, resist the movement toward frequent amending of the nation's premier document. In this regard, Perot voters may find common ground with the impatient far-right Republicans, at least on some structural issues.

4. Perot voters tend at present to be anti-establishment, anti-incumbent. This is why they supported Republicans in the 1994 congressional elections after helping to dump a Republican president two years before. To the extent that they identify the Democrats as the "in" party, they may instinctively trend Republican. But Republicans will also be defending their control of Congress in 1996, and some of their incumbents may feel the wrath of Perot voters, especially if the GOP leadership has failed to deliver.

This anti-incumbent posture does hurt President Clinton, whose negative ratings outweigh his positives by two to one among the Perot supporters. However, a tired old horse like Robert Dole, who was elected to Congress the year John F. Kennedy won the presidency, is unlikely to receive enthusiastic support—if he receives it at all—from the Perot sector.

There are also a number of negatives that Republicans face in their attempts to win over the Perot voter.

5. The most significant negative—the Achilles heel—is the veto power of the Religious Right in the Republican party. Perot voters are decidedly secular—in the political sense of not wanting a political system suffused with religion. Their church-going patterns and religious interests are sharply at odds with evangelical and social conservatives in the Republican party.* Another Republican platform like that adopted in 1992 will not be a positive selling point among Perot fans. Restrictions on abortion rights and family planning, crusades to restore "family values" to prominence as a divisive political issue, a crusade to reestablish formalized school prayer or classroom devotional activities, or harsh attacks on artistic freedom will leave Perot voters cold. Perot voters are economic-issue voters; social issues are of less concern to them. The only hope for Republicans on this issue is that Perot voters may temporarily ignore them and choose whichever party is considered better on the economic and government-reform issues. But Republicans, assuming they win both the presidency and Congress in 1996, will have an extremely difficult time trying

---

*Perot received 24.2 percent of the vote in the twelve most secular states, where the largest number of religiously nonaffiliated individuals reside.

to implement a social-issue agenda that pits one religious community against others or any type of lifestyle or family pattern against others in a multicultural, pluriform society.

6. The question of special interests and lobbying also hurts Republicans because Perot voters see no change under a Republican Congress. In fact, the situation has worsened. *Time* reported in 1995 that lobbyists from key special interest groups—including the Christian Coalition—meet every Thursday with major Republican congressional leaders to shape legislation and to press for concessions to certain special interests. This smacks of corruption to Perot voters (and to many non-Perot voters, too) and is far from the ideals advocated by Perot in his several books. Republicans may routinely accuse Democrats of being beholden to special interests such as labor unions, civil rights groups, feminists, and environmental groups. But Republicans have their own congeries of special interest—the gun lobby, the tobacco interests, big business, and the Religious Right. Little has been accomplished regarding foreign lobbyists in Washington, about which Perot railed during his campaign.

7. Attempts to restrict the electorate are deeply offensive to Perot supporters. Perot himself advocated making voting requirements looser and simpler in order to expand the potential electorate and thus grant greater legitimacy to the party that wins. Perot has excoriated attempts to limit voter choices and to retard participation. But Republicans are doing just that. Three Republican governors—Wilson of California, Ridge of Pennsylvania, and Beasley of South Carolina—are refusing to implement a law passed by Congress—the so-called "motor voter" law, which requires states to allow or encourage people to register when they apply for a driver's license. This opposition, which seems irrational and destructive of our federal system, seems motivated by a Republican desire to limit the electorate to those groups it feels are most sympathetic to its message. Republicans in Congress were also strong opponents of the measure when it passed in 1993.

Perot advocated a two-day voting—on Saturday and Sunday—to encourage and to make it easier for more working people to vote during his August 1995 conference in Dallas. Republican opposition to measures encouraging a higher voter turnout makes many Perot supporters suspicious of GOP motivations. This reinforces the image of the GOP as the party of the wealthy and privileged, who want to limit the turnout of average citizens.

8. The hard-edged partisanship of the Republican-dominated Congress may turn off many Perot voters, though Democrats are also somewhat vulnerable on this point. Perot voters are fed up with the rancorous divisiveness that has characterized national politics in recent years, and they believe this has impeded the nation's ability to tackle serious problems effectively. The Republican Senate's refusal to hold public hearings on charges against Oregon Senator Robert Packwood—on party-line votes—is a glaring recent example of the kind of destructive partisanship abhorred by many Perot partisans.

Some factors hurt both parties. The most serious is probably economic. Perot voters, who were so disproportionately angry about their own economic decline, are still unsatisfied. With so many in the lower-middle-income area, lacking some of the educational and technical skills necessary to the complex ailing economy, they are unconvinced that the economy is improving, as the raw data indicate. This hurts President Clinton, who should be benefiting from the relative increase in jobs, the upward turn in general economic indicators, and the rise in the gross national product and gross domestic product.

The majority of Americans, however, are not experiencing any personal feelings of well-being, if the polls can be believed. Nearly 70 percent believe the nation is on the wrong path. The majority do not believe their economic fortunes have improved. There is a major gap between objectivity and subjectivity in the economic debate.

The persistent and continuing gap between the rich and everyone else continues to anger the Perotistas and many other voters. U.S. newspapers and magazines were filled with articles during 1995 showing that the United States now has the worst inequality of any large industrial nation, the greatest gaps in income between the upper and upper middle strata of society and the struggling middle- and lower-income groups. The lot of the average skilled and unskilled workers has worsened since the 1970s under both Democratic and Republican administrations. Poverty is tenacious. Nearly one-fourth of U.S. children live in poverty, while the wealthiest citizens luxuriate in unparalleled wealth and corporate profits soar. The time is ripe for the kind of populist movement that coalesced around Ross Perot. Uncertainties in the economy, the bitter feelings about NAFTA and GATT, a disillusionment with politics as usual, a receptivity to a third or more political parties that represent the forgotten Americans are all likely to remain central to the drama which will unfold in 1996 and in the years to follow.

As the 1996 election draws close, it appears that the time is increasingly propitious for a serious independent party challenge to the long-dominant Democrats and Republicans. Disaffection has reached such a high level that a serious disengagement from the established political order is possible.

University of Virginia political scientist Larry Sabato suggests that a third party has its best chance of success if it coopts the middle-ground voters who feel abandoned by the major parties. Voters who believe that both the Democrats and Republicans are too subservient to special-interest groups are inclined to support a third-party alternative. Polls consistently show that between 45 percent and 60 percent of voters want more options. A Lou Harris and Associates survey indicates that 30 percent of weak Democrats and 26 percent of weak Republicans are dissatisfied with their party's leadership and positions. Writes political journalist John F. Persinos, "Recent polls show that the two major political parties are vulnerable to encroachment from a new centrist force. At least one-third of the electorate is dissatisfied and up for grabs."*

The possibility that the major parties will move toward the center may be limited by interest-group politics. Says Dr. Gordon S. Black, a pollster and market research specialist,

> If one of the two parties moves to the center—as Clinton now appears to be doing—it co-opts the momentum for a centrist third. However, both parties have powerful constituencies deadset against moving to the center. A lot of this "moving to the center" is often lip service. The Democrats are beholden to public unions and the black vote—those two blocs alone make it impossible for the Democrats to become a centrist party. The Republicans, meanwhile, must pay deference to the National Rifle Association, the Christian coalition, and the military defense lobby. The parties talk like they want to be centrist, but they don't behave that way once they get in power.†

---

*John F. Persinos, "Third Party Rising?" *Campaigns & Elections* (September 1995): 20.
†Quoted in Persinos, "Third Party Rising?" 25.

Both parties are looking longingly at the Perot voters. Republican National Chairman Haley Barbour is convinced that the Perot enthusiasts will back his party.* But Democratic pollster Stanley Greenberg believes that the Republican Party's adoption of issues central to the Religious Right agenda will lead to an inevitable clash with Perot's followers. "Perot voters are secular, libertarian and cautious—putting them into direct conflict with the increasingly powerful Christian Right,"† says Greenberg.

Many Perot voters have taken steps to insure ballot access for a third-party alternative. In April 1995 *New York Times* reporter B. Drummond Ayres, Jr., summed up the mood of the Perot voters:

> What is clear, both from the meetings and recent polls, is that a great many of the Perot faithful, along with many other independents who have supported the Texas billionaire in the past, have not been politically co-opted by the Contract With America. They are still fed up with the American political system and in a mood to punish, an ominous development for the Republicans.‡

By August 1995 Perot assembled thousands of politically informed citizens to a convention in Dallas, to which politicians of virtually every persuasion came to pay court. Observed David S. Broder:

> The attention that prominent Republicans and Democrats lavished on them last weekend was not misplaced. It was, if anything, a necessary plea from the political establishment to the people who may help save the system of self-government from the corrosive cynicism that is undermining it.**

Broder added that the Perot partisans are "the radical middle, the most significant and fastest-growing element in our politics."††

E. J. Dionne, Jr., author of *Why Americans Hate Politics,* warned that the professional party leaders dare not ignore the Perot movement.

---

*Major Garrett, "Survey Finds Perot Backers Will Vote Republican in '96," *Washington Times,* July 18, 1995.

†Quoted in Persinos, "Third Party Rising?" 25.

‡B. Drummond Ayres, Jr., "Perot's People, Still Angry, Consider Third Party in '96," *New York Times,* April 9, 1995.

**David S. Broder, "The Perot People," *Washington Post,* August 15, 1995.

††Ibid.

Republicans and Democrats would do well to think more about how they have failed to deal with the problems that made Perot possible. Washington's sloth in dealing with political reform only reinforces his followers' beliefs about Washington's corruption and lethargy. The appeal of his attack on free trade bespeaks the depth of economic insecurity in the country and the failure of government to do much to relieve it. . . . The disaffection Perot has organized around the deficit will not evaporate, even if the budget is balanced in seven or 10 years.*

Perot has built a solid, if contradictory, base. Dionne says:

His angry anti-Washington themes and economic nationalism helped him do well among the disaffected on the right and far right in rural areas, particularly in the Rocky Mountain states. But Perotian economics also appeals to urban and suburban blue-collar constituencies. Tough talk on trade and a steady focus on declining living standards draw voters who were once the Democratic Party's bedrock.†

In October 1995 Perot launched his Independence Party. Within a few weeks it had qualified for the most important state, California. Considerable enthusiasm was generated nationally, and Perot received 21 percent in a *Newsweek* poll of 590 registered voters conducted by Princeton Survey Research Associates in late September. (Clinton led Dole 39 percent to 35 percent in the same poll.) Another poll of a thousand voters, conducted at the same time by Yankelovich Partners Inc. for *Time*/CNN, found a favorable view of the Independence Party. By 54 percent to 31 percent, voters called the formation of the Independence Party "a good thing for the country," though only 27 percent wanted Perot to be its candidate.‡

Perot remains the quintessential anti-establishment candidate, which is why he received little support in the high status, prestige subgroups of the electorate in 1992. Perot blamed the establishment—an admittedly amorphous term which has both conservative and liberal branches—for his defeat. In an interview with *Newsweek* reporters Howard Fineman and Joe Klein, Perot said angrily, "If all that propaganda hadn't hit at the end, with

---

*E. J. Dionne, Jr., ". . . And Pandering Pols," *Washington Post,* August 15, 1995.
†Ibid.
‡Dan Goodgame, "This Time, Perot Wants a Party," *Time,* October 9, 1995, 52–54.

both candidates and both parties and all the establishment pouring on the propaganda, they [the voters] would have elected me. It was the impact of propaganda. Those are the facts.*

When all is said and done, *Newsweek*'s Joe Klein put it succinctly, "American politics seems ready to be transformed."† If that transformation occurs in 1996, Perot's voters will be central to the process.

---

*Howard Fineman, "Let the Party Begin," *Newsweek,* October 9, 1995, 37–39.
†Joe Klein, "Stalking the Radical Middle," *Newsweek,* September 25, 1995, 33–36.

Appendix—55 Maps

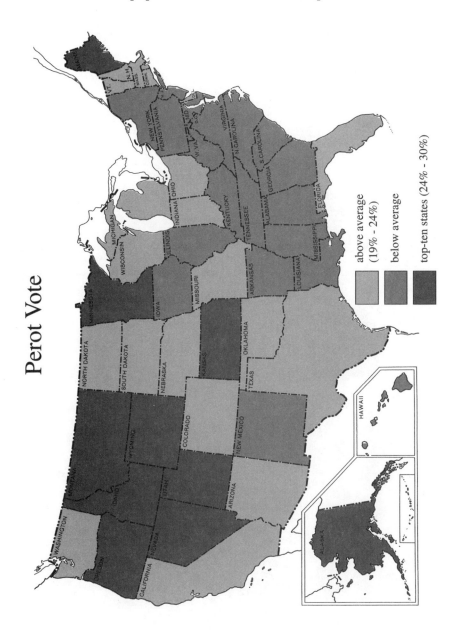

Perot Vote

above average (19% - 24%)

below average

top-ten states (24% - 30%)

223

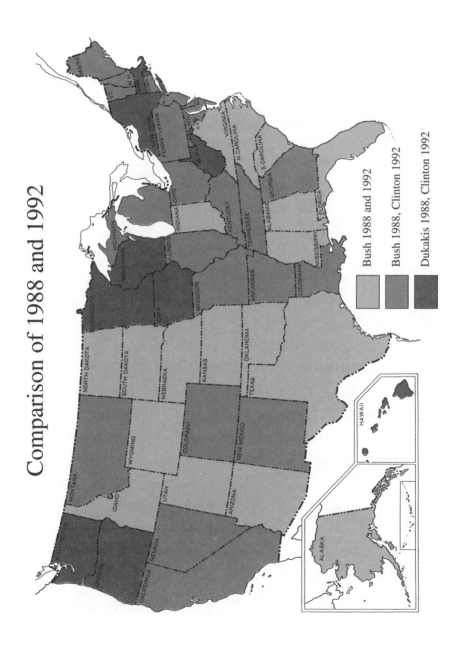

Comparison of 1988 and 1992

Bush 1988 and 1992

Bush 1988, Clinton 1992

Dukakis 1988, Clinton 1992

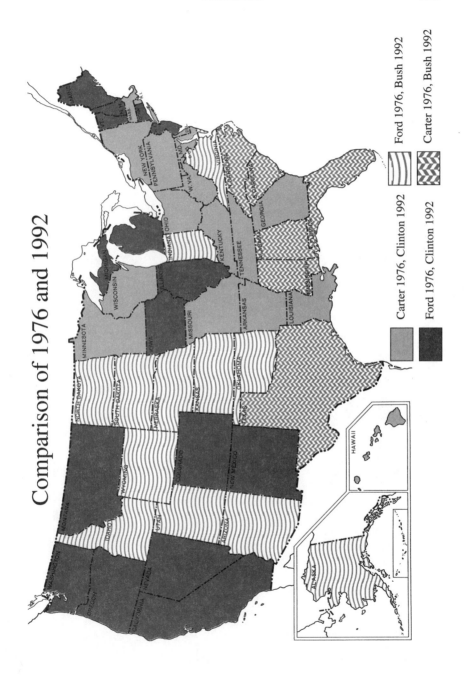

Comparison of 1976 and 1992

Ford 1976, Bush 1992

Carter 1976, Bush 1992

Carter 1976, Clinton 1992

Ford 1976, Clinton 1992

Comparison of Top-Ten Gain States: Dukakis, 1988; Clinton, 1992

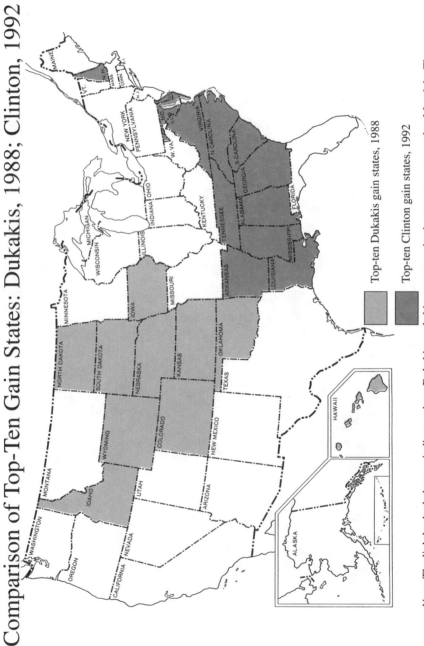

Top-ten Dukakis gain states, 1988

Top-ten Clinton gain states, 1992

Note: The lightly shaded states indicate where Dukakis made his greatest gains in support compared to Mondale. The darkly shaded states are the ones where Clinton made his most significant gains in voter strength compared to Dukakis.

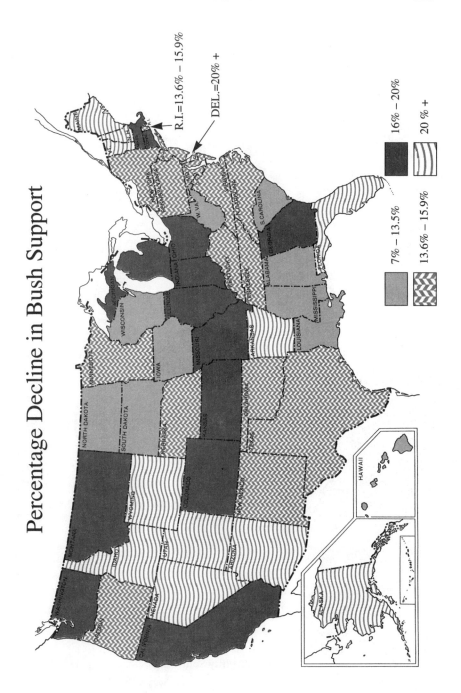

Percentage Decline in Bush Support

R.I.=13.6% – 15.9%

DEL.=20% +

7% – 13.5%

13.6% – 15.9%

16% – 20%

20 % +

ALABAMA

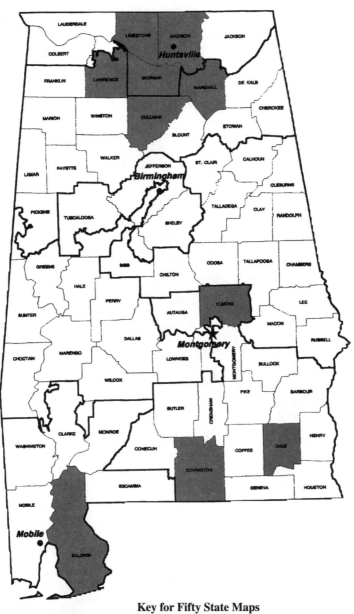

Key for Fifty State Maps

Counties where Perot's support was highest

ALASKA

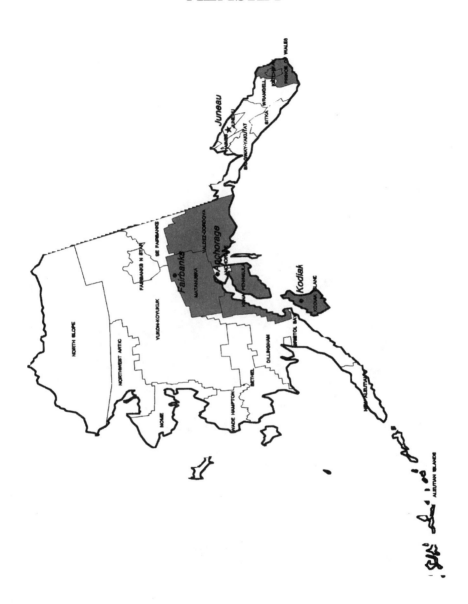

ARIZONA

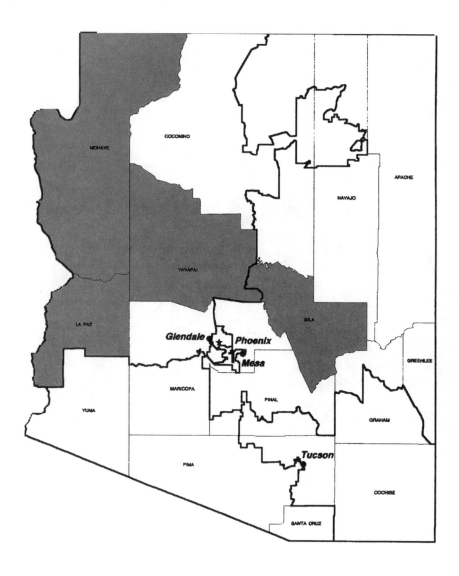

ARKANSAS

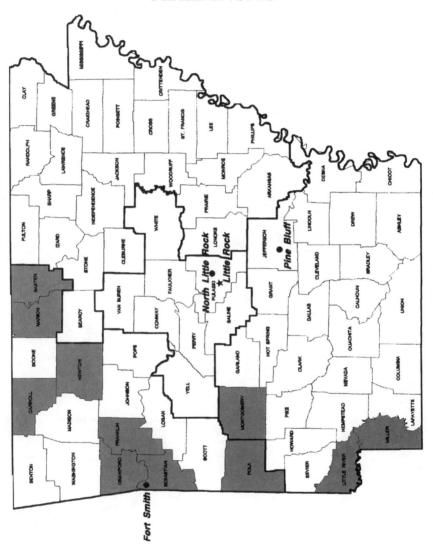

CALIFORNIA

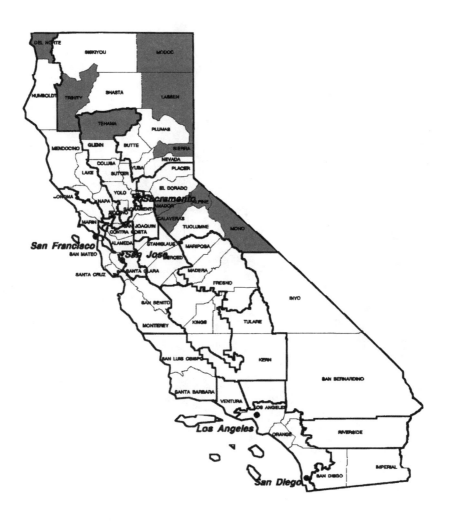

COLORADO

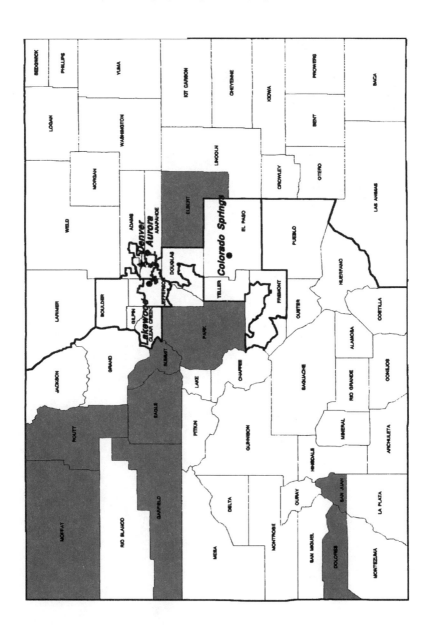

CONNECTICUT

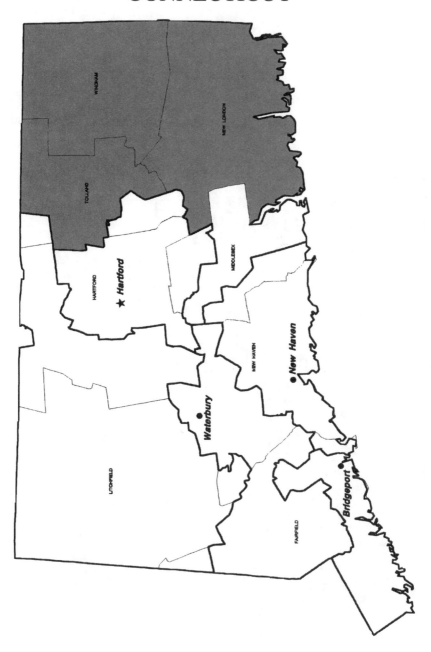

DELAWARE

FLORIDA

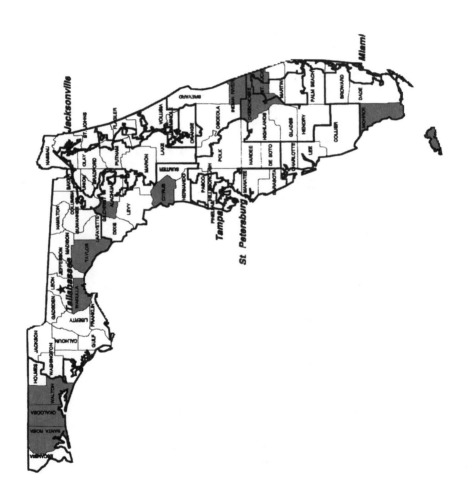

GEORGIA

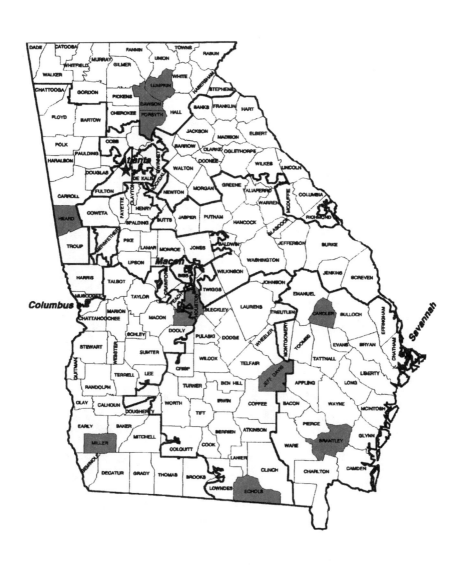

HAWAII

IDAHO

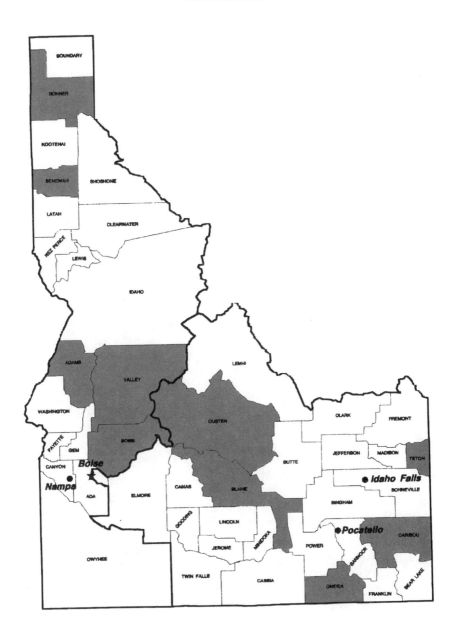

ILLINOIS

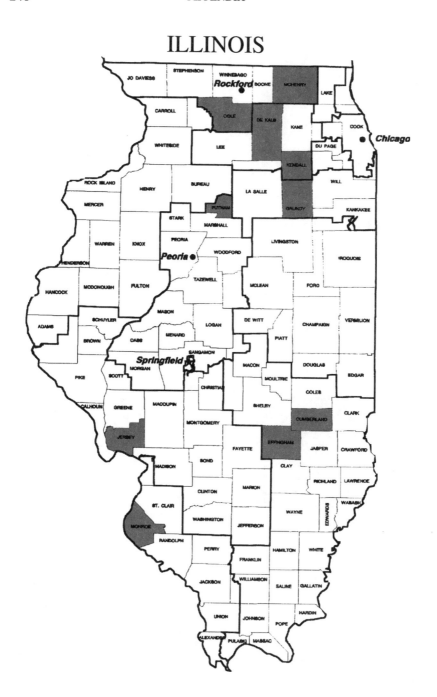

INDIANA

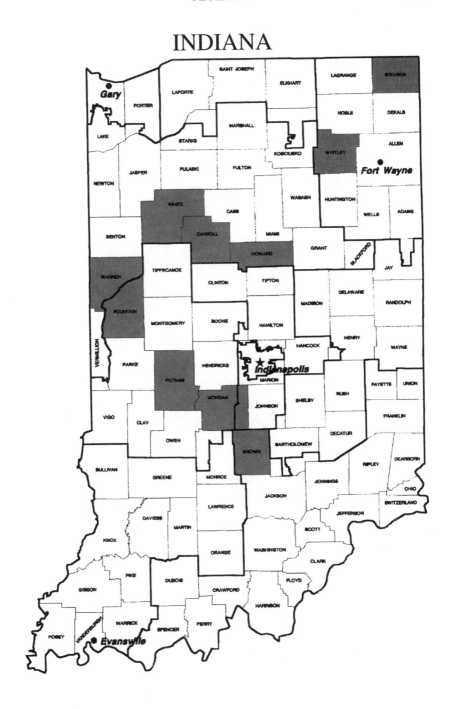

IOWA

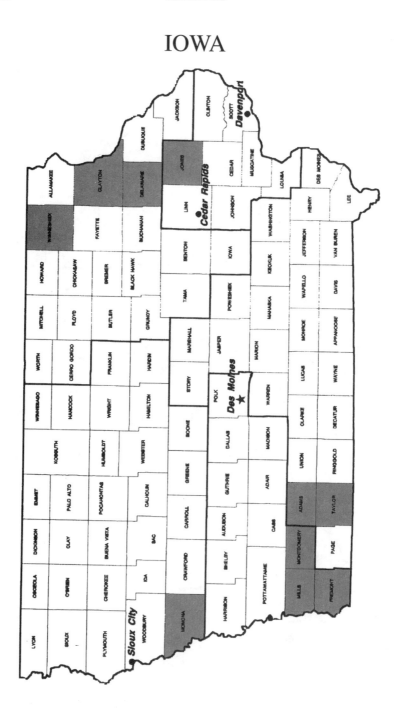

KANSAS

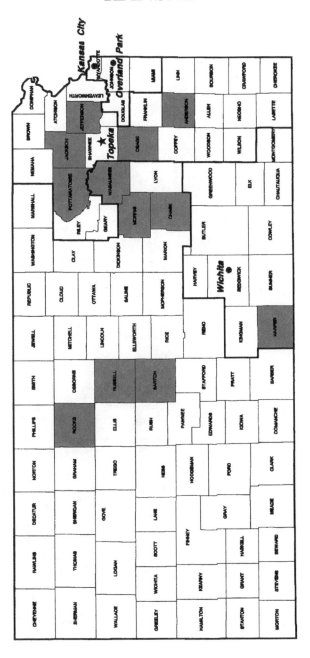

KENTUCKY

LOUISIANA

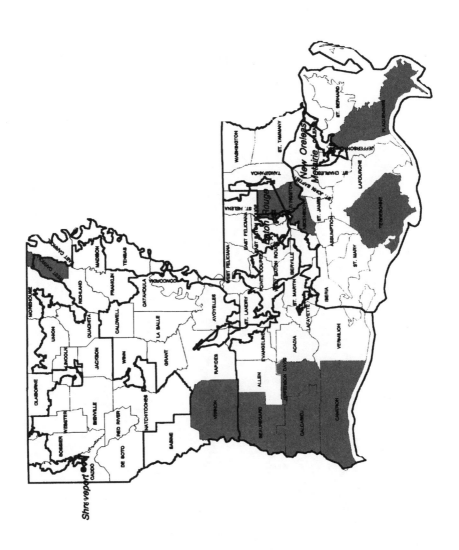

MAINE

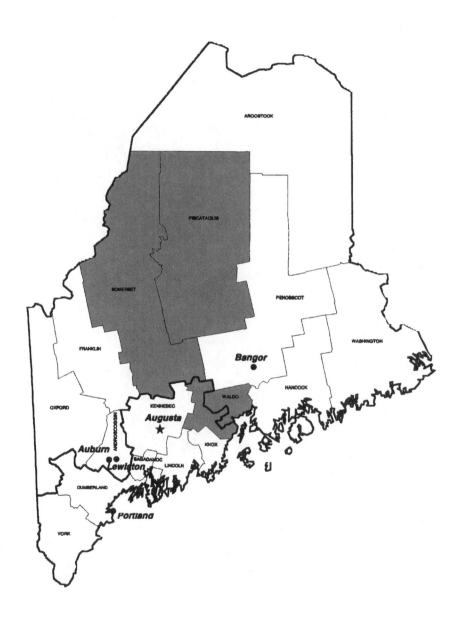

MARYLAND

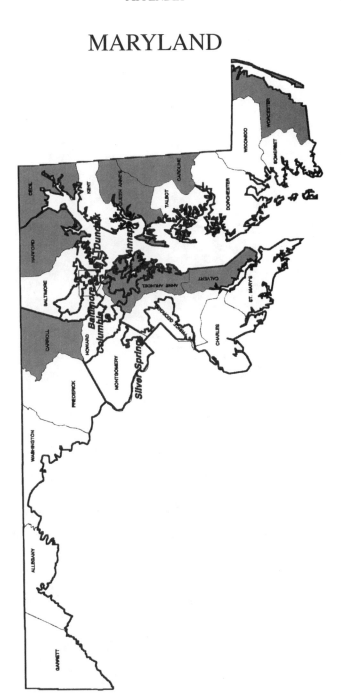

MASSACHUSETTS

MICHIGAN

MINNESOTA

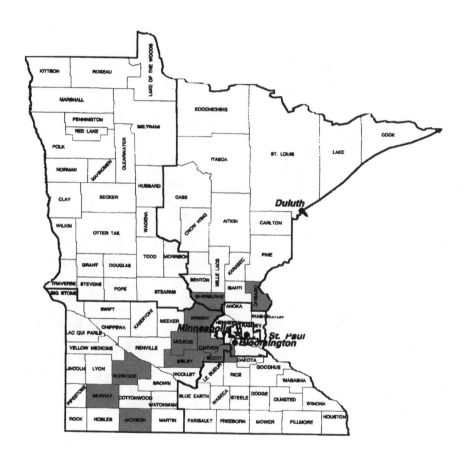

MISSISSIPPI

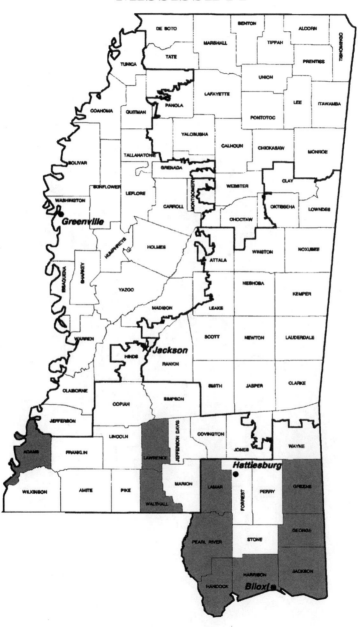

MISSOURI

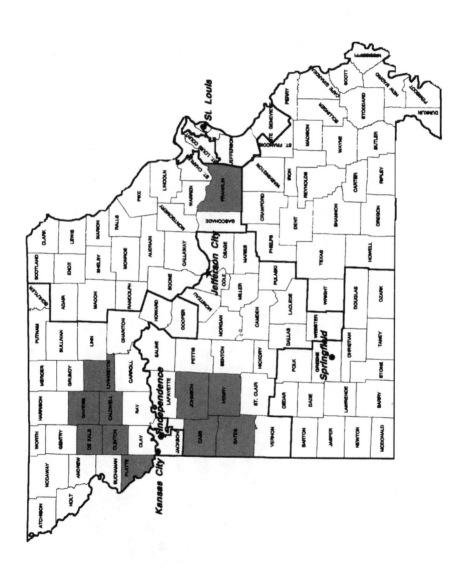

MONTANA

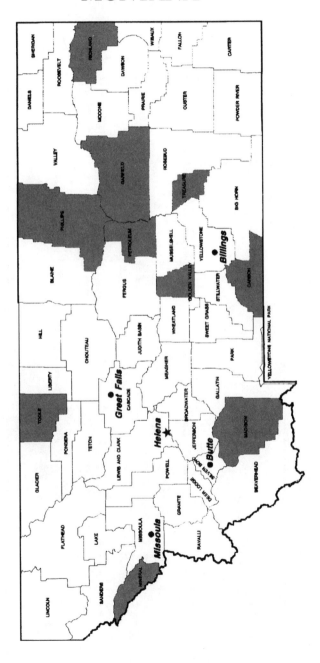

NEBRASKA

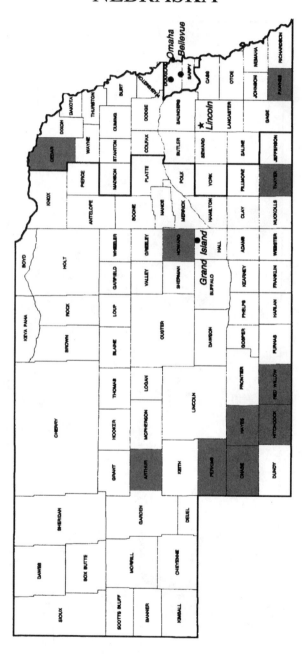

NEVADA

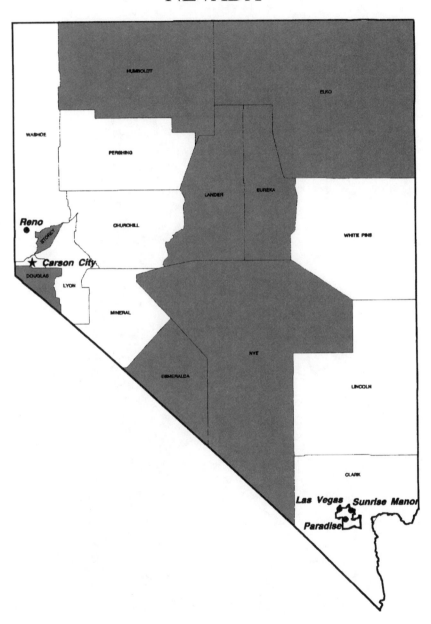

NEW HAMPSHIRE

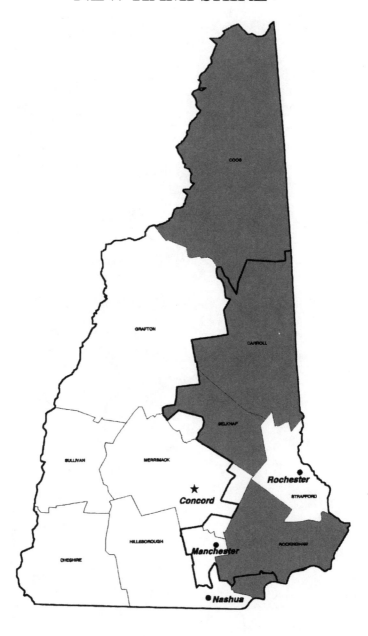

NEW JERSEY

NEW MEXICO

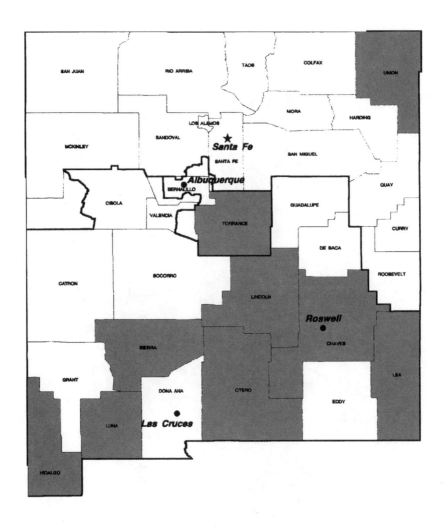

NEW YORK

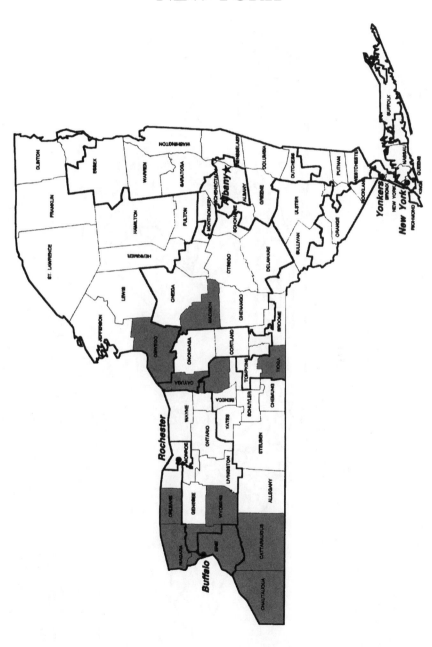

NORTH CAROLINA

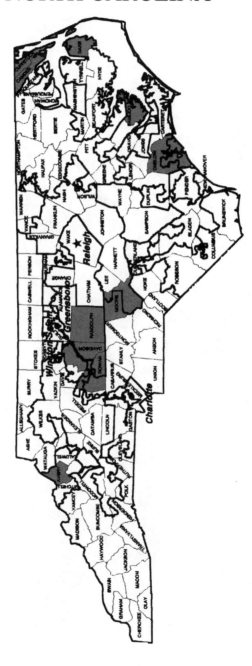

NORTH DAKOTA

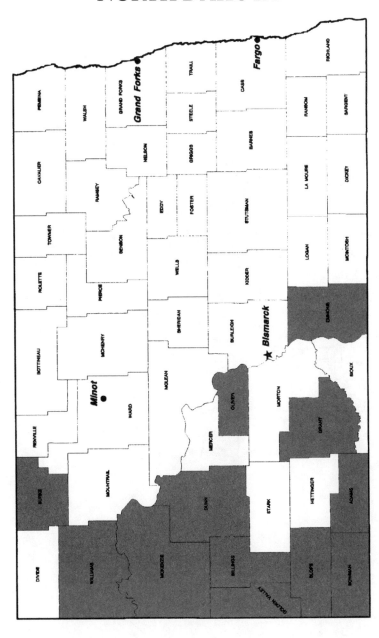

OHIO

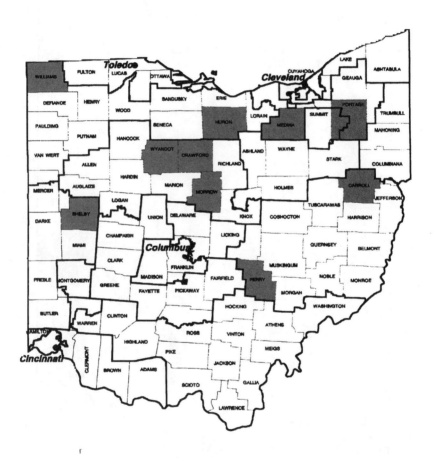

OKLAHOMA

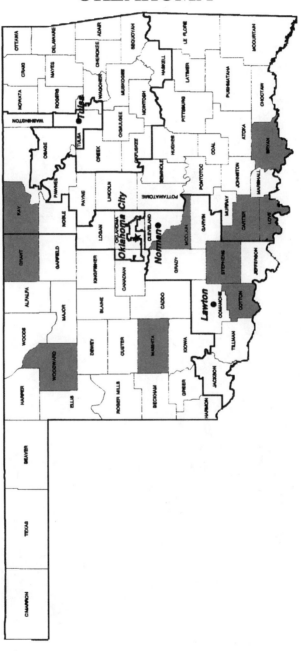

OREGON

PENNSYLVANIA

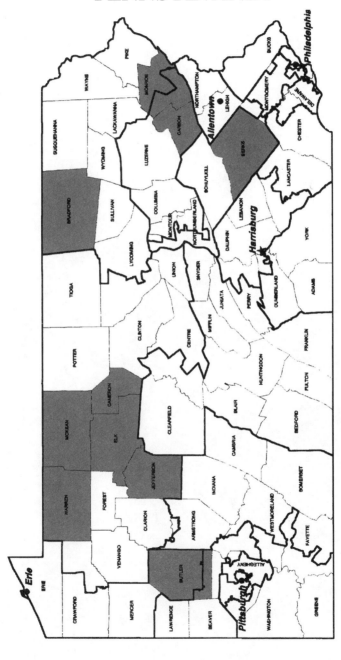

RHODE ISLAND

SOUTH CAROLINA

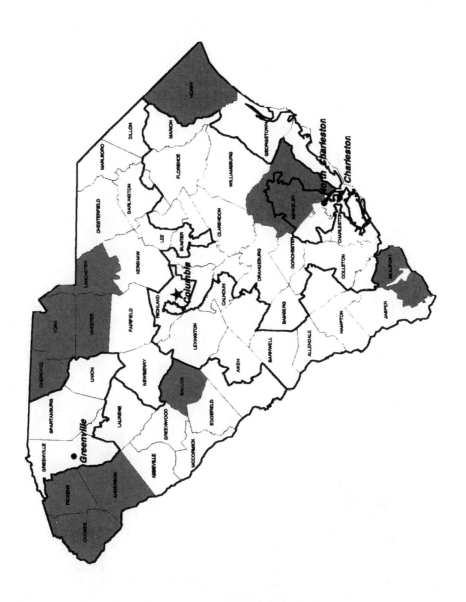

SOUTH DAKOTA

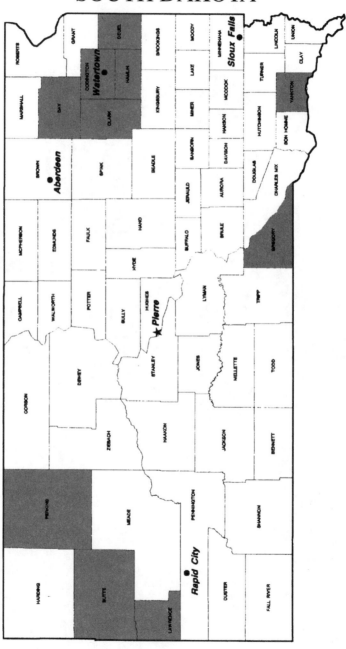

TENNESSEE

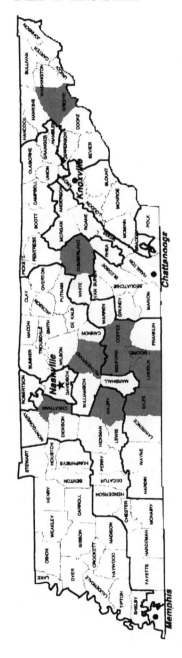

TEXAS

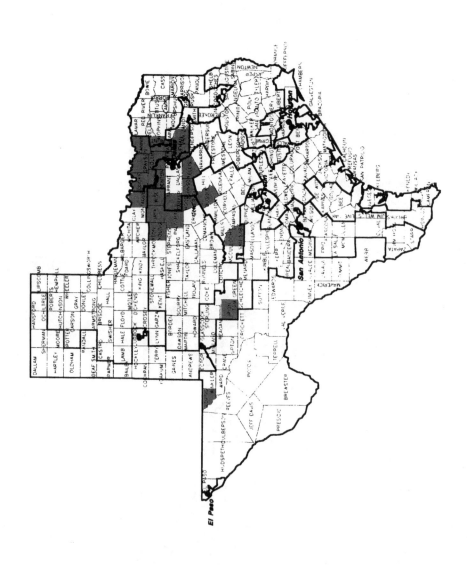

UTAH

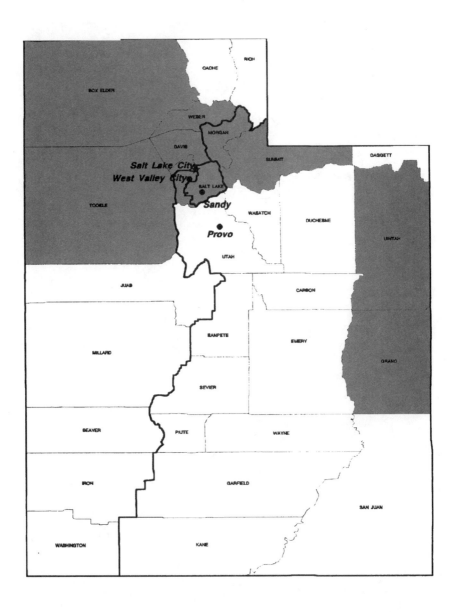

VERMONT

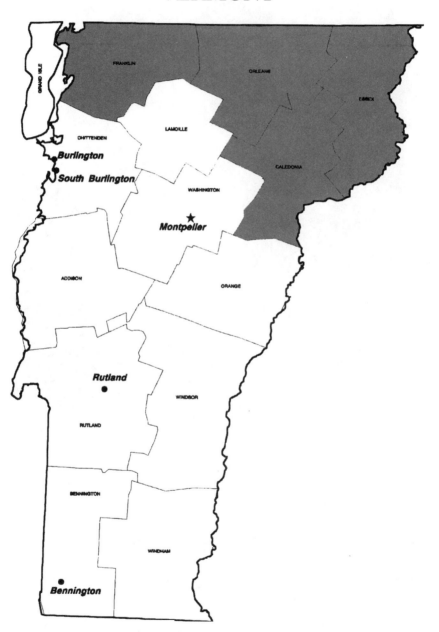

VIRGINIA

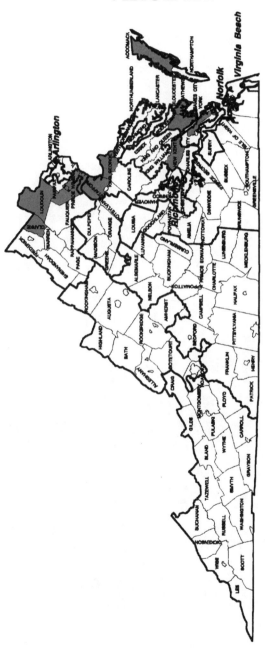

WASHINGTON

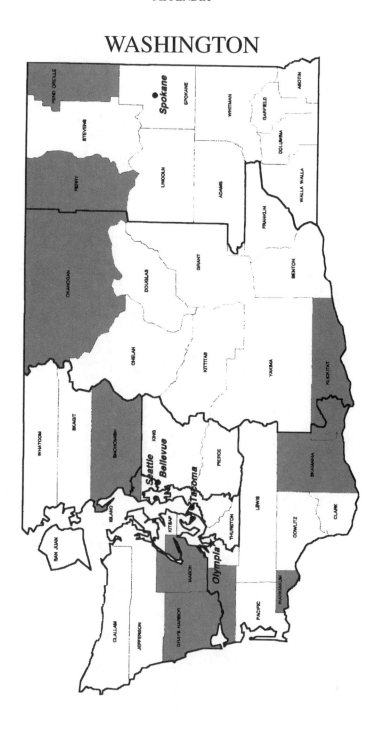

WEST VIRGINIA

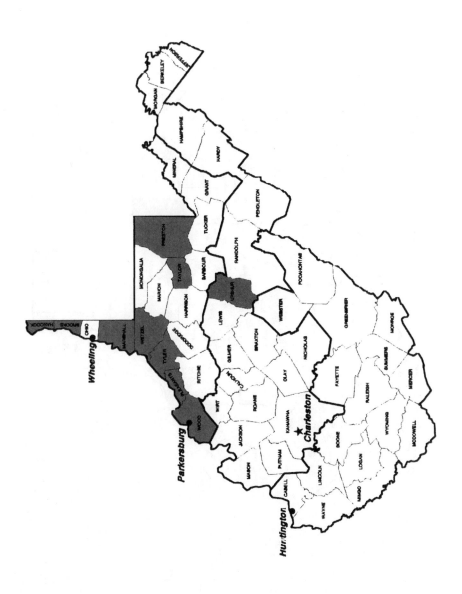

WISCONSIN

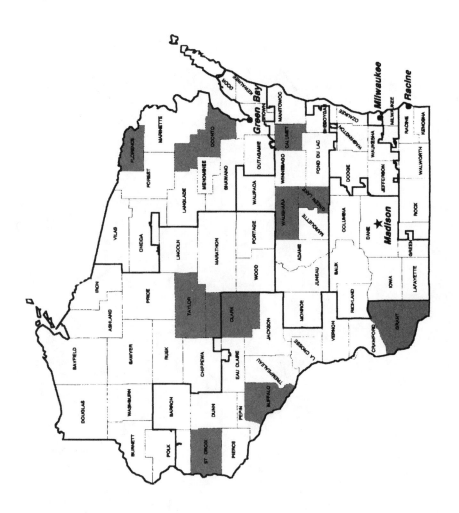

WYOMING

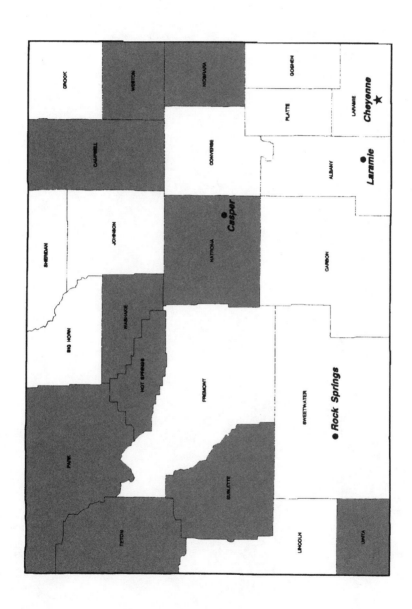